CONFESSIONS OF A TACTICAL DRIVER

(A Beginner's Guide to Offensive Driving)

The Driving Game

C. G. KNIGHT

Disclaimer

This book, "Confessions of a Tactical Driver," is <u>not</u> a Driving-Instruction-Manual; it is not intended for use as an instructional tool for driving or for driving techniques. The author is not a driving expert.

The author's goals with this book are:

1. To entertain.

2. To point out, through humor and satire, how people actually drive and, as a consequence of those people's actions, what to watch for on the road.

3. To get drivers to **"pay attention"** to the road and to the vehicles around them.

Driving is dangerous. Do not break any driving laws. Do not do anything to endanger yourself or others while driving or otherwise. Live to drive another day. Participate in your own health and wellbeing.

Disclaimer

All <u>web addresses</u> listed in this book were valid at the time of publishing. But with the speed-of-change of all things internet-related, those addresses could have changed or no longer be in existence.

Copyright – All Rights Reserved

ISBN: 0615868266

ISBN 9780615868264

*This book is dedicated to my wife Carla
who believed in me when no one else did.*

ACKNOWLEDGEMENTS

Special Thanks to
Marshall Griggs & Mike Bossert
of the Lexington Fire Department
for their time and invaluable input.

My Gratitude to
Officer Contact & The Shadow
of the Lexington Police Department
for taking time to answer my questions.

My Thanks to
my family and friends
Ray, Dean, and Philip for their stories.

My Thanks to
Dave for his input, and who, in a fit of wisdom,
told me to imagine what could be.

TABLE OF CONTENTS

BONUS SECTION

CONFESSIONS OF A TACTICAL DRIVER

(A Beginner's Guide to Offensive Driving)

"The Driving Game"

© 12/09/2012 C.G. Knight LLC

"Bless me, Father, for I have sinned." No, wait, wrong kind of confession. Old habits, I suppose. At least that's what Sister Estelle told me. Just a distant childhood memory. Probably brought on by the fact that I am going to make a few unvarnished admissions as we cruise this twisted road we're about to share. "Yes, Father, I have drivingly sinned." "Yes, I will try to behave better while driving." "No, Father, I don't have my fingers crossed."

I have lots of "dirt" to share with you – confessions - funny stories - secret stuff - personal insights - privileged information really - at least up to now. I've even thrown in a few driving tips. If I had to sum it all up, I'd say this book is an accounting of my lifelong addiction to The Driving Game. I'll explain as we go.

You will see yourself in these pages. I'm sure you've lived some of what I'm about to tell you, but I think you'll find some of it surprising. Most of all, I hope you find it entertaining. So, sit back and relax. Put your feet up. Make yourself at home. Let's talk. Confidentially (and I know *you know* who I'm talking to here), I think that maybe we're among the few sane drivers out there on the road.

Right out of the gate I want to say that this book is mostly a humorous and satirical look at how we drive. Occasionally it's serious. It is <u>not</u> a How-To-Manual for stupid driving stunts, don't treat it as such. Though, I am going to talk about some stupid drivers. There are some disturbing trends you should be aware of. This book is about the *unspoken driving game* that takes place every day, on every road, everywhere. But please don't read it while you *are* driving.

While you are driving, I recommend that you always wear your seatbelt, keep your eyes on the road, and above all, drive safely. This is of great importance to me because I'm out there on the road with…*you*. And although I'm sure *you're* a good driver, the rest of **the morons**, in all those other vehicles, **are out to get us,** so pay attention.

You might even see me on the road. That's me shaking my head in disgust and wagging an extended index finger at some idiot who narrowly missed me while texting some mundane thought to his OMG BFF. "Might I point out," my extended finger speaking for me, "you're careening down the road in 3,000 pounds of life-changing carnage. You came within inches of having my blood on your hands. Look where you're going, dumbass."

I suppose that's what this book is really about – paying attention.

I suggest you pay particular attention to **Rule One – Participate in your own health and well-being.** Yes, the Game has rules; three as a matter of fact. It also has an Ultimate Goal and a little white lie, but don't worry, you'll have no problem understanding any of this. You're as smart as me, probably smarter.

Along with learning, living, and loving the Rules and the Ultimate Goal, the Game involves knowing how to properly assess any given driving situation, thereby taking the proper action and accurately determining your score. This book will help you do just that. Of course, your score is the only one that counts. You will, however, be required to give Penalty Points to Morons you observe on the road.

So sit down in your easy chair and buckle your seatbelt because, trust me, *there are morons among us.* Your easy chair doesn't have a seatbelt? Then move it away from a wall that faces a road. Here's one of those disturbing new trends I mentioned: There's an increase in morons-in-vehicles-crashing-into-buildings. There's a moron-in-a-vehicle out there right now waiting, unwittingly, to make an appearance in your living room. Don't sit near a front wall. But we'll get to that. Let's talk about the Game.

THE DRIVING GAME

When you strap into your vehicle and pull into traffic you *are* part of the Game. Like it or not, you're just another vehicle-game-piece in the maze of roads that slice up the landscape, caught up in traffic like a bug in a stream. You might think you're safely driving along minding your own business, but that only lasts until some Jerk cuts you off and takes your right-of-way. You were third in line, now you're fourth. "I don't think so. Nobody's going to get in front of me." Then it's Game On. You have your honor to reclaim and your rightful position in traffic. You start watching for an opportunity to get back in front of the Jerk. He can't mess with you and get away with it, right?

You could become an angry driver and risk life and limb to regain your coveted spot, screeching around the Jerk with careless abandon, forcing him with threat of vehicular contact to relinquish *your spot*. You could do that, but I know a better way. Learn to be a player, learn to read the traffic (I will explain this concept in more detail) and you'll get your opportunity to get back in front of the moron.

4

Wait for your moment. Why just "get back in front" when there's the possibility you might regain the lead, whisk through the next yellow light, smiling and watching your rearview mirror as the Jerk gets caught by the red light while you sail off victorious. Much more satisfying than crude screeching and risking vehicular contact.

And if you don't get an opportunity to regain the lead, oh well, some days are diamond and some days are stone. Life goes on. You'll get over it. I believe, however, that the insights you'll gain reading this book will tip the scales in your favor; you'll get more of those diamond days. You will get your share.

Never be an angry driver. You lose judgment when you're angry. You're more likely to do stupid and dangerous stuff. Be a player. Let the anger go. It's okay to shake your head in disgust. That's a universal sign for "Beware, there's another Moron on the road that we, as great drivers, have to deal with." Besides, you automatically lose if you let another driver see that you're angry.

I don't usually mess with other drivers unless they're doing something irritating like riding right on my ass, wanting to get by. Ride too close to my bumper and I'll keep you back there a while. Then, when I finally do get over and *let you go,* I consider it Bonus Points if you blow your horn and throw a curse my way. It always makes me smile.

I play the Game incognito, like I'm clueless as to why you're upset. When someone blows their horn and flips me off, I just smile, oblivious, and wave like, *do I know you?* Sometimes it's hard not to laugh when I see some of the looks I get. But I'm always a player. I always wear my game face. I never laugh until they're well out of sight. Don't get angry.

However, the Driving Game is about more than just being a player. It's a combination of things. It's about avoiding The Referees (the police) should you decide to "break the law" and "bend their rules" (definitely not recommended). It's about the process of messing with the minds of other drivers who, for whatever reason, have intentionally or unintentionally messed with you. It's about living to drive another day. Not that you can't have a little fun. I didn't say that. Like I said, if you're driving next to me and doing something stupid, I will have some fun at your expense. Believe me, I know how to play the Game. I wrote the book.

I guess the best way to understand the Game is to describe the participants.

THERE ARE TWO BASIC TYPES – MORONS AND PLAYERS

Players are always aware of what's going on around them. Morons are usually lost in their own little self-centered world. Of course there are subtleties and nuances to either definition. You'll know exactly what I'm talking about by the end of this book, but here's a quick sampling:

If you speed up so another driver can't get over, in front of you, in *your lane, because the road belongs to you*....you're a Player.

If you swerve in and out of traffic on a busy multi-lane highway, barely missing other vehicles, so you can get ahead of one more driver before your exit, a hundred yards down the road ...you're a Moron

If you intentionally hesitate when a *turn-signal-light* turns green, then proceed *so slowly* that you get through, but the cars behind you get caught *again* and have to wait through yet another cycle of lights….you're a Player and a Moron.

If it was me behind you in the just-mentioned turning lane, you'd strictly be a Moron and my car horn would shout out that fact in no uncertain terms. I know you've heard a horn blow and translated the sound to its actual meaning. Here are a few common horn phrases: "Hang up and drive, Moron." "Do you need help? Green means Go." "Move it, Dumbass. It's the pedal on the right; the skinny vertical one." If your car horn speaks to Morons….you're a Player.

I suppose this is starting to sound a little like "you might be a redneck if." However, morons and players are a multi-cultural phenomenon. Rich and poor, young and old, yellow and brown, black and white, red man and redneck alike contribute equally to the spectrum of morons and players that infest our city streets, our highways, our back roads, and our parking lots. How long do you have to wait to see a Moron? Oh look, there goes one now…so, not long.

Of course I'm never a moron, I'm always a player (I suspect that's true of most of you as well). I constantly survey the situation and the vehicles around me, and I drive to stay alive and unhurt, but I don't always embrace the safest of driving practices - I'm a little heavy-footed.

However I drive, I would never break **Rule Two – Your vehicle cannot collide with any other object**. This means you can't hit trees, telephone poles, fire hydrants, people, other vehicles, animals, or buildings. And you can't, by your actions on the road, cause another driver to break Rule Two. But that being said, I'll be the first to admit that playing the Game and bending the rules a little does add a degree of entertainment to *the boring task* of driving.

Did I say boring? Let's be honest, you were doing something entertaining before you got in your car, and you'll be doing something entertaining after you get out. But in between, while you should be paying attention to driving, you're in limbo, lost in your thoughts, waiting for the journey to be over, anxious to get where you're going. You have to entertain yourself somehow, don't you? Of course you do.

"Being a player" is the most entertaining thing you can do while driving; for one thing you get to point out morons. That's one of my favorite games. They're everywhere. In fact that brings us to **Rule Three – Everyone on the road is a Moron but you.** And you know that's true. There's just a few of us good drivers out there.

The hard, cold reality is that everyone on the road wants to hit you. They're all morons. They're not aware that they want to hit you; they're just busy doing other things and are unaware of you. At least once during every trip someone will change lanes without looking and you'll have to brake and swerve. Or they'll wait until you're right on them, then pull out and you'll have to screech to a halt. Trust me, morons are everywhere.

A benefit of believing Rule Three is that it makes you both judge and jury. When you *point out a moron* and *render a ruling*, it's a matter of fact. If only the rest of the world could drive as well as me and you.

And Pointing Out Morons is a safe driving game. You are paying attention to the road and the drivers around you. And you get to point out what the moron did wrong and how much better you would have handled the situation. It's a great self-esteem builder. "Did you see that, Carla? That moron just made a left turn from the right lane. Almost caused an accident. Minus a thousand points at least. You'd never see me pulling a stunt like that."

I come home the same way every day from work and recently I've noticed this one particular moron several times. Apparently, he needs to turn left onto Limestone (local street) on *his* way home from work. He gets in the left-turn lane and speeds up to the light. If the signal turns red before he gets there, he brakes suddenly, then turns right from the left-turn lane across two lanes of oncoming traffic. He drives a short way up Limestone going opposite the direction he needs to go, makes a quick U-turn then heads the other way.

He knows the traffic-signal pattern and knows he can catch the crossing green light and not have to wait for the left-turn signal to cycle through one more time. He's a complete moron. This is the Ultimate Goal (which I'll explain shortly) gone horribly awry. Everyone on the road is a moron but you. I wish a cop would see this guy. Give it a rest, dumbass; you can wait for the next green left turn signal.

THE GAME REFEREES

The Game Referees are "Law Enforcement Officers" who are ready, willing, and able to impose Game Penalties such as speeding tickets, a night in the local jail, and vehicle impoundment, perhaps all three – they're full of fun stuff. Always pull over if a Cop signals you to do so. Getting a speeding ticket is much better than getting killed trying to get away.

However, it is a violation of the Game to get caught by the police. Remember, this is not a team sport. You are an island. When you see "the dreaded blue lights" in your rearview mirror, you are in your own **you-ni-verse**. "So, Mr. Phelps, I will disavow any knowledge of your existence should you get caught." The cops are not going to care that you read and misinterpreted this book.

A quick review of the Rules so we're all on the same page:

Rule One – Participate in your own health and well-being.

Rule Two – Your vehicle cannot collide with any other object.

Rule Three – Everyone on the road is a Moron but you.

You never want to get caught if you're one of those people that bend the rules a little. In your hometown, as a local, you know where the police hang out. You know their *speed traps* and such. So you can usually navigate your area without getting *snagged for a ticket* should you have a slightly heavy foot and travel faster than the *suggested speed limit* posted along the side of the road.

A note of caution: The police don't think of Speed Limit signs as *suggested speed limits.* To the police, and in actuality, these Posted Speeds are absolute and the police will pull you over to let you know that's true. I'm sure you've seen their latest campaign, "Ignore the sign. Pay the fine." And the police have been known to change things up and be in places unfamiliar to you. Keep it close to the suggested speed and you should do okay. "Remember, Jim, I don't know you."

It's when you're an "out of towner" that you really have to watch. Nothing spoils a vacation like a speeding ticket. Let's say you're on open road in unfamiliar territory. You're traveling south and going 5 mph over the suggested speed limit and suddenly you pass a radar-toting police officer who has a 5 mph-over-the-speed-limit tolerance, what should you do?

First, after you realize that he's not coming after you because you didn't break his "5 mph tolerance," and your adrenaline starts to subside, you have a couple of choices. Depending on your mood you may want to signal the drivers headed north that they're approaching a speed trap. You do this by flashing your headlights. (Danger, Will Robinson.) I recently read that in some states the police are issuing tickets for this flashing of lights ritual. They see it as "obstruction of justice." Others claim it's "freedom of speech" and should not be ticketed. Either way, consider yourself forewarned.

Another choice is to do nothing. Let the other drivers negotiate the road unassisted. Nobody signaled you. Besides, it's a little bit funny to see somebody else get a ticket, right?

Now let's suppose you're on open road in unfamiliar territory and you're traveling south and going 5 mph over the suggested speed limit and you haven't seen a cop all day. If, because you're bored and you want to play the Game, you might decide to signal north bound traffic that there's a speed trap in their near future even though there isn't one. This keeps the other drivers on their toes. And you're doing your part to slow down speeders. What do you think of that, officer? Would you give me a ticket for that? I'm sure you would.

Now that I've divulged this game of mine, when someone flashes their lights, you'll have to decide if there is a speed trap or if their flash is a bluff. You are an island. It's best to keep your eyes on the road. Speed along at your own risk.

Before we get to other driving games, and different driving situations, we need to discuss the various kinds of drivers. This discussion might take a serious turn here and there, but sometimes the truth hurts.

THE MORONS ARE OUT TO GET US

Tiskets

A Tisket, a Tasker, a waiting disaster!

The most dangerous morons on the road are the **Tiskets**. [Tisket definition: a distracted driver; oblivious; a multi-tasker; the one most likely to kill you.] You'll see them reading a newspaper or a book, going over a business proposal, putting on makeup, reading their email or texting, or having sex, all while driving. The list goes on and on. (A quick side note about having sex and driving – coming and going don't mix. Tsk, tsk, tsk, shame on you and a strange way to die.)

The latest version of a Tisket is the **Cell Assassin.** That's what I call them. Has a nice ring-tone to it. Cell Assassins are the morons who believe they can pilot 3,000 pounds of life-changing carnage (weight of the average car) while "texting." It's fast becoming the leading cause of accidents and vehicle-related deaths. Kentucky, my home state, will soon assess "penalty points" on anyone caught texting while driving.

I can't imagine what someone might need to "text" while trying to drive. [hi bff im drvng 70 rte nw, I shld prby b lookin up {: o]] Can't it wait until you've parked your vehicle? Do you really need to be in constant contact with the rest of the world? Are you so boring that you can't just be lost in your own thoughts?

I wish I could tell you what to do if you see a Cell Assassin but I can't. Stay out of their way. Pay attention. Try not to be in front of them. That's the one place they're not looking – in front of their vehicle. They are easy to spot at a stop light. They're the ones with their chins buried in their chest; the ones that don't move when the light turns green because they are oblivious to the world around them, texting their OMG BFF. AWTTW, put the cell phone down and drive, Moron.

I recently heard a report of a 9-year-old girl that was injured as she plowed the ATV she was driving into a tree because she was checking her email on her cell phone. Really? Why does a 9-year-old need a cell phone? And why was she driving an ATV without supervision? All moot. A future Cell Assassin in the making. The problem is only going to get worse. Someone should invent a text-blocking app for cell phones in moving vehicles.

I did read about an app that turns "text" into speech and speech into "text" so you can drive and "text." Isn't that just talking on the phone? Isn't that a bit redundant? Am I missing something here?

It's my opinion that Cell Assassins have a death wish; they apparently want to commit suicide or, if you like, Cellicide. If they only killed or maimed themselves that would be one thing (fewer morons on the road and I'm all for that), but they take innocent lives, maim innocent people, and ruin families forever.

Just today, before writing this, I saw in my local paper that a man had run a red light, T-boned another car, and killed the driver. The victim was a 17-year-old girl. Her family will be forever damaged. He was charged with Reckless Homicide. He ran the red light because he was "distracted by his cell phone." Don't tell me that Cell Assassin is not an appropriate name.

Remember Rule One. If you have to use your cell phone while driving, make a call, hold the phone up to your ear and "talk" to your BFF; keep your eyes on the road. You'll still be distracted, but *maybe* you won't cruise through the red light and hit me. I don't have a death wish. Oh wait, sorry, **i dnt hv a death wsh**.

There needs to be a Hot Line where Players can report Cell Assassins they see on the road. "Texting drivers" are 20 times more likely to be involved in a personal-injury crash than those who don't text, and about 6 times more likely to be in a serious accident (multiple deaths) than our next category, The Impaired Drivers.

"SHUT UP AND HAND ME THE KEYS"

Only slightly less dangerous than a Tisket is **The Impaired Driver (Stoned, Medicated, or Drunk Drivers).**

Stoned drivers (potheads) are usually paranoid so they're the most likely to be driving slowly. They have thoughts like: *Oh my God, that cop over there knows I don't have shoes on, and I'm going two miles over the speed limit. He knows I'm stoned. Must drive exactly the speed limit.* As a side note: it's an urban myth that it's illegal to drive barefooted. You have a right to bare feet.

C. G. KNIGHT

And stoners are the ones most likely to forget where they were going. So be on the lookout for that stoned driver who suddenly realizes he needs to turn right, but he's already past where he could safely turn, then decides to make an attempt at the last second, hits the brake, jerks the wheel, hits the gas, and makes an amazingly-wide right turn barely missing oncoming traffic. *Oh my God. Act normal.*

The trouble with Drunk or Overly-Medicated Drivers is they're fearless and stupid and many times barely aware of what they're doing. They *are* on the road with you. I have some very personal ties to this category of driver. I have a friend that's an alcoholic. I let him live with me for a few months (big mistake) when he was homeless. He's this wonderfully funny, very intelligent man when he's sober, but when he starts drinking (straight vodka) he turns into a belligerent (cursing me and my family) falling-down drunk. That's the scary thing. The alcohol so depresses his senses that he literally just falls over, sometimes face first sometimes backwards.

The breaking point for me was the night I heard a terrible crashing noise coming from the stairs that lead down from the room I was letting him use. When I opened the door to the stairwell, there he lay at the bottom, in a crumpled heap, obviously hammered. I helped him to his feet and led him to a chair in my living room. He wasn't injured. I don't know how he wasn't injured, but he wasn't.

He sat there for a moment, twitching and jerking, his head bobbing this way and that, then he looked at me and slurred, "I'm going to the liquor store, you want anything?" I told him he wasn't going anywhere but to bed. He got angry and started cursing me and saying everything was my fault, and "fuck

15

you, I'm going anyway." He stood up, turned, took one step and fell face-first with his arms at his sides. With a loud sickening crack, like a bat striking a ball, his head caught the edge of my marble-top coffee table, ricocheted and snapped sideways. He then hit the floor unconscious.

I quickly went and rolled him over. I thought he was dead. And in truth, for an instant, I almost hoped he was dead so he could escape the life he was living, (if you've never seen the face of alcoholism it's a sad and terrible thing), but then he started to come to. There wasn't even a mark where his forehead had hit the marble table; again, uninjured. I finally got him to his feet and led him upstairs and put him in bed. The next day I checked him into a homeless shelter that specialized in treating alcoholics. I've only seen him once since that day.

I've been told by friends that I saved his life by putting him in that treatment program. But it wasn't some magnanimous gesture on my part, it was self preservation. I wanted him gone so he wouldn't actually die in my home, or burn my house down; he was a smoker as well. I thought later that I should have made a video of him when he was drunk so he could see what he turned into (alcoholics are unaware of their Mr. Hyde transformations). Maybe that would have helped him. For those of you living with alcoholics, I'm so very sorry for you.

That was a long story just to make a point. But people like him are on the road with you every day. They are not in control. "Shut up and hand me the keys." Of course, not every drunk on the road is an alcoholic, some are just weekend partiers, but alcohol affects them the same as it affected my friend. Their awareness and reactions are depressed. According to an article I read on LifeTips.com, one person is killed every half hour in the U.S. due to drunk driving; that's 48 people every day. Couple that with all the over-medicated drivers and you have a lot of impaired drivers on the road with you.

The second most-abused category of drugs after marijuana is prescription pain killers. They depress the senses much the same as alcohol. According to a recent report, forty-two tons of hydrocodone is dispensed yearly by pharmacies in the U.S. I wonder how many hydrocodone pills it takes to weigh forty-two tons.

I worked with a fellow for a short period that had a pain pill addiction. He'd come to work and you could see how messed-up he was; he had slurred speech, his knees were weak and his legs wobbly. You could see in his eyes that he wasn't quite there. Management gave him several opportunities to straighten up but to no avail and they were forced to let him go. A few weeks after his termination he was found dead from a pain pill overdose. He was 45-years-old; a sad and senseless death. The scary thing was he drove to work in that semi-conscious state. He was on the road with me and you.

Report every Impaired Driver you see. Call 911 and report their location, vehicle description, and license plate number before they kill somebody. Get them the hell off the road before they hit me or you. And you seem like such a nice person. I'd hate to see you get hurt or killed.

JEEPERS CREEPERS

Creepers are those drivers that for whatever reason drive 5 to 10 mph slower than the suggested speed limit. They're not particularly dangerous. They're just frustrating to be behind. Which brings us to **The Ultimate Goal**

- Every time you get in your vehicle you must safely get to wherever you are going as fast as possible with the least amount of resistance and the fewest amount of stops. Creepers are "in the way" of achieving that Goal.

THERE ARE SEVERAL VERSIONS OF THE CREEPER

The Safe Creeper: They believe that if you drive very slowly you are being safe. Maybe that's true, maybe it's not. That's why there's a minimum suggested speed limit on interstate highways. Drivers that are moving too slowly can cause accidents. If you're cruising the highway at 75 mph and you suddenly come upon a Creeper doing 45, bad things can happen. If a Tisket going 75 comes upon a Creeper doing 45, bad things are likely to happen. "Hypermilers" fit this category as well, but more on that later.

The Handicapped Creeper: They drive slowly out of necessity. It should be obvious that you leave Handicapped Drivers alone. Life is tough enough for some people. Give them some space. And don't park in a Handicapped parking space unless you're handicapped; even if it's just for a minute. I used to keep business-card-sized notes to stick under the windshield wiper of unauthorized vehicles parked in Handicapped spaces that simply read, "Stupidity is not a Handicap."

The Over-Cautious Creeper: I hate to get behind an overly cautious driver. They start slowing down as they approach a green light because they're afraid that the light might change to yellow just as they get there. Oh My God, what would happen then? They slow down to go up a snow-covered hill, then get stuck halfway up and start sliding off the road because they've lost their forward momentum. (Driving tip: You reduce speed going down a snow- or ice-covered hill. You need forward momentum going uphill to get over the top when you don't have adequate traction.) They sit at Stop signs for way too long before proceeding. They won't go at a right turn on red because they see an approaching vehicle a half mile down the road. I know everybody has their own driving comfort level, but these people drive me crazy.

The Blue-Collar Creeper (Semis, construction vehicles, delivery trucks, school buses, that sort of thing): Sometimes these vehicles are Creepers, and sometimes they're not. I have seen more than a few Jerks driving semis. I was once run off the interstate by a semi changing lanes because the driver failed to get over soon enough for his exit. I didn't get hurt, thanks for asking. I did get angry after I skidded to a halt and the "scare" wore off.

Try to keep in mind that Blue-Collar Creepers are working. Give them some space.

The Elderly Creeper: If someone is still above ground and kicking at 80-years-old and wants to drive slowly, get off their ass. I know there's some debate about when driving privileges should be taken from elderly drivers, and I know there are some elderly drivers that shouldn't be on the road, but I'd rather be on the road with an Elderly Creeper than a Cell Assassin. I don't have a death wish. I'll take the Creeper every time.

[I have to tell this joke, though: Two older individuals were out for a Sunday drive, enjoying the countryside, getting away from the bustle of the city, when they came into a small rural town with one traffic signal. As they approached the traffic signal, the passenger noticed that the light was red, but the driver never slowed and drove right through the red light and right on out of town. He just shrugged and assumed that the driver must have been familiar with that road and that little town and knew it was safe to cruise right through that red light.

A little while later they went through another small rural town with one traffic signal. Again, the same thing happened. The driver cruised through that red light as well. The passenger finally spoke up, "Didn't you see that red light back there? That's the second light you've run today." The driver blinked and replied, "Oh, am I driving?"] I know, I shouldn't poke fun at the elderly. That *is* where we're all headed.

Besides, an elderly person could have a Driving Phobia. My grandmother had a fear of oncoming traffic. It kept her from ever getting a driver's license. She could ride with someone driving next to oncoming traffic, she just couldn't do it, bless her heart. Though, Driving Phobias are not limited to the elderly.

A Driving Phobia is where you start becoming afraid to drive because you think you're going to be killed. You start worrying that the driver coming at you on a two-lane road might have a heart attack or a stroke then veer across the centerline and kill you in a head-on crash. Drivers have heart attacks, and strokes, and seizures on the road every day. You never know what's coming at you.

I can sort of identify with people who have driving phobias. I get it. I've been driving for years. I've driven through thousands of intersections, where I had the green light, unscathed. It turns into a phobia when all you can think about is that "sooner or later" something bad is going to happen. Like rolling "snake eyes" if you keep rolling the dice.

Haven't you done that? Start wondering as you approach an intersection where you have the right-of-way, that maybe this is going to be it. That a Cell Assassin is going to run his red light, T-bone you and you're going to die. Did you tell your children that you loved them this morning? Who's going to water your plants? Did you pay the water bill? Have all those unanswered thoughts run through your mind as you approach a beckoning green light? No? I bet it'll cross your mind now.

It's a lot like telling someone to not think about their tongue. (Thinking about your tongue, aren't you?) Sorry, I've been told more than once that I have a twisted sense of humor. I just want you to be aware that there are people with driving phobias driving right next to you. Consider this: If you're riding right on the ass of a Driving Phobic it might cause them to have a panic attack. Personally, I don't want to be on the road with someone having a panic attack. It's best not to ride too closely to another vehicle anyway. I'm not sure, but I might have just created Driving Phobic Phobia.

The Intentional Creeper: The Intentional Creeper is someone who's playing the Game. They're hoping to frustrate you by driving slowly. They enjoy watching Ultimate Goal practitioners squirm in their rearview mirror. They're the worst kind of Creeper. They belong to a group I refer to as the ICU (Intentional Creeper Underground), *a secret society* of drivers bent on keeping us from "making good time." To my knowledge no ICU member has ever admitted to the existence of their organization. Apparently, they have no leader or newsletter. They operate as single sluggish cells, like some road bacteria, with nowhere to go and plenty of time to get there.

If you find yourself behind an ICU don't get frustrated. They're bottom feeders; they thrive on your frustration. If you want to mess with one, just drive slower than they're going. I did exactly that recently when I found myself behind an ICU. It was actually quite a bit of fun.

I knew he was an ICU because he was driving very slowly and he kept checking his mirrors trying to leach all the frustration out of me. I kept reducing speed and he kept trying, with no success, to keep me right on his bumper. It was like some backwards race. I could feel his pain as his lead grew and he realized that a "superior creeper" was behind him. He had to surrender when the two-lane road we were traveling split into four. I re-engaged my warp drive and went on, smiling, fully enjoying myself. I love the Game.

Personally, I think Creepers should have a warning label on their bumpers that says CAUTION! CREEPER! Maybe with a picture of a smiling tortoise as a universal image.

THE JERK

The Jerk is really just an immature driver, "an excitable child" behind the wheel. Though it has nothing to do with age. It's all about attitude. You'll see him on every outing. He's the one most frustrated by Creepers. In fact, to him, everyone is a Creeper. He flies up right behind you and rides inches from your bumper, sometimes flashing his lights, anxious to get around you. He has a need-for-speed. He has a need-to-be-in-front. If a Creeper is a Tortoise, then the Jerk is a Hare.

When I find a Jerk on my bumper, I use a formula to determine how fast I go. My speed is inversely proportional to the distance between my bumper and the Jerk. The closer he gets, the slower I go. Huge satisfaction factor here. It's a Creeper thing. I can feel his frustration washing over me like a soothing breeze.

So Jerks, if you get behind me, keep a respectable distance. Sit on my ass and you'll be there a while. And when I do get over, I'll do it so slowly that you'll most probably crowd another lane to get around me quicker. The more you crowd another lane or shoulder, the more points I get. That means your frustration level was so high that you couldn't wait the two seconds more it took me to change lanes. And, as you go by, if you blow an angry horn (Points), or call me some name (Double Points), I'll just smile, oblivious, and wave like, do I know you?

On multilane highways you see Jerks attempting to pass an entire line of drivers who are trying to get past a Creeper Semi in the right lane as I've demonstrated here.

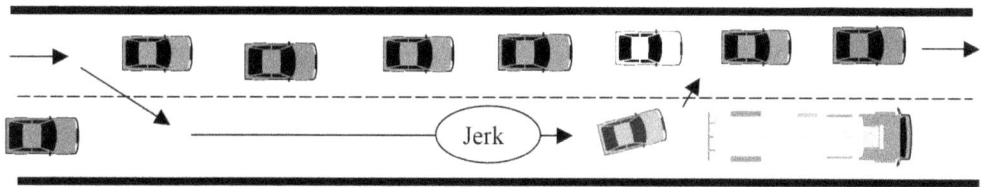

Okay, pop quiz. If you're in the white car, what should you do when the Jerk in the gray car tries to cut in front of you? This should be obvious. You close the gap and you hope that the entire line of vehicles behind you close any gaps where he might squeeze in. And, as a plus, if things go perfectly, maybe more cars will fall in line where he jumped out and keep him stuck behind the Creeper Semi until everyone has cleared. Even though the Game is not a team sport, I love the sense of fellowship when an entire line of cars team up to prevent some Jerk from cutting in at the front. Stay strong, Players! Don't let him in.

A less obnoxious version of a Jerk is a **White Rabbit**. You know, from Alice in Wonderland. "I'm late, I'm late, for a very important date." They're the ones that don't include traffic problems when calculating the time it's going to take to get to the 2:00 movie. "Let's see, it's ten miles down the interstate, then take the mall exit. The Movieplex is behind the mall. It's Saturday, so it might be *a little busy* but you can *always* find a parking spot behind the mall. We should probably leave by 1:45. I wouldn't want to be late."

Then they get on the interstate and wouldn't you know it, there's been an accident. With all the emergency vehicles blocking the road it's down to one lane of traffic moving 15 mph. And somehow, inevitably, they end up behind me.

I'll have to admit that torturing a White Rabbit is more fun than torturing a Jerk. Jerks are just speed freaks. White Rabbits actually have someplace to be. You can see it in their anxious faces; their shoulders hunched up, their children in the backseat screaming, "Mommy, we're going to be late. Hurry!" Same rule applies; the closer you get to my bumper the slower I go. Poor planning on your part, does not affect me in the least.

I will admit, however, that I've been a White Rabbit, and you have too. You're late and traffic sucks. You're missing an important meeting at work. Your kid needs to make the school-trip bus or get left behind. Mom, Hurry! Or you're late to church. Oh My God, you can't be late to church. That's when time changes, it slows down.

Traffic signals seem to take twice as long to change. Come on, come on, come on. You try to "psychically will" a green light to appear before you. You look at the clock to confirm that ten minutes have passed, but it's only been one. Then, Finally! Everyone starts to go. Everyone but a Creeper in front of you. Damn it, move! You're riding inches from the Creeper's bumper; your hand reaching for the horn… That's why White Rabbits are so easy to torture. They're trapped in a time warp. Allow plenty of time to get where you're going or risk getting stuck behind me.

THE ANGRY DRIVER

The angry driver is to be avoided at all costs. They are extremely danger-ous. Nothing is off limits to an angry driver. They will speed out of control, swerve in and out of traffic just to "get even." By God, you're not going to cut them off. It's where the term Road Rage comes from. I witnessed two very an-gry drivers recently. I didn't see the infraction or the perceived infraction, but I did see the aftermath.

I was sitting at a red light when, across from me coming the other way, two cars, one hot on the other one's tail, came screeching to a stop at the red light. The moron in the front car was trying to turn right, but couldn't because of traffic. The moron in the trailing car jumped out, ran up to the front car, jerked open the door and pulled the other moron out. A fist fight ensued.

Because the extracted moron didn't have time to put his car in Park, his unpiloted 3,000 pounds of life-changing carnage proceeded to roll into mov-ing traffic. As push came to shove, one angry moron ended up on top of the other angry moron and was choking him. I started to get concerned when it appeared that no one was going to intervene and that the moron being choked might actually die right in front of me.

In my mind, I planned to pull through the intersection and head right for the morons, pretending I was going to run them over in an effort to stop the ridiculousness. But before I could put my plan into action, apparently the murderous inclination abated and the top moron got up, cursed and kicked the one on the ground, ran back to his car and left.

The other moron, after getting to his feet, saw his car in the ditch across the road. Miraculously it hadn't caused a collision, but crossing traffic had to swerve and stop to miss the unpiloted vehicle. A very dangerous situation for everyone.

What can be learned from this incident? Let the anger go. I can't believe that someone would risk going to prison for murdering another driver. Really? You want to become somebody's prison-bitch because you killed a moron that cut you off? You're willing to change your life forever?

Get a grip! Go to anger management classes. There's nothing that happens on the road worth going to prison for. Let someone else drive if you can't handle the stresses of the road. Shit happens. Get over it. If you see an angry driver, get over and let them go. Live to drive another day.

DRONES

A Drone is a tired driver. They're just getting off a twelve hour shift and they "don't give a hoot about nothing." You can be a White Rabbit or a Jerk right on his ass; a Drone is in no hurry. He's barely aware that you're even there. I have to admit that I've been that person. And I'm the worst version you've ever seen.

The interstate highways in my area are all six lanes, so each side has three lanes. I often go hiking in the Daniel Boone National Forest in a very geologically interesting area about forty minutes from my home. My friends and I hike three or four hours on each visit, and it's strenuous. I'm usually tired for the drive home. When I get on the interstate I get in the center lane, set my Cruise for 5-over and go into Drone Mode. I turn on my stereo, sink back in the seat, and let my subconscious drive me home.

If you've done any long distance driving, you've been in Drone Mode - one moment you had 100 miles to go, and the next you only have 15. You get lost in your thoughts and you ignore the road signs because, well, you have 100 miles to go, no need to pay attention right now, then suddenly, where'd the time go, you're almost home.

Sometimes this can be a blessing, and sometimes it can be disconcerting. Like, OMG, I'm missing forty minutes of time. How did I get here so quickly? Was I abducted by aliens? Did my Cruise Control secretly take command and gradually accelerate to 88 mph and I traveled through time? I am wearing a stainless steel watch.

When I'm in Drone Mode, a Pod of semis, several in each lane, each with a Jerk behind the wheel, all bearing down on me, wanting me to Get Over because I'm being a Drone Creeper, it doesn't matter; I'm not moving. I'm not going to touch my Cruise Control. I'm in the center lane going 5-over, you'll just have to go around.

I am amused by drivers who get on my ass and stay there hoping I'll see them. Hoping I'll get over. Hoping. Some of them stay there for miles. Finally, they all give up and go around. And I always get that dagger stare as they go by. I get Double Points if they actually flip me off. I just look surprised and wave like, do I know you? Some of the looks are priceless.

Another Drone is an elderly driver. The eighty-year-old I mentioned before is set in his ways. Dern fool behind him anyway. By God, he's eighty and that entitles him to drive any damned way he pleases. He's in no hurry. Hell, he's retired and life is good.

A common Drone Mode moment is when you're driving along lost in your thoughts, and you make a turn by habit at an intersection where you turn daily on your way to work, even though that's not what you needed to do. Then, slightly confused, you snap back to reality and realize that it's Saturday and you're headed to the grocery store, not going to work. We are all creatures of habit, particularly when subconsciously driving in Drone Mode.

THE NEW DRIVER

Ah, the Newbie. I don't like being on the road with Newbies. I always want to mess with them but they're like a one-legged man in a butt-kicking contest; it's just no fun, no challenge. I have to force myself to ignore those Student Driver vehicles; though I suppose they have to learn about the realities of the road sometime.

I guess that a few of you Newbies are surprised to hear that other drivers might be messing with you; some of you fresh from Driving School where you've been taught proper procedure and the "order of things" that makes the road safe. And they're correct, there is a safe order to driving on the road. I suggest that you learn everything in your driving manual. Can't hurt to know the rules. And I'm sure you do. Well, I hope you do. I don't have a death wish.

I try to avoid Newbies because of their lack of experience and their belief that they are indestructible. They drive the same regardless of road conditions. You'll find them in a wreck in a rain storm because they failed to factor in water on the road. Always be a player. Be aware that you change how you drive according to weather conditions. Water, snow, ice, and wet leaves on the road are slick.

One dry, sunny day in my youth I took a shortcut across a neighborhood street that was hill-shaped, up one side to the top, then down the other side where the street ended at a Stop sign at one of the busiest streets in our town, Broadway.

As I cleared the top of the hill and started down towards the Stop sign, I discovered that city workers were flushing fire hydrants and water was flowing down the middle of the street where I was driving a little more than the suggested speed limit. Well, I was young and dumb, it was probably more like 15 mph over, and I panicked because a very busy Broadway was only seconds away. I hit my brakes and started sliding out of control on wet pavement, on a dry day, towards traffic whizzing by on Broadway.

That's when I got that *sinking feeling*, when you think you're going to die. I was in 3,000 pounds of life-changing carnage, I had zero control, my adrenaline had kicked in, and my heart was racing as I started to dread the possible outcome. But I wasn't going down without a fight.

I started pumping my brakes and turning into the skid. I finally came to a stop a little sideways and a little too much out into Broadway. Luckily, at that moment, no traffic was coming. I was able to put my car in Reverse and back up to the Stop sign, embarrassed, but glad to be alive and uninjured. Your tire's connection to the road is your lifeline. Pay attention. Don't drive too fast when road conditions are anything but perfect.

THE OUT-OF-STATE DRIVER

I guess my favorite category to discuss is the out-of-state driver, or as I sometimes refer to them, "Fur-in-ners." Not foreigners in the traditional sense, just anybody from another state. And if you're from Canada, well, you're a Ca-knucklehead if you cut me off. I read recently that Canadians refer to Americans as Upper Mexicans or Continent Hogs. Too funny.

Out-of-state drivers are the easiest to make fun of. It seems to me that most states have some sort of *border war* when it comes to driving. For some reason, drivers from any-given-state don't like the drivers from any-other-state (particularly from an adjacent state), and they usually have creative names to call these offending drivers.

For instance, if a driver from Florida cuts me off he's a Floridiot. More name calling occurs when, in my area, we denounce "a Buckeye," from Ohio. There's nothing particularly insulting about the word Buckeye. Here, though, it has to be said with such venom that there's no question as to its meaning. Buckeye - rolls off the tongue like fiberglass.

Anyone from the South can be called a Hick or a Hillbilly. I'm from Kentucky and my favorite term for a local moron is a Hickamy (hick-a-my). I coined the term after a friend of mine from Eastern Kentucky said something with his backwoods up-in-the-holler accent. He said, "Then it bounced ryte (right) off the wall and hit me ryte in the ford (forehead). "Ryte in the Ford?" I laughed. When he realized what he'd said, he looked at me, laughed and said, "What kind of <u>hick am I</u>?" Thus, the birth of the Hickamy.

Did you know that a Hickamy invented the tooth brush? Anyone else would have called it a Teeth Brush. Do you know what a Hickamy divorce and a tornado have in common? Either way somebody loses a trailer. I can take these jokes to a level that would shock most of you so I'll just leave things… ryte where they are.

Okay, I lied; I have to tell this story. It has nothing to do with driving but it's a worthy Hickamy tale. One of my first summer jobs was with a sink manufacturing company. My job was to mix marble dust with an epoxy compound, pour it over a mold smeared with a little paint and voila, once the epoxy hardened; a faux-marble sink.

I had only been working there a week when another employee, an older gentleman, came up to me and asked (while I was mid-sink) if I had a Stanchon Cord. Being new to the company, I assumed that Stanching was something you did to a sink, and it involved a cord. So I said, "No, I don't think I do. What is a stanchon cord?" He looked at me frustrated and said, "You know. You plug one end of it into a wall," his hands smoothing the thought for me as he looked over the top of his glasses, "then you plug something else in the other end. A stanchon cord." I laughed and said, "Oh, an extension cord. No, I don't have one." That was my first close encounter with a Hickamy. He was a nice guy, he just talked funny. Hell, I talk funny. It takes all kinds. Where was I? Oh yeah. Out-of-state drivers.

Another great other-driver nickname comes from a poem I saw in a bathroom stall at a rest area in Oklahoma. Apparently there's no love lost between an Okie and a Texan (adjacent states). Anyway, neatly printed in my stall were these words; "Here I sit my buns a flexin', giving birth to another Texan." It's rare that I see a Texas license plate in my parts, but when I do, I affectionately call them Texas Turds, inspired by that great little rhyme. I'm sure you have your own inappropriate terms of disrespect for your least favorite drivers. You'll have to share them with me sometime. I can always use the extra input.

And, of course, this is all in fun. I have nothing against Texans, Floridians, Buckeyes, Canadians, Mexicans, or anybody really. The reason that out-of-state morons seem to do more stupid stuff than local morons is that they're not as familiar with the local road layout as you. So cut them some slack. But feel free to sling these insults at will. Because I know one day you're going to get stuck behind me when I'm in Drone Mode and Hickamy is going to be the nicest thing you call me.

THE BACKSEAT DRIVER

I've been driving for more years than I care to admit. I've seen and done some dumb stunts on the road, but the thing that irritates me more than getting stuck between a Creeper and a Jerk is a Backseat Driver. Of course, Backseat Driver is a relative term and has nothing to do with their actual position in the car. It's a title given to any passenger who believes that you, as the driver, need help driving. They can see that your driving skills are woefully inadequate and it's up to them to *help you drive.*

If you're going to ride with me, you have to *let me drive* or I'll pull over and *let you out.* I don't want to hear that I'm driving too slowly or too fast. I'll change lanes when the opportunity presents itself. I'll drive the speed I want. I'll use my turn signals when I want. I'll take the route *I think* will quickly get me where I want to go regardless of whether you think it's the best way or not. I'm behind the steering wheel, it's my foot on the gas pedal; I'm the one driving. I don't need any help. If you don't like how I drive, don't ride with me.

The worst of the Backseat Drivers are the Gaspers. They gasp when you make a turn in front of oncoming traffic. They'll scare the bejeezus out of you. You'll be driving along, fully in control, begin to make a turn, when, "Gasp! Look out! Don't you see that car coming?" Their arms flailing about as though death is imminent, their foot mashing an imaginary passenger-side brake pedal. You look to see if you missed something. A hundred yards away you confirm a Creeper inching up the road and your assessment that not only can you make the turn safely, but the two semis behind you can make the turn as well.

I suppose it's acceptable that you, as my passenger, are participating in your own health and well-being, but please save your gasps for actual emergencies. Believe me, I try to be aware of all that's going on around me and I promise I'll try not to put you, or more importantly, me in any danger. I do, however, want you to speak up if you see an actual emergency, so I guess it's a double-edged sword.

Case in point: a group of friends and I were leaving a local restaurant. I was behind the wheel, sitting at a red light waiting for the green. When the light changed, I started into the intersection. My passenger in the front seat, Ray, hollered, "Stop." And I did. Then I saw what he saw; a Tisket, cell phone in hand, running the red light. The Tisket must have glanced up at the last second because he swerved barely missing my front bumper, the wind shock from his passing vehicle shaking my car.

If I hadn't stopped when Ray spoke up, I would have been T-boned and probably killed. So I'm not opposed to any input from my passengers. I did learn one thing: when I get a green light, I now look to see if anyone is running their red light before I proceed. The morons *are* out to get us.

THE COURTEOUS DRIVER

I'm all for being courteous. The world is a far cry from being courteous these days. You can't go into a fast-food restaurant or a convenience store anymore and expect to be treated with anything but contempt. Apparently, the employees at these places hate their jobs and they take it out on you. I suppose good help *is* hard to find.

As far as courteous driving, I'm all for letting another vehicle "in" when traffic is at a standstill. It's five o'clock, no one's moving, fine, let in all the vehicles you want. They want to get home, too. But don't stop moving traffic so you can "be courteous."

I've seen courteous drivers stop one lane of moving traffic and signal a waiting vehicle to turn in front of them across a moving-adjacent-lane that the signaled driver can't see, putting everyone at risk. The rule is: the waiting vehicle will proceed when the way is clear. You rule-changing courteous drivers are not supposed to suddenly stop moving traffic to let someone in or to turn left. If you get rear-ended, you deserve it.

If traffic is moving, keep it moving. Don't change the rules of the road so you can "feel good about yourself." Get a job at a convenience store or a fast-food restaurant. Do some volunteer work. You're an accident waiting to happen.

There should be a warning label on the back of courteous drivers' vehicles that reads; Danger! This vehicle makes Sudden Stops for self-esteem building.

I let vehicles "in" all the time when traffic is at a standstill. The thing that gets me is when I do grant right-of-way to another driver and they don't give a nod or a wave that says *thank you.* I didn't have to let you in. I could have left you trapped until all that traffic piled up behind me gets past you. Always say *thanks.*

THE OVER-CONFIDENT DRIVER

I consider myself to be an excellent driver, maybe not so much in my youth, but now that I have lots of experience, definitely so. And considering all the close calls I've survived, I feel that I can handle most situations. I do handle emergency situations well. Always have. I feel confident in my driving abilities. But being over-confident can put you and others in danger.

Jerks and Drunk Drivers are examples of over-confident drivers. Although over-confidence, arrogance, and risk taking are usually associated with new, young drivers who have an exaggerated sense of their own capabilities, it's been my experience that there is no age limit for stupidity.

There's nothing worse than a driver who feels that they can drive faster than everyone else in poor weather conditions because they've driven fast before and all the Creepers are just Weenies for driving slowly in the rain or on snow and ice. *Heck,* they think, *I know what I'm doing. The steering wheel makes the car go left or right. The gas pedal makes the car go fast, and the brake pedal makes the car stop. What else do you need to know? Shut up and hand me the keys.* (We'll discuss Driving Skills later.)

One study I read said that 98% of drivers feel that they are safer drivers than everyone else, and 90% of drivers claimed to be very confident conscientious drivers. Somebody is lying to somebody. You've seen all the morons on the road, right?

Much closer to the truth is another study I read claiming that 90% of drivers admitted to speeding, 74% admitted to driving tired, 35% admitted to driving after consuming alcohol, and 34% admitted to texting or reading email while driving. All over-confident activities. Even considering all this over-confidence, only 1% thought that they were being less safe than other drivers.

You know what they say about one bad apple. Though, in my opinion, the road is covered in bad apples. It's the good apple that's a rarity. You and I, of course, are good apples. The rest are rotten to the core. Just remember Rule Three and you might make it to your next birthday. Well, enough talk about the various kinds of drivers. It's time to talk about....

CITY DRIVING

C ity Driving is a complication of Stop signs and Stop lights and one-way streets. You have to deal with Creepers and Jerks and White Rabbits. And let's not forget Rush Hour Traffic. On the bright side, however, there are endless opportunities to play the Game. Keeping all that and the Ultimate Goal in mind, any trip through the city requires careful planning and execution. Can you get from Point A to Point B with no stops and make it in record time?

The problem is there are too many obstacles, too many places where you *have to stop.* You must learn to read traffic and react correctly to be a true aficionado of the Ultimate Goal as I've demonstrated in the next diagram. If you're in the white car, which of the two vehicles do you get behind when you have a choice at a red light? Which driver in which lane is the most likely to move first?

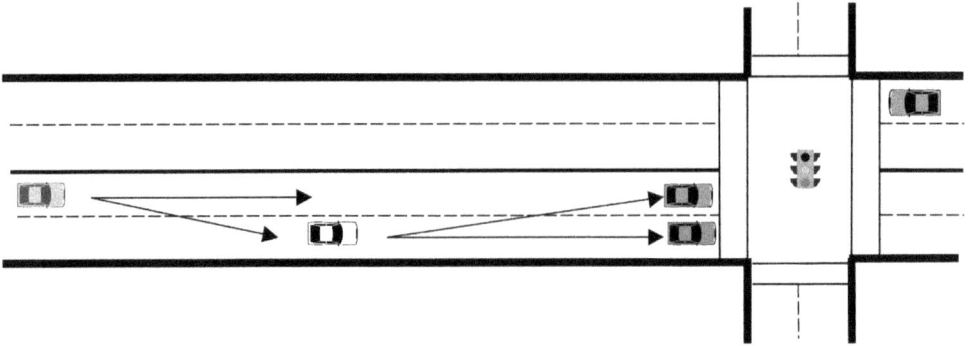

If you'd been paying attention and had been able to observe the two drivers as they approached the light, you'd know that the driver in the right lane is a Creeper, so the correct move is to take the left lane before the car coming up behind you beats you to that spot. This does two things: it hopefully puts you behind a Player, and it puts the approaching car in third place in pole position at the light.

You get Points for taking the second-place slot from the approaching car. Although, if it was me in that car, I would see your move and I would take the right lane in hopes that you chose incorrectly. I would then get your Points because you failed to deny me a second-place slot. Then we'd see who was correct when the light changed. Some days are diamond and some are stone.

However, if you came upon the two cars already stopped at the red light and you had no knowledge of their driving characteristics prior to the light, you must make a decision based on experience or logic. Both vehicles have a front slot, so either could be a Player. Consider the make and model of the two vehicles. Which might belong to a Player? Which one is inching forward as though anxious for the green light? Sometimes you just have to roll the dice and pick one.

It's always better to be behind a Player. They're the most likely to quickly go when the light turns green, giving you a chance to pass the Creeper and gain a better pole position at the next light. The given example is fairly simple and the reality of most situations is more complex, but the strategy is sound. Evaluate both lanes, look for obvious Creepers such as large trucks, RV's, or buses, then pick a lane and live with the choice.

The most frustrating thing that can happen is you chose a lane because the other has several semis, then, when the light turns green, a Creeper in your lane goes slower than the semis. Makes you want to scream. Creeper 1, you 0.

In city driving the Game is usually played in segments, one light to the next, Players jockeying for pole position at each intersection, hoping to get a front spot at the light. If you are Ultimate Goal oriented, it helps to have a front spot. However, don't break Rule Two just to get a good pole position. Sit back, relax, and don't take dangerous chances.

But be aware that there are plenty of Jerks who *will* take dangerous chances; Reckless Drivers that will cut in and out of traffic, barely missing other cars just to "get even," or gain a few seconds, or get that front spot. Keep your eyes open and live to play another day.

A quick discussion of my point system: The way I play you get Points, Double Points, or Triple Points. I give numeric values to Pole Positions (that's when you're stuck at a red light in position, waiting for the-race-to-the-next-light to begin); they are valued: 10 points for a front spot, 9 points for the second spot, 8 points for the third spot, etc.

Minus Points are awarded to other drivers (morons) you see doing something, in your opinion, stupid. I usually just say, "Minus Points," when I see a moronic driver, just as I would say, "Points," when I, as usual, do something good. You can, however, give a numeric value to a negative judgment. Something like, "minus a thousand points," when you see an extreme moron.

And though it rarely happens, I will award Points to another driver if they handle a particular situation well, even if they leave me stuck at a red light as they cruise off victorious. Sometimes you just have to say, "Well played." Though I would never award Double Points to another driver; it just isn't done. And in truth, I seldom actually say, "Minus Points." I usually say something much more graphic. Triple Points are for very special occasions. I'll get to that.

LAST ONE THROUGH, PLEASE CLOSE THE DOOR

Another popular Game I see is "the last one through the yellow light." Better than getting a 10-point pole position is being the last one through the yellow light. In a 1984 movie called "Starman" an extraterrestrial takes a human form, ends up driving a car and says to his human passenger, "I know how the traffic lights work. Red means Stop. Green means Go. And Yellow means Go Faster." Ah, from the mouths of aliens.

It's great to get through the yellow light at the last second; to be the last one through (definite Points). But don't run a red light to save a few seconds on your errand to the grocery store. Running a red light is a Tisket thing, a Cell Assassin stunt; it's how you get killed or kill someone else or both.

I'm not saying that I don't try to get through yellow lights, I do. And I've cut it close and had lights turn red just as I pass under. But if I see I'm not going to make the yellow light, I stop and wait for the next green light. With alarming frequency I see Jerks and White Rabbits running red lights, plowing through intersections well after their light has turned red. So be on the lookout for these morons. Again, I'd hate to see you get hurt. You seem like such a good person.

SOME DAYS ARE STONE

Okay, let's say that you chose correctly in the last example. You got behind the correct car at the red light, which let you finally get around the Creeper and you have open road in front of you. Your job now is to get-to-and-through-the-next-light before the group of vehicles from which you escaped catch up. You enjoy seeing them at a distance in your rearview mirror. You want them to get caught at the red light after you pass under the yellow. Points if it happens, Double Points if you're the only one from your group to get through. This doesn't always work out the way you want.

Sometimes you jump out to a big lead, hoping the above scenario happens, but instead you get caught at the next light and have to sit and wait as the group you left behind slowly catches up. What should you do then?

The best you can hope for is that the next light turns red well before you get to it. When this happens, lift your foot off the gas and let the momentum of your vehicle slowly carry you to the light. In other words, you become an Ultimate Creeper.

You don't want to give any satisfaction to the group you left behind. You don't want them to slowly catch up and again be equal with you. And you definitely don't want to be sitting at a red light through most of the cycle, and then have a Creeper get there just as the light turns green and not have to wait at all (a moral victory for the Creeper).

So you keep letting your car gradually slow down until the group you left behind almost catches up before you actually stop at the red light. At this point, however, you've lost any points for having a front pole position. Maybe you'll do better at the next light. You get Minus Points if, light after light, you speed ahead but get caught by the Creepers anyway. You may want to rethink this strategy.

TRAFFIC SIGNAL PATTERNS

Traffic signals are synchronized to allow groups of vehicles just enough time to get from one signal to the next before changing and stopping them, thereby moving traffic in chunks and controlling the speed of the drivers. That's why city driving is called Stop and Go.

Your goal is to always have a front pole position, immediately go when the signal turns green, quickly get up to speed, and make it through the next signal while the rest of your group gets caught by the red light. It happens, even in cities that you're unfamiliar with. However, the longer you live in an area, the more familiar you become with traffic signal patterns. And that can work to your advantage, particularly in pursuit of the Ultimate Goal.

As a local you know which light at which intersection turns green first; the straight lane light or the turning lane light. I've taken some very circuitous routes to get somewhere simply because I refuse to sit and wait at a light; because the turning light changes first, because the Ultimate Goal dictates that I keep moving. Sometimes I get there faster; sometimes it takes a bit longer, though I keep moving.

There are several places in my town where the traffic signals are timed such that if you drive exactly the suggested speed limit you'll catch eight or nine green lights in a row. That is if you're the lead car and you don't find a Creeper in the way. I love those sections.

Knowing the signal patterns also comes in handy if you've been passed by another player and you want to regain your honor while he's stuck at the next light in the straight lane. So you get in the turning lane, get the first green, then sail off victorious while he's has to wait for the straight lane green light.

TURNING LANES

Another place to be in Moron Lookout Mode is Multiple Turning Lanes. Increasingly traffic engineers are designing intersections with parallel turning lanes in order to move traffic more effectively through each signal. What you need to watch for at these intersections are **Drifters**. These are the morons that choose the wrong lane. For instance, they get in the inside turning lane but really need to be in the outside lane once they've turned, then, mid-turn, they drift into your lane. They don't look; they just change lanes.

Drifters are so self-absorbed they are unaware of anyone on the road but themselves. It's up to you to avoid a collision. You can blow your horn but that seldom changes things. That just makes the Drifter glance in his rear-view mirror and wave, "so sorry, I didn't see you." No, dumbass, you weren't looking. You got in the wrong lane to start with. You failed to plan ahead. You're why car insurance is so high. You're why accident attorneys make so much money.

The reality is that no two objects can occupy the same place at the same time. Apparently Drifters can't seem to grasp that concept. It's a simple law of physics. It's the very foundation of Rule Two – Your vehicle cannot collide with any other object. Nothing messes up your day like an accident. It's the antithesis of the Ultimate Goal.

In my opinion, an accident is a very rare occurrence. I know what you're thinking. What? Accidents happen every day. No, morons such as Drifters and Tiskets happen every day. Accidents are: a tire suddenly going flat and you lose control and hit another car; or you round a corner and there's debris or an animal in the road that you swerve to miss and hit a light pole. Accidents are caused by circumstances beyond your control.

Most *wrecks* are caused by *driver inattention* and by *driver error* and should not be called Accidents. They should be called Faults and most could be avoided if the drivers were simply paying attention. The Big Story at 6:00 should say, "Tisket causes a Huge Fault on the interstate; ten vehicles involved. Stick around for five minutes of extra-loud commercials and we'll have all the gory details right after the break."

Let's say what's really going on. "Moron driver is to blame for Fault on bypass." "Blunder by Cell Assassin kills fifteen." Some states have No-Fault car insurance. No-Fault insurance was invented so you can't sue the driver who caused the accident. Proponents of No-Fault insurance claim that *accidents are inevitable*; therefore, *at-fault drivers* should not necessarily be punished. *Accidents are inevitable?* I will agree that the road is infested with morons, but accidents are not inevitable. Get the morons to simply pay attention.

I say let's have At-Fault insurance. At least pass a <u>Three Faults and You're Out Rule.</u> If you are found at-fault three times you lose your driver's license. They do that with drunks. Why not do the same with inattentive drivers? I guess I'm getting way too worked up. I do that sometimes. Where was I? Oh yeah, turning lanes.

RIGHT TURN ON RED

You'd think that right turn on red is a simple concept to understand. You'd think that, but you'd be wrong. How many times have you been behind someone who just sits and waits for the green light before turning? The whole point of right turn on red is to save on fuel consumption. With gas prices constantly going up, sitting and waiting to turn, with your engine running is costing you money, but more importantly, you're in my way. I have the Ultimate Goal constantly in mind, so when it's clear, go. Don't make me blow my horn.

Okay, let's say you're waiting to turn-right-on-red, and behind you, second in line, is a Jerk. What should you do? If he rode your ass all the way up to the red light, sit there for a moment and enjoy being alive, then look to go.

But beware, because of his need-for-speed, a Jerk will sometimes watch oncoming traffic, determining, at least in his mind, when *you* should go. He projects his driving personality onto you (I call this auto-projection). He hits the gas because you should have hit yours. Then he smashes into your rear-end. "Heck, there was a two-car gap in front of that semi. The way was clear," he'll explain to the officer later. "The other guy should have gone."

This is a pretty common Fault of a driver second in line. The problem with "auto-projection" is everyone's comfort level is different. What looks like a mile to you looks like death to others. Your job as second in line is to watch the ass-end of the car in front of you. When there is no car in front of you, then look to go.

When I want to turn right on red and it appears that I'm going to have to wait a while, I start looking for a gap in traffic wherein a Creeper lies. There's always a gap caused by a Soft-Start (I'll explain later) or a Creeper. These gaps are usually not a good place to have a Gasper in the car.

I wouldn't turn into a gap that would cause an oncoming vehicle to hit their brakes. I like my gaps somewhat comfortable. I have, sometimes, cut it close. Jerks don't care, they'll jump into any gap, cause a Gasper to grab hold of their heart and the Oh, Shit! handle (you know, that little handle on the ceiling just above the car door).

There are vehicles that only a Moron would pull out in front of; for instance, a semi or a cement truck barreling down the road. Here in Kentucky, we have coal trucks and they're huge, loud, and heavy. Recently, I was waiting to turn right when I saw a comfortable gap in traffic coming at me. Problem was, the gap was in front of a coal truck, and he was picking up speed.

The gap kept getting closer but smaller, and just when it reached me and I had to decide if I should jump in there, the coal truck driver put the pedal-to-the-metal. Black smoke poured from his muffler with a loud BBBBRRAP. It sounded like machine gun fire. I half expected to see bullets ricocheting off the road in front of me. Coal truck 1, me 0. I decided not to turn in front of the scary oncoming coal truck.

You've no doubt made one of those uncomfortable right turns onto a four-lane road where the right lane is clear but the left lane has loads of traffic. I suppose it's the drivers in the oncoming left lane that are the most uncomfortable with this turn. They're not sure if you'll turn into the right lane or you'll not see them and cross into their lane. If I'm in the left lane and someone is turning right just as I drive past them, I always slow down; I make sure they are not crossing into my lane.

And I know you've seen those drivers that steer a little bit left to make a right turn, or a little bit right to turn left. What's that all about? It's like they think they're driving some huge vehicle that needs extra turning room. They swing out in a large arc as though the lane they want is somehow difficult to access. Most cars have a fairly tight turning radius; no need for wide arcing turns. Being behind these drivers is confusing. You're not sure which way they are actually going.

As a final note, once you've turned, and the road you've turned onto is a multilane road, make sure the way is clear, then get in the lane you need. Don't drive a hundred yards, let traffic build up beside you and behind you, then change lanes because, oh yeah, you need to turn left in a minute. Plan ahead. Know where you're going.

RIGHT-OF-WAY

M ost drivers know the right-of-way rules, or at least I hope they do. Right-of-way is usually a common sense sort of thing. It is the crux of city driving. It's the thing most drivers get angry about; having their right-of-way impinged upon.

I know you've been driving along when you see a vehicle at a Stop sign on a side street ready to turn into *your lane.* The Stop-sign-car is suppose to wait until it's clear, wait until you pass, then pull out because *you* have the *right-of-way.* But what you're about to find out is that it's a Jerk in that vehicle. He doesn't respect your right-of-way. He pulls out and you have to brake just so you won't violate Rule Two. The Jerk has stolen your right-of-way.

Jerks always need to be in front. If there's the smallest window of opportunity, a Jerk will jump in front of you, even if it means that you have to brake, even though the Jerk knows that you'll have to brake. He knows you won't hit him, unless you're an Extreme Moron. If you're willing to sacrifice your vehicle because another driver has taken your right-of-way, you need help. Park your vehicle and let someone else drive.

FOUR-WAY OR ALL-WAY STOPS

Four-way Stops can be a bit of a challenge. They are a first come, first served sort of thing. If you come to a full stop at your Stop sign before I come to a full stop at mine, you have the right of way. This sounds simple, but apparently it's a concept that eludes some drivers.

The first vehicle to a four-way Stop goes first, the second goes next, the third one follows him, and so on. If two vehicles stop simultaneously at their respective Stop signs, the driver on the right goes first. Does this system get messed up when there's a line of vehicles at each of the four Stop signs? You bet it does. What if four vehicles stop simultaneously at each Stop sign, who goes first then? He who hesitates is lost.

When I pull up to a four-way Stop, I look immediately to see where I am in the pecking order and I wait my turn, unless the driver that's supposed to go next sits there indecisively and hesitates. I have no respect for your right-of-way if you don't know you have it. I'm not going to wait or politely signal you. The Ultimate Goal dictates that I take your right-of-way because you're baffled. I will not babysit you. Learn the rules.

Now let's say that you're approaching a four-way Stop and behind you is a Jerk that's been riding right on your bumper. What should you do? I love these moments. I become one of the baffled. I hesitate like I don't know who's next until several out of sequence drivers go ahead of me or until the Jerk behind me blows his horn. I can feel the Jerk's frustration washing over me like a cool breeze. Don't sit on my ass and you won't have a problem.

LEFT TURNS

In most situations, turning left means you don't have the right-of-way. However, there are a few intersections where left-turning vehicles not only have the right-of-way; they also don't have to stop as I've demonstrated in this diagram.

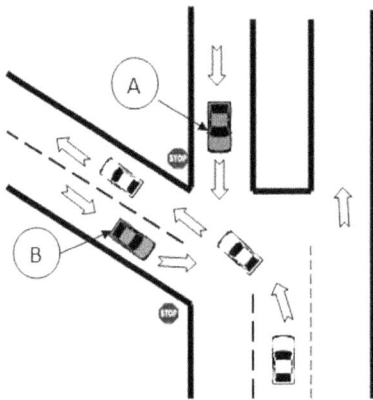

This is an intersection in my hometown. As you can see, cars A and B have to give right-of-way to the white car. Be aware that intersections like these exist.

More than once I've been in the white car, and car A will pull out almost hitting me, then the A-car driver will look at me angrily like I'm the one at fault.

Just a note to you morons that stop where car A is shown; there's another sign under the Stop sign that states "Yield to Left Turn." It might help if you read that sign.

There are signs at every intersection that give instructions for that intersection like "No Turn on Red," or, "Right Turn must Yield to U-Turn." You would be amazed by the information available at each intersection if you were to simply pay attention. That's all I ask – pay attention.

SHOOTING THE GAP

In the illustration below, you're driving the white car approaching a busy intersection where you need to turn left. You have a green light, but you have to wait for oncoming traffic to clear. How would you handle this situation?

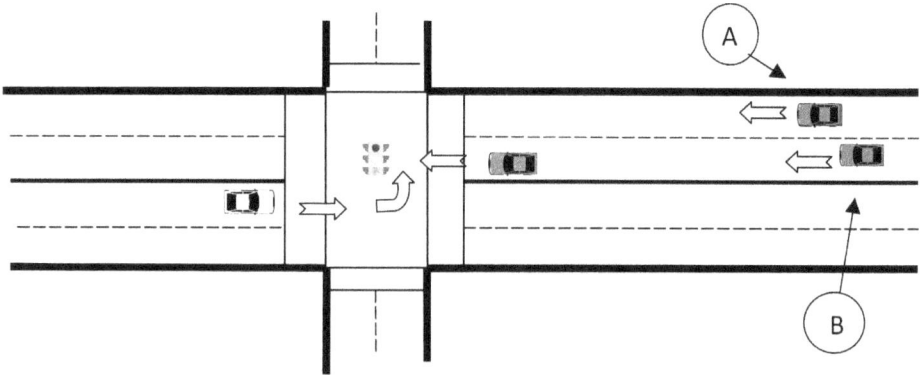

The cars coming at you are traveling 30 mph, 5 mph under the suggested speed limit. You *have to wait* for the first car to pass, but do you shoot the gap between the first car and cars A and B? That depends on how confident a driver you are. Everyone's comfort level is different.

Some drivers won't shoot any gap. Me? Once the first car has passed and it looks like A and B are Creepers, I probably *would* shoot the gap. Unless I had a Gasper in the car, then it's not worth the trouble. If I see that A and B are closing the gap, I'll wait until they pass.

Side note: Often times Jerks will shoot a gap very slowly. They want to demonstrate that they are not impressed with oncoming traffic. They turn just fast enough to show their disrespect for your right-of-way, hoping you'll have to slow down as they do what they please.

Back to the illustration: Now let's say that you're in car A. What should you do? If you're a Player you are already aware that the white car is planning to turn left. It's your job then to close the gap by speeding up just enough so there's no gap to shoot. It's your job to make the white car wait until you pass. You get Points if you center yourself between the front car and car B so the white car has to wait on B as well.

You'll notice that the white car is positioned where you're actually sup-posed to wait to make a left turn. Would I stop there and wait? It depends on traffic. If it's Rush Hour, then yeah, I would wait there. If not, I would probably pull into the intersection, but not so far that I couldn't see the traffic signal. If I couldn't get a gap, I'd want to go when the light turned yellow.

Be forewarned; because of an increase in Jerks and White Rabbits running yellow and red lights, sitting in an intersection waiting to turn on the yellow is becoming more hazardous. Make sure no one is going to run the light before you proceed. I never pull into an intersection if I see that I might get stuck and end up blocking the intersection.

BLOCKING AN INTERSECTION

The just described scenario is a common right-of-way violation. You regu-larly see drivers pulling into intersections even though it's obvious that they can't get through on their light. They end up blocking everyone's right-of-way. These are, again, Jerks and White Rabbits.

To those of you who block intersections, you accomplish two things: you cause more delays and traffic snarls than normal because, apparently, you can't sit through one more light cycle; and you piss-off all the drivers you end up blocking and they, in turn, end up blocking the intersection as they try to squeeze through because of your dumb ass.

Just the other day I was sitting at a red light waiting to turn left when several cars from a cross-flow turning lane completely blocked the intersection. No one could go when the light changed, except for, and I loved this, a police car sitting behind me. He turned on the dreaded blue lights, pulled around me, instructed all the cars blocking the intersection to pull to the side of the road, then gave them all tickets. Needless to say, for a while at that intersection, no one else blocked anyone's right-of-way. Keep up the good work Mr. Traffic Cop.

My favorite "blocking an intersection" story happened one day when I was minding my own business and caught, with a front pole position, at a red light. The road in front of me sloped downhill for several hundred yards where a side street intersected, and then the road sloped back uphill several hundred yards to the next traffic light.

As I waited for the green light I could see all the way to the next intersection and my path was clear. Not a car in sight. It was then that opportunity struck. Suddenly, at the Stop sign on the side street at the bottom of the slope, two cars appeared that proceeded to turn left across my path, as shown in the next illustration.

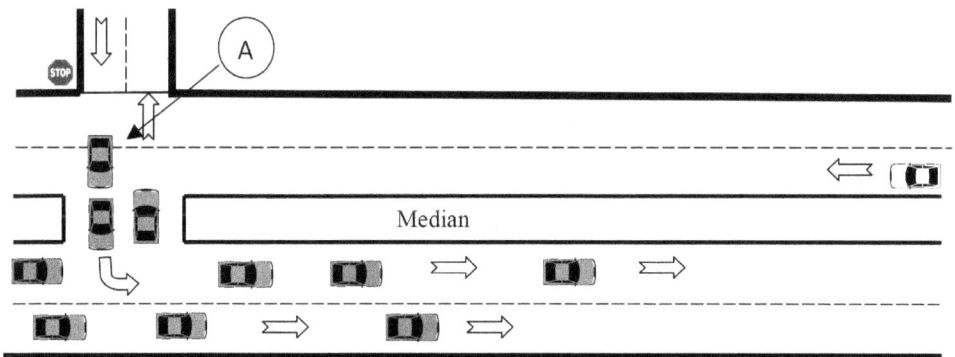

I was in the white car and the driver of car A was blocking my path as I started down the road towards him. He shouldn't have pulled out until he could have cleared the intersection. To be fair, when he pulled out, no cars were coming. I suppose he thought, *no problem*. And, as I was picking up speed, he was so otherwise occupied that he wasn't even looking in my direction - big mistake.

Luckily, I had gotten a quick start and was well ahead of the Crunch of Creepers (term used to indicate a group of Creepers) that I had shared pole position with. I was alone on the road as I approached car A. I was almost on him when he finally glanced my way.

What he saw was me heading straight for him, my hands off the wheel waving frantically, my eyes wide with false fear, my face contorted in a scream of panic as though impact was certain. I startled him so badly and he flinched so dramatically that I swear his head hit the ceiling. I swerved, passed behind him and went on, laughing so hard that I thought I might pee my pants. I'm sure he had to change *his* underwear.

To the guy in car A, if you're reading this, in retrospect I guess I apologize for scaring you, but I'll bet you look now before you block an intersection. Another priceless moment in the Game.

EMERGENCY VEHICLES

If you're suddenly confronted with an Emergency Vehicle, lights and siren going, don't panic. Look around to see what you can do to let the Emergency Vehicle get safely past you. Most probably someone's life is at risk. It could be someone dear to you. If you or a loved one were in the back of an Ambulance dying, you'd want traffic to clear a path, to give right-of-way. You'd want every chance to survive. Sometimes every second counts. I interviewed a few local Emergency Vehicle Drivers and learned some interesting things.

Their main concerns are Time and Safety in emergency situations. When on a run, Emergency Vehicle Drivers prefer, on four-lane roads, to use the inside lane (the fast lane) because it's the most effective passage; safest for them and you. So, if you see them coming up behind you in the left lane, get in the right lane and let them pass.

Another system for their safe passage they call "Parting the Wave." This is where you, the public, on two-lane roads pull off to the closest curb or shoulder. For example: on a two-lane road with traffic going both directions, you would pull over to your right and leave the center of the road open for the emergency vehicle. I can see how this would look like a "parting wave." If you're on a multilane highway, pull off to the nearest curb or shoulder (right or left) and give the emergency vehicle the center of the road.

A new problem for emergency drivers is other drivers being unaware of their presence because they're not paying attention (cell phones), or not being able to hear the siren because they're wearing headphones (illegal in some states), or they have their stereo up too loud. A recent innovation in siren technology called a "Thumper" was designed to deal with this problem. It directs a loud thumping sound at the ground so you can *feel the presence* of an emergency vehicle, rather than just see and hear it.

I have not personally experienced one of these new sirens, but if they catch on and you know they will, how will I know the difference between them and one of those cars with a thumping stereo? Will I have the urge to pull off the road when someone's "jammin'" down the highway?

Okay, let's say you're stopped at a red light, when you hear or feel a siren (pronounced Sigh–reen if you're a Hickamy) and you look in your rearview mirror and see an emergency vehicle (V-hick-le) coming up behind you. What should you do?

First, look to see if there's an open lane at the intersection. If there is, sit still and let the Emergency Vehicle use the open lane. Don't confuse things by moving into the intersection. And don't be indecisive. If you do move, find a spot out of the way and stay there until the emergency vehicle passes. Don't change your mind and move again because you're uncertain about where you're supposed to be. You're supposed to be "out of the way."

However, if there's not an open lane when an Emergency Vehicle comes up behind you, look to make sure it's safe, then pull through the intersection and move out of the way. Don't go if it's not safe. Emergency Workers do not want you to endanger yourself or others.

Another interesting fact I learned from the Battalion Chief of our local Fire Department is that vehicle-hitting-structure collisions are on the rise. This means there's a new trend where moron drivers are hitting buildings.

I can see how collisions happen on the open road with vehicles moving and interacting; surprises happen. Buildings, on the other hand, don't move. They just sit there. Sooo….what? How did a building end up in your path? How is it possible that you didn't see a building in front of you? It's a building. It's one of those great big things made of concrete, brick and steel. They are extremely predictable. I've never *ever* had a building get in my way. Never had to suddenly swerve because a Jerk Building cut me off. Do you really have to hit your head against a brick wall to figure this stuff out? Apparently so. Sounds like a texting thing to me.

THE JERK AND THE EMERGENCY VEHICLE

One emergency vehicle driver told me that nothing irritates him more than seeing vehicles pulling over to get out of his way, and then some Jerk takes advantage and passes the pulled-over vehicles before he gets over. When you see an emergency vehicle, treat the moment like a NASCAR "Red Warning Flag," keep your position, pull over, and stop.

A common misconception is that Emergency vehicles drive fast. That's not necessarily true. Police Cars, Ambulances and Fire Trucks try to drive comfortably fast - safely fast. Fire Trucks seldom travel over 60 mph.

Another problem for emergency vehicle drivers is Jerks passing them on the right because, apparently, the emergency vehicle is not going fast enough in the left lane. Do not pass Emergency Vehicles. Stay a safe distance behind them and don't use their wake as an opportunity to pass other vehicles. These people are working. Get out of their way and let them do their job.

Lastly, don't drive through an accident scene or a fire emergency scene unless instructed to do so by Emergency Workers. Don't Rubberneck. Proceed with caution. Don't become so enamored by the flashing lights that you quit paying attention to the road and cause a wreck or a safety issue for the Emergency Responders. They're out there risking their lives to save your life, or your loved one's life. They're saving your home or business from fire. They're arresting drunk drivers. They are keeping us safe. That's what we pay them to do. Respect their work space and keep them safe.

RIGHT-OF-WAY ON NARROW ROADS

Narrow roads such as subdivision streets with parking on one or both sides can prove to be tricky right-of-way situations. In the next illustration how would you handle right-of-way?

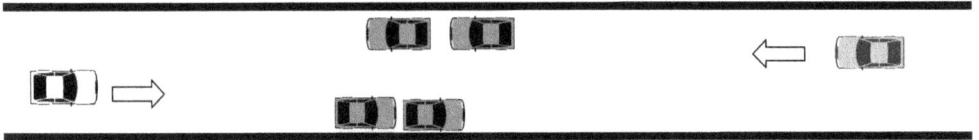

This is any neighborhood street with cars parked on either side. You're in the white car with a car coming towards you as indicated by the arrow. One of you is going to have to surrender right-of-way and let the other driver pass between the parked cars first. Usually, whoever gets there first, goes through first.

But let's say there's a Jerk in the approaching car and he sees you in your white car and he knows you're going to win this race, so he speeds up, forces the situation, and takes your right-of-way. What should you do then? The first option is to concede, pull to the right, as I've demonstrated below, and let the Jerk pass.

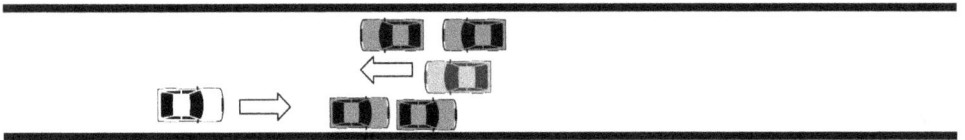

The second option is to concede, but align with the opening between the parked cars and wait there for the Jerk to pass. This way, even though he took your right-of-way, he has to steer around you (a moral victory for you). Which way would I handle this situation? Depends on what kind of mood I'm in and who was coming the other way.

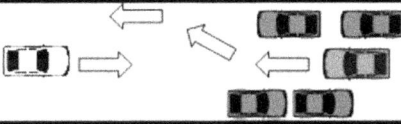

ENTRANCE AND EXIT RAMPS

If you live in a town or city of average size you've experienced Bypasses, Interstates, Beltways, and Parkways, and you've gotten on and off these road systems using entrance and exit ramps.

The Entrance Ramp is called an Acceleration Ramp. Its purpose is to allow you to accelerate and match the speed-of-traffic that you wish to merge with. If you're on an interstate acceleration ramp wanting to merge into traffic that's cruising by at 75 mph, by the end of the ramp, when you need to merge into traffic, you should have accelerated to at least 70 mph. This, I know, seems like another simple concept, but apparently it's not understood by many.

How many times have you been behind a Creeper on an entrance ramp who apparently believes that merging into 75 mph traffic is much safer if they don't exceed 35? They slowly drive down the ramp with their blinker going to let other drivers know that they're coming. Thanks for the heads up. Then once they've reached the end of the ramp, when it's do-or-die time and they see slews-of-cars and pods-of-semis roaring by at 75 mph, what do they do? They slow down, of course. Then they start to run out of ramp as they approach the shoulder in a panic, because they can't seem to squeeze into traffic. Finally, interstate traffic has to react to the moron half on the road and half on the shoulder, driving 25 mph, and a dangerous time was had by all.

I don't know what to say except, "It's an Acceleration Ramp! Accelerate!" Accelerate up to an acceptable safe speed for merging into traffic. This is not difficult. If you can't handle this task, let someone else drive.

And of course, once you've merged into traffic, you should give yourself a grace period, a minute or so, where you observe the new pack of vehicles that you're now running with. Look to see where the Jerks and the Creepers are. Don't jump into the middle of the pack and consider yourself the alpha. Adjust to the pack and let the pack adjust to you. Don't do the following...

THE JERK AND THE END AROUND

In this illustration I show the just-mentioned acceleration ramp situation with a Creeper in car A leading a line of cars merging onto a four-lane highway (I call this a Creeper Parade). There's a Jerk in the white car near the back of the parade ready to execute a dangerous move I refer to as an End Around.

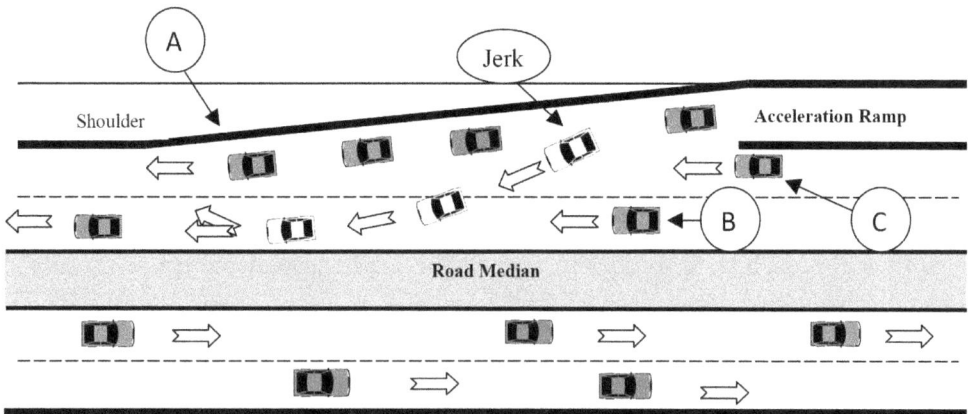

As you can see, the Jerk in the white car was not happy with the Creeper in car A, so he pulled an End Around, whisking around the front three vehicles and straight into the fast lane, and in the process, cutting off car B. Though illegal, the End Around is commonplace. Have I ever had the urge to pull an End Around? Sure.

When I'm behind a moron creeping down an acceleration ramp it's frustrating. It's an acceleration ramp, accelerate. I have, with Extreme Creepers, shot around them, but only if the way was clear. I would never cut off another vehicle. Usually I just stay in line, wait until I get on the road, then look for my opportunity to pass the Creeper Parade.

Now let's say there's a Jerk in car C as well. He didn't get into the left lane so oncoming traffic could merge. He never gets over so cars can merge. He wasn't involved in the white car drama. But if he'd been up close, he would have sped up, stayed in the right lane and got beside the Creeper to keep him from getting in front of him, even if it meant running the Creeper onto the shoulder. I don't have a cute nickname for these assholes, but I do have a few choice words. Get the hell over! What's the matter with you? This is not a Death Match. Don't endanger everyone by being a Jerk. I've seen lots of these merge-blockers lately. I suppose I could call them Blockheads but that's not a deep enough insult. This is Jerkism at its peak.

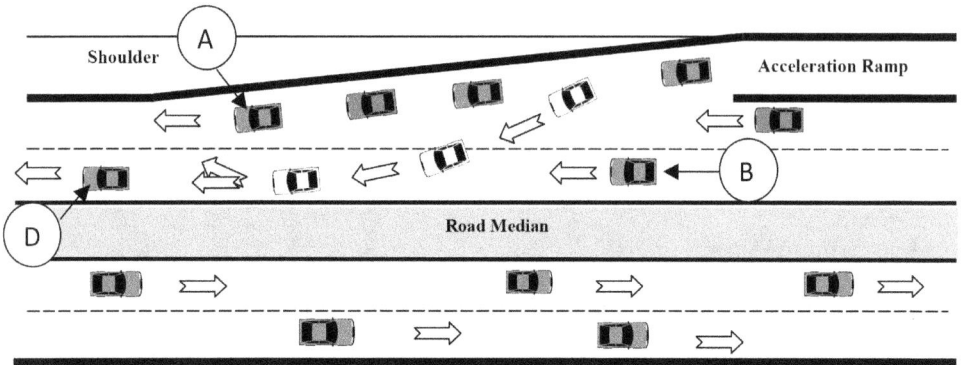

Okay, now let's say you're in car B and the white car just cut you off. What should you do? You should probably forget it and thank your lucky stars that you didn't get hit by the Jerk. But if you are otherwise inclined, if you feel you've been slighted, if you're at all like me, it's your job as the offended driver to get in front of the white car because he took your spot in traffic. You got over so he could merge but then the Jerk cut you off.

If he double-jerks and recklessly cuts between car A and car D, let him go, he's probably crazy. You're better off staying away from Jerks that have no concern for safety. But if you end up behind him, stay there and wait for your moment.

Being a Jerk, he'll constantly be looking to get "one more car ahead." He'll be cutting in and out of traffic because everyone's a Creeper, and sooner or later he'll screw up, get stuck in the "slow lane," as you drive past him and on to victory. And if you don't get a chance to get in front of him, that's okay, some days are stone. You'll get over it.

Once, a few years back, I had a Jerk in a pickup truck riding on my ass as I drove *a little over* the suggested speed limit in the left lane of our four-lane bypass. I was eventually going to make a left turn and I wanted to stay in the left lane because of heavy traffic.

The Jerk was extremely unhappy about my choice to stay in the left lane, so he rode inches from my bumper. I could feel his frustration washing over me like a cool breeze as I applied my inverse speed-to-bumper-distance formula and began to slow down to the suggested speed limit. Finally, after a half-mile or so, he got his opportunity to pass me on the right.

His plan was to quickly pass, then, in an effort to "show me," he was going to cut as close to my front bumper as possible. Just as he sped by I came to my turn lane and I merged left just as he jerked his truck into the lane where I'd once been. The moment was priceless. I watched as he looked into his rearview mirror to gloat about "cutting me off" and I had disappeared. You could tell by his actions that he was dumbfounded. He had no clue as to where I had gone. I had spoiled his plan. Another wonderful moment in the Game.

PEDESTRIANS AND RIGHT-OF-WAY

Pedestrians always have the right-of-way at marked crosswalks with Stop signs or Yield signs. Pedestrians are supposed to wait for a green light at intersections where there is a signal. But always be on the lookout for pedestrians. You're driving 3,000 pounds of life-changing carnage. There's no place you need to get to so quickly as to put a pedestrian in harm's way.

Even if a pedestrian is going against the light and crossing in violation of Rule One, do not try and get around them. Let them cross the road safely. Besides, how would you deal with hurting or killing a pedestrian? I read a sad story the other day about a young man that had killed a pedestrian because he was texting and wasn't paying attention. Apparently he couldn't live with what he'd done and ended up taking his own life; two senseless deaths. Pay attention.

TRAFFIC CIRCLES AND OTHER CHALLENGES

The world of Traffic Engineering has brought us new and wonderfully intricate road interchanges so we'll constantly be entertained and left wondering who has the right-of-way. Though, if you pay attention and follow the signs, most interchanges work reasonably well.

There's a myriad of creative interchange names. We're all familiar with the Cloverleaf, but in doing research for this book I found some names I was unfamiliar with, like a Far Side Jughandle and a Basket Weave. How about a Turbine? An overhead view of a Turbine looks like the spiral on a hypnotist's dangling coin. There's a Windmill and a Divided Volleyball. In my town we now have Traffic Circles (Roundabouts), and the latest craze, the Double Crossover Diamond. Now there's a mouthful.

You've no doubt driven on a Traffic Circle. That's where drivers get caught in a counter-clockwise merry-go-round traffic-flow, desperately hoping to see their exit, and where, apparently, everyone has to yield to everyone else. Well, the rule is: incoming traffic is supposed to slow down and give right-of-way to vehicles already in the circle. But it's been my experience that very few drivers get this concept. I've seen plenty of near misses. Overall though, because everybody thinks they have the right-of-way or vice versa, Traffic Circles seem to work and keep traffic moving smoothly. I suppose that's all anyone can ask. It's the Tisket that makes these interchanges a delight for ambulance chasers.

The Double Crossover Diamond is an extremely interesting design that crosses the lanes of a minor road where it intersects with a major road; the minor road intersecting as an underpass or overpass. Its purpose is to make entering the major road, left and right turns, safer and easier. Right turns are as usual, exiting to the right, no stop necessary because they occur before the crossover. Left turns happen after the crossover so they're essentially the same as right turns, except exiting to the left, no stop necessary because they're not crossing in front of oncoming traffic.

Apparently, you only have to stop at this intersection if you're going straight through. Somehow that just seems wrong. Was there a vote to take away the straight lane's right-of-way? Why weren't we apprised of this situation? That was the best part; I enjoyed being able to go straight through an intersection, left-turning vehicles having to surrender right-of-way to me, as nature intended it.

If you do get a green light to go through the Double Crossover Diamond, it's a very serpentine straight-through, with several lanes of traffic swerving through the crossover together like slot-cars on a curvy track. Since its unveiling here in late 2011, the Double Diamond (local slang) has relieved congestion, even with a 30% increase in traffic, and reduced accidents by over 40%; a very successful modern traffic solution.

The other side of that coin is an outdated interchange near me where oncoming traffic and exiting traffic have to cross through each other. There are always two rows of seven or eight vehicles, one trying to merge right and exit, and one trying to merge left and enter, each line passing through the other like a zipper. And they're all in each other's way.

Seems like every time *I'm* at this intersection and exiting, there's a line of semis coming on just a few feet apart and I have to squeeze in between two semis and hope for the best. I often feel like one of those hapless humans being trampled by dinosaurs in some Jurassic movie. I'm sure these prehistoric interchanges exist elsewhere besides here. I guess I'm just complaining now.

I will have to confess that with my somewhat twisted sense of humor, I conceived my own intersection. I thought it would be fun if they put a Traffic Circle at each end of a Double Crossover Diamond as I've demonstrated here. I think I'd call it a Double-Stitch Injury-Lawyer Bow-Tie.

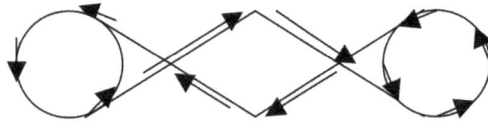

Heck, I could install cameras and make a Reality Show. Call it "Whose Fault is it anyway?" I know, sort of goofy. Even I was only mildly amused until I did some research and found an actual interchange similar to my design called, no kidding, a Dumbbell. You can't make this stuff up.

So I changed my reality show to a game show, "The Double-Stitch Dumbbell & Shyster Show." Tune in each week to see accident attorneys mud wrestle for the right to represent the weekly output from the Double-Stitch.

I guess I shouldn't give accident attorneys such a hard time, but they are easy marks. Plus I hate their commercials. "Hi, I'm Dangerous Dan. If you've been injured in an auto wreck, call me and we'll 'spank' that insurance company into submission. If anyone can get you the money, Dangerous Dan can." A little rhythmic tune going on in the background with lyrics like, "Dan can, yes he can, Dan can," playing over and over as Dan holds out a phone with Dollar

Signs spewing out like confetti. His phone number flashing like an ambulance light. "Call Dangerous Dan, cause Dangerous Dan Can."

Wouldn't it be great if everyone paid attention and we didn't need accident attorneys? But that's not likely to happen. It would be my guess that, with the Rise of the Cell Assassin, being an Injury Lawyer is probably very lucrative.

I feel like we're getting to know each other a little better. I suppose I can tell you my favorite lawyer joke: A man had just left his attorney's office with the outcome of his divorce ricocheting around in his head – he got the shaft, she got the gold mine. He was having very negative thoughts about his lawyer as well as his ex-wife's evil counsel. He decided that what he needed was a good stiff drink so he headed for a local bar.

He entered the bar intending on drinking himself into a better state of mind. But as he sat there drinking, his thoughts got darker and darker until he couldn't stand it anymore. He jumped up and announced to the room, "All lawyers are Assholes." A hush fell upon the crowd. Finally, a drunk near the back of the bar spoke up. "I take offense at that remark," he shouted. The disgruntled man turned, surprised, and shouted back, "Why? Are you a lawyer? "No," he answered, "I'm an Asshole."

All in fun; I have nothing against attorneys. Like I say, they're easy marks.

TURN SIGNALS

If there was ever a subject that inspires adamant opinions, it's Turn Signals. If you don't believe me, just mention in a group that some moron was turning and the dumbass didn't use his turn signal and you almost hit him. Then sit back and listen. *"Ooo, I hate those people. Why have turn signals if no one uses them? They're evil those drivers that don't use turn signals. Oooo, just makes me so angry.*" Faces turning red as blood pressures rise.

I have a different take on turn signals. It's sort of that thing, if a tree falls in the forest and there's no one there to hear it, does it actually make a sound? If I give a turn signal and no one's there to see it, did I actually give a signal? By definition a signal is intended for someone else. A turn signal is not for you. You already know you're turning.

"*But you should always be in the habit of using your turn signal.*" If you're just driving by habit you're not paying attention. It's why most Faults happen within a mile of a driver's home. They were driving by habit, accustomed to things as usual, then Bang something changes. Whose Fault is it anyway?

If I'm approaching a street where I'm about to turn and there's no one there to see me turn I do not use my turn signal. Yeah, I know it's against the law. I use my signals if there's a cop around. Otherwise, I don't use them unless my actions are going to affect another driver. If I'm going to cross someone's right-of-way, it just makes sense to let them know that's my plan, so I use my signal.

And I don't sit at a red light with my signal on. I flip my turn signal on when the light turns green. I hate listening to the tick, tick, tick. The way I see it, I'm saving wear and tear on my turn signals. Light bulbs only have so many hours of life before they have to be tossed. So in reality, I'm being environmentally conscious. I'm being green by not creating more trash.

Plus I'm saving energy. Your turn signal puts a tiny bit of an extra load on your vehicle's electrical system, which in turn puts a tiny bit more load on your engine, which in turn uses a tiny bit more gas. Think of all the gas we could save if no one used their turn signals. How's that for a bit of twisted logic? If

I ever get pulled over for non-signal-use I think I'll try that thought process on the cop. "But Officer, I was trying to save energy, trying to save the planet. Can't we just forget it this time?"

I hate getting behind people who use their signal then leave it on. I call these people **Flickers**. They drive for miles apparently anticipating a *future* turn. If you're behind them, you're not sure what their plan is. In actuality they don't have a plan; they're not paying attention.

I thought about having a loud-speaker system installed on my car so I could alert them. "Hey, Flicker, in the blue car, turn off your blinker. You're wasting energy." But then I thought, if a turn signal is an energy siphon, imagine how much gas a loud-speaker system would use. So I scrapped the idea. Just as well. Can you imagine what it would be like on the road if everybody had their own P.A. system? HYD!

A quick note: Some people use their turn signals as a tool to extract money from insurance companies. They flip on their turn signal hoping you'll think that they're turning. Then you pull out in front of them and they flip off their signal and plow into you, then sue your insurance company. I always wait to see if someone is actually turning before I pull into their right-of-way. But we'll talk about "driving scams" later. It's time we shine a light on a new subject.

HEADLIGHTS

Speaking of adamant opinions, let me expound on Headlights. Headlights are for seeing and for being seen. Did you catch that last part? The "being seen" part? There's a gaggle of drivers that don't seem to get this concept. They drive around in the dim predawn light and the dim post-sunset light with no headlights because *they can see.* "Why do I need my headlights on if I can see?" So you can be seen, moron. I call these dimwit, lightless people the **Grays**.

They drive gray vehicles on gray rainy days down dark gray roads, then are surprised when someone pulls out in front of them and they narrowly miss a collision. They blow their horn and shake their fist, "Hey, didn't you see me?" No, dumbass, you didn't have your headlights on. You blended in to your surroundings like a chameleon. I didn't see you until the last second. Good thing *I was paying attention* or we both might be dead.

Just the other day I was waiting to turn right and it was one of those gray misty rainy days. I looked to see if anyone was coming and apparently no one was so I proceeded to turn. Suddenly, a Gray came out of the mist and whipped past me doing well over the suggested speed limit. I did manage to stop in time, but it was close. If I had pulled out he would have hit me going at least 60. That might have been it for me and for him as well. Turn on your headlights so people will see you coming. It's a Rule One tactical thing.

To all you Grays out there, read Rule One several times and try to remember it. I was going to suggest that you stick a little note on your dash that reads, "I'm driving 3,000 pounds of life-changing carnage. It would help if other people could see me coming so I won't get killed," but then I thought better of it. You'd be busy reading the note and cause some other problem.

Turn on your headlights in dim daylight or on gray cloudy days. If you have your windshield wipers on you should have your headlights on. There are places now where it's the law. The police can ticket you for not using headlights when your wipers are on. Thought you might want to know. (My mom told me that as a child learning to speak I called windshield wipers "win-shypers." Is that too cute or what?)

Headlights can be dangerous things as well. Let's say you're on a two-lane country road at night, no street lights, just dark road. You have your Brights on so you can see well ahead to look for animals or sudden curves in the road, when you notice, in the distance, a vehicle coming towards you. You'll soon have headlights in your eyes and your headlights will be in the eyes of the oncoming driver. Two-lane country roads are prime real estate for head-on collisions.

A little head-on collision non-math: There's a common belief that if you're going 60 mph and you collide head-on with another vehicle going 60 mph, it's the same as you hitting a brick wall at 120 mph. That's not true. If equally-weighted vehicles, each going 60 mph, collide head-on, it's like each vehicle hitting their own brick wall at 60 mph. Twice the energy is produced in the crash, but each vehicle only experiences half of it.

If the vehicle hitting you head-on weighs considerably more than your vehicle, you're not only going to instantly stop, you're going to change direc-tions and slam backwards - a very violent event. What happens is your vehicle instantly stops, but your body keeps going forward 60 mph until the steering column instantly stops you. Then your internal organs rip loose and they keep going forward 60 mph until they're stopped by your chest wall. Then you and your jumbled mess of innards start moving backwards. Has that got your at-tention? You're driving 3,000 pounds of life-changing carnage.

Now, you're back on that dark country road with a vehicle coming at you, what should you do? As soon as you see that there's oncoming traffic, you should dim your lights and slow down (improves your math) because you never know who or what is coming at you. It could be someone with terrible night vision, someone who might swerve into your lane if your lights blind them.

Now let's say that you dim your lights, but the Jerk coming at you doesn't dim his, what should you do? You can try flashing your lights, which works sometimes. You can turn your brights back on and hope to pass each other no-harm no-foul. Unless he has those new high-intensity-discharge headlights, the ones that have that irritating blue color, then all you can hope for is to escape the moment without having your retinas seared by those strange alien-blue lights. (They won't actually sear your retinas; it just seems like it at the moment. I hate those new headlights.)

If he does dim his lights and you dim yours, you're supposed to wait until you pass each other before flipping your brights back on. But there's always the Jerk that flips his brights back on in that half-second before he actually gets past you and you get that flashbulb effect. You see spots before your eyes and have to slow down until your vision returns.

I read in my October 2012 edition of Discover magazine about new and interesting headlight-safety technology. Apparently BMW has developed headlights that help to illuminate pedestrians, and a researcher at Carnegie Mellon University has developed headlights that make rain drops all but invisible. I wonder what irritating color those lights are. I could expand exponentially on headlights, but let's move on. Take a bathroom break if you need one, but we got to keep moving.

RURAL DRIVING

I f you decide to take a drive in the country you're likely to encounter farm equipment (tractors and such) going anywhere from 15 to 30 mph. Here in Kentucky, our country roads have lots of hills and curves, so it's common to come around a curve or over a hill and find a tractor creeping down the road. In my youth that exact thing happened and I was lucky to escape with my life.

I was driving on a rural road that I was very familiar with, driving by habit, going well over the suggested speed limit. I came around a curve and suddenly, in front of me, was a tractor going no more than 15 mph. There was no way I could stop so impact was imminent. My only option was to pass him using the oncoming traffic lane. I swung out and passed him on a curve. Luckily for me no traffic was coming so I managed to get around him and back into my lane without causing a head-on collision.

Thinking that you "know a road" and that it's always going to be the same (driving by habit) is a good way to get killed or to kill someone else. If you can't see around curves or over a hill, slow down and enjoy the scenic drive.

Another danger on rural roads is a Jerk looking for an opportunity to pass a Country Creeper coming your way, which means he'll be whipping in your lane head-on at the first opportunity. And that's okay if there's a clear straightaway and he has time to pass. But there's always the Jerk who can't wait for a straightaway and will pass on a hill, or around a curve; another reason not to drive too fast on country roads. Head-on collisions are a nasty way to die.

Another thing to be aware of on rural roads is the bicycle enthusiast. If you see one, you'll probably see more, they usually ride in groups. And there's seldom a shoulder where they can ride, so you always have to be on alert. A friend of mine who drives a lot on rural roads can't stand these people. He sees them, of course, as Ultimate Creepers that you can't pass if there's a vehicle coming the other way. It frustrates him. I have a different take on these bicycle enthusiasts.

To me, they're out there enjoying the country air and scenery while getting some exercise. In our "obesity crisis" era where people park in the Fire Lane so they don't have to waddle all the way from the parking lot, it's nice to see someone getting their exercise, riding their bike. Bicyclists are definitely participating in their own health and well-being. Give them some room on the road.

Though, the outfits cyclists wear leave little to the imagination. I understand the aerodynamic aspect of it; less wind resistance if you're banded in spandex. But really? Don't you have a nice pair of khakis? I suppose I don't mind the feminine version of the cycling body wrap.

I have to tell a story about some bike riders I encountered in the city a while back. These weren't adults trying to get exercise; these were three pre-teens on

20-inch bikes. And they were riding three-across, intentionally blocking both lanes of a neighborhood street I was traveling.

They were taking their time, coasting, talking back and forth, laughing and glancing back at me, being little snots. I stayed back a fair distance because I didn't want to endanger the boys. I was a kid once, I remember being obnoxious.

It had rained the night before. The street gently sloped downhill and ended at a Stop sign. At the bottom of this slope, near the Stop sign, was a depression that always filled with rain water creating a large puddle, probably five-feet wide, twenty-feet long, and four-inches deep.

The mistake these boys made as they relinquished the right-of-way was stopping on the wrong side of the large puddle, grinning like they'd just won the obnoxious-lottery. Imagine their surprise as I steered through the deepest part and drenched them with a large spray of water. And "drenched" is the correct word here. In my rearview mirror I could see them sputtering like wet hens and shaking their little pre-teen fists at me. You know what they say about payback. One of my favorite driving moments. It still makes me laugh.

BACK TO CITY DRIVING

Another driver to watch for is a **Left Turn Jumper**. He's a Jerk sitting at a red light, with a front pole position, hoping to make a left turn exactly when or a half-second before the light changes. He doesn't want to wait for through-traffic to clear. He wants to beat them to the punch, hoping to Jump-the-Left-Turn before they have time to react. You'll see him intently anticipating the green, constantly inching forward.

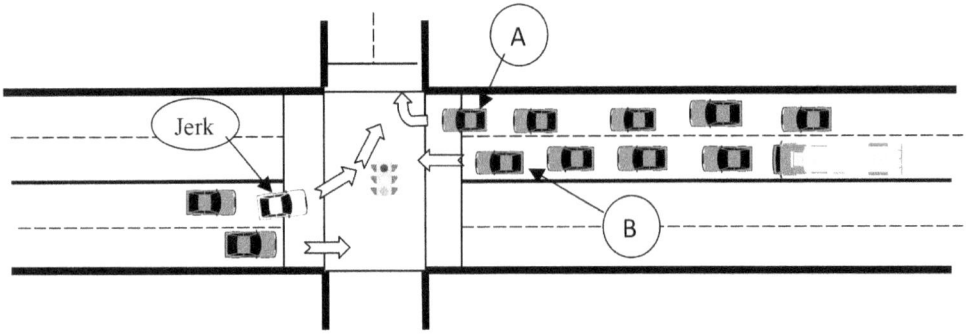

The Jerk in the white car is a Left Turn Jumper. You can see that he's already pulled into the crosswalk. He's watching the traffic signal, studying the cross-flow side, waiting to see the yellow so he'll know his green is about to turn. He's hoping that cars A and B are Creepers, slow to react so he can pull off his Jump.

Now, let's say you're in car B. What should you do if you suspect that the driver of the white car is a Jumper? You should start inching forward so he can see that you're not a Creeper and he'll just have to wait. That might work. Some Jumpers will go anyway. The car with all the power here is car A.

If you're in car A you should flip on your right-turn signal even though you're not actually turning. If the Jumper thinks you're turning, he *can't* Jump because he believes you will be filling the lane with your car thus blocking his move. I've lost count of all the times I've used this trick, flicking my turn signal off at the last second. I know, illegal use of a turn signal. I did say I was going to make a few confessions.

RAILROAD CROSSINGS

Now here's a place where Rule One should strictly be applied. Apparently there are quite a few drivers who gun-it across train tracks when the warning lights are flashing and the safety gates are closing. I suppose if I had to nick-name these morons I'd call them **Mangles**.

According to a www.tdi.texas.gov publication, a train hits someone every 115 minutes in the United States. That's 12.5 people a day. How can you have half a person? Get run over by a train, that's how.

The average train weighs 12 million pounds, that's a 4,000 to 1 weight ra-tio between the train and your car. Who do you figure is going to win in that equation? It's approximately the same weight ratio as your car running over an aluminum soda can. The word "squashed" keeps coming to mind.

Also according to the publication, 25% of all collisions between cars and trains happen while the train is already in the intersection. What? This goes back to cars colliding with buildings. How did you not see a train in front of you? It's a train, 12 million pounds of car-grinding fury. They're huge. They're loud. It's a train. Hang up and pay attention, Tisket. You're 40 times more like-ly to die in a collision with a train than any other type of collision. Ya think? What part of mangled don't you get?

Here's a few of the thirteen safety tips from said publication:

1. Any time is train time; meaning a train can come by at any time.
2. Watch for vehicles that must stop at all railroad crossings; such as school buses or trucks carrying hazardous materials.
3. Always yield to flashing lights, whistles, closing gates, crossbucks, or Stop signs.

An interesting point also made in the publication was that if a train is coming and you insist on being a Mangle and your vehicle stalls on the tracks, get out and abandon your vehicle, and (here's the part that I found interesting) move towards the train; not on the tracks, obviously, but in that direction.

The reasoning here is that when your vehicle shatters from 12 million pounds of train smashing in to it, the shrapnel from the collision is going to spread downstream in the direction of impact, so it's best to be upstream. Even if you do get out and away from your vehicle, you could still be killed by the sharp pieces of what was once your vehicle as they fly through the air.

Although I'm going to tell on myself here. There's a railroad crossing near me that at one time (it's not like this now) had no safety gates, plus it had trees and thick bushes that grew down either side of the tracks all the way up to the road. You could not see down the tracks either direction until you were right on them. There was a warning sign at the crossing, one of those X's with two red lights that flashed if a train was coming.

I had to cross these tracks everyday on the way to work, and for a while, a month or so, the warning lights would mysteriously flash as though a train was coming even though there wasn't one. I would pull up to the crossing, stop, look up and down the tracks until it was quite clear that it was safe, then go.

There must have been a malfunction in the warning system. I reported the problem to local authorities, but for that month, every day I would come up to those tracks and the lights would be flashing and there'd be no train. By the end of that month I was driving "by habit" and I would hardly slow down when those lights were flashing because I was young and dumb.

One afternoon, coming home from work, the warning lights were again flashing as I confidently proceeded across the tracks. When I was mid-track,

I looked to my left and saw, not twenty feet from me, the enormous face of a locomotive. I almost jumped out of my skin, and I do mean literally. I know my heart skipped several beats. Luckily for me, the train was just sitting there, not moving, twenty feet from the road, hidden from view by the trees and bushes.

The best part was I made eye contact with the train engineer just as I jumped out of my skin, and he started laughing, gave me a thumbs-up and blew his horn, because he knew what had just happened. I felt like a fool, and I'm sure he told the story to his friends. Which I can't blame him. If we were to trade places, I would be laughing and telling the story about the guy who most certainly had to change underwear when he got home.

Do not take railroad warning lights for granted. Do not try to "beat the train." Don't chance an encounter with 12 million pounds of car-grinding fury. Squash, Mangle, then Squash again.

BE PREPARED - PLAN AHEAD

The safest way to drive through any situation is to be observant and plan ahead. Look to see what's in your near future. Look to see what vehicles are behind you, beside you, and in front of you, so you'll know how to react and keep yourself safe. Check your mirrors and don't fall for a Blind Man's Bluff (that's where a vehicle is riding in *your* blind spot and *you* don't check, then change lanes and cause a collision). Though, I think anyone riding in a blind spot should be partially responsible.

The danger in a Blind Man's Bluff is proportional to the speed you're traveling when you hit the unobserved vehicle. In town, at 30 mph you might only need body work done to your car. On the interstate at 75 mph it could be your body that ends up needing work, or worse.

You check your blind spots by glancing back over either shoulder. For the driver's side blind spot, lean forward and check your side-view mirror. Leaning forward changes your visual perspective on the mirror and allows you to see more of the road beside you.

Don't ride in somebody's blind spot. Get up beside them so they know you're there, or drive a little behind them so when they pull a Blind Man's Bluff they'll miss your vehicle. You'll probably still have to brake, but at least you'll avoid a collision. You'll live to drive another day.

You can, as I can testify to, get carried away with looking ahead. In my case, for a while, I watched so far ahead that I would be sitting at one red light and I would react to the signal change at the next intersection. Not that I actually went, but I definitely flinched. I'd feel my foot start to come off the brake and I would have to contain the urge. I'm much better now; at least that's what my therapist and the voice in my head keep telling me. Though I still look well out in front of me as I drive. (You just said that.) No I didn't. (Yes you did.) Shut up, I have other stuff to talk about. (Fine.)

SOMETIMES YOU JUST HAVE TO BLOW YOUR OWN HORN

The car horn is supposed to be an instrument of safety, an alert to danger and close proximities, but you and I both know it's used for much more than that. As I said in the opening, our car horns "speak" for us.

Your horn is not a substitute for your brakes. Apparently Jerks don't get that. They whiz by as their horn blares, "Get out of my way, Creeper! I'm not slowing down." And it's not so much what the Jerk means with his horn, it's his tone of horn. He uses a very rude tone. You can tell, by the sound and duration, what the horn said.

For example, you're sitting at a red light and in front of you is a Cell Assassin joyfully texting about how his thumbs are sore. Then the light changes to green and he fails to launch because his chin is buried in his chest. You blow your horn to let him know it's time to move. Everyone at the light knows what you said. You said, "Move it, Dumbass."

Proper etiquette requires that you wait anywhere from two to four seconds before *lightly blowing your horn* to let the *moron not moving at the green light* know that it's time to *please move.* Yeah, right. Do you know the definition of a New York Minute? It's the time between the light change and the first horn blow. By that definition, two to four seconds would be a New York Hour. It would be my guess that the time between the light change and the first horn blow is less than a second. Maybe I can get a government grant. Do a New York Minute study.

I personally don't use my horn much. I don't put myself in situations where I need to use my horn. I don't ride in blind spots. I watch so far ahead that I'm rarely surprised. Not that I won't use my horn. It speaks up if there's a Tisket sitting in front of me and he doesn't move when the light turns green.

It's my opinion that the duty of blowing, "Move it, Dumbass," falls to the vehicle directly behind the offending Tisket. However, if the cars between me and the Tisket fail to speak up, I *will* use my horn. I've been as far back as fifth in line, started blowing my horn which triggered the car in front of me to blow their horn which caused the cars down the line to blow their horns, which got the Tisket moving that lived in the house that Jack built.

What the car horn *is not* is a Traffic Jam Reliever. It never fails, traffic can be backed up for miles and some dumbass will start blowing his horn. Yep, that'll help. The Emergency Responders miles down the road are going to speed up the process because you blew your horn.

Blowing your horn is also not a good way to pick up a date. Get out and go up to the door, Romeo, or Juliet, whichever the case may be. And to all you rednecks, blowing your horn and screaming, "Woo Hoo, baby," is not an effective pick-up line. If you wish to procreate, you may want to rethink that strategy.

A car horn can be a signal that your car is malfunctioning and you're not in control, as in your brakes are gone. It can be used as an insult, we've covered that, or as a request to merge, or as a show of solidarity. You know what I mean, you've seen those people on the side of the road with signs that want you to "honk if you love Jesus," or "honk if you think government is corrupt," honk for this and honk for that. I suppose it's the automotive equivalent of a high-five or a handshake. I've never wanted anyone to honk for anything. Sometimes I think I've led a sheltered life.

I suppose my biggest misuse of a car horn occurred in my teens and maybe a bit into my twenties when I played a game I called Drive-By Waving. I would drive around a random neighborhood looking for an unsuspecting participant; someone out doing yard work or walking their dog. Then I would drive-by, blow my horn and wave like I knew them. The payoff was their expression. I always got that pitiful little *do I know you wave* and that scrunched face of unsolved mystery.

Sometimes I would yell things like, "See ya on Sunday," or, "It was great seeing you the other night." Then they were obligated to wave back. What if they did know me? What would they say the next time we met and I asked why they didn't wave? What am I, chopped liver? I haven't played Drive-By Waving in a long time. I'd probably be much better at it now. I have one of those I-might-know-you faces.

MAKE 'EM WAIT

Make 'em Wait is about when *you* control *Right-of-Way*; when another driver has to wait on you before they turn, wait on you at a Stop sign, wait for you to pass because you have the right-of-way, you have the power.

A simple version of this concept is illustrated here:

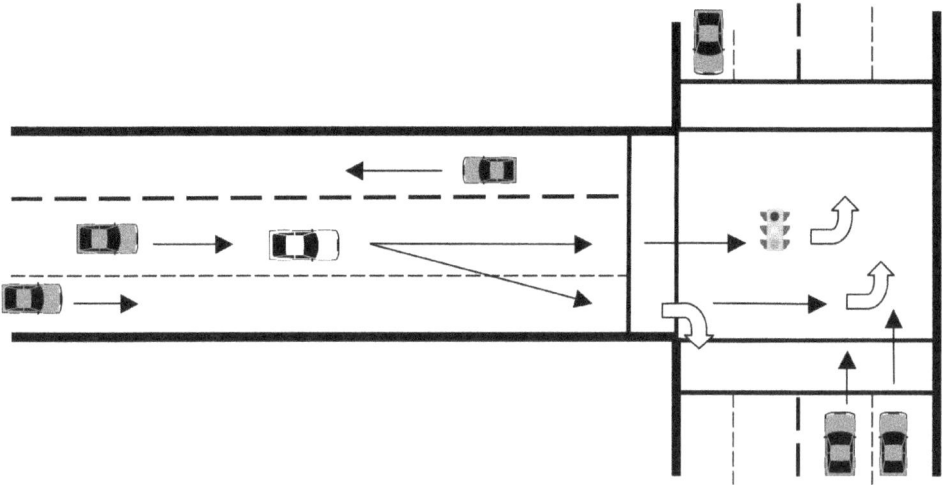

You're in the white car approaching a red light. You're going to turn left. Both lanes can be used for a left turn. Do you stop at the light in the left lane or the right lane? If you're playing Make 'em Wait you would choose the right lane because if the car coming up behind you, in the right lane, wants to make a right turn on red, you can "make him wait" until the light turns green. Points if he actually turns right. No Points if he turns left and follows you. Double Points if there are multiple cars waiting to turn right; I call that Releasing the Right-Turn Floodgate.

Make 'em Wait is a common driving game. I see it all the time. Put a little power in people's hands and they'll use it. In a society where few people have any real power, Make 'em Wait provides a little recompense. It's why pedestrians sometimes intentionally saunter across an intersection, particularly if they're walking because they don't own a car. You can see the resentment in their eyes and body language as they slowly cross in front of you, enjoying their moment of control.

A popular Make 'em Wait spot is a left turn lane. You've experienced this left turn moment. You have a front pole position, then the light turns green, and suddenly it's officially your right-of-way. Everybody has to wait on you to go.

A standard left-turn lane Make 'em Wait play is the "delayed-start." The light changes to green and the front car fails to launch. Sometimes it's simply a Cell Assassin not paying attention; but often, it's an ICU playing Make 'em Wait.

You'll see him checking his mirrors, then fiddling with an imaginary object in the passenger seat, casually ignoring the traffic signal. He's hoping for a line of White Rabbits behind him (Torture Points) because he's the leader of the pack. He decides when it's time to go.

The light changes. The ICU, checking his hair in his vanity mirror, doesn't move. Tension builds. A White Rabbit somewhere in line succumbs to the pressure and blows his horn, which prods the ICU to finally launch, freeing *most* of the White Rabbits behind him.

A delayed-start usually snares a couple of White Rabbits; the weak ones near the end of the line, who get caught as the turn light changes back to red because the dumbass in the front car didn't go. You've seen the delayed-start guy. You've been behind him. What was it you called him?

If I'm the front car I have a play I like better than a delayed-start. I'm always hoping to catch cars coming towards me that want to turn right onto the road that I'm turning left onto and make them wait. We're both turning into the same lane, but I have the right-of-way.

When I see a car approaching the intersection, wanting to make a quick right turn on red, hoping to beat the tide of turning vehicles, I put my play into action. I know his light *just turned red* because mine *just turned green*, and even though he can make a right turn on red, he's supposed to wait because *I have the green light*. So I quickly go. If I'm into my turn, he has to wait.

Here's the beauty of it. Instead of keeping my White Rabbits penned behind me, I herd them through the intersection so the right-turn guy not only has to wait on me, but he has to wait on the line of cars behind me. Points if I trap a right-turn guy. Double Points if I trap more than one right-turn guy.

Some drivers make their opening move very slowly, a "soft-start." You have to be careful here. Turn too slowly and the right-turn guy gets away, too fast and there's no White Rabbit Torture Points. Sometimes it's a delicate balance. You get Double Points if a White Rabbit behind you blows his horn, plus the right-turn guy has to wait. Like I say, be careful here. If I'm the right-turn guy, I'm gone if I see a moment's hesitation. He who hesitates is lost.

Triple Point Plays are rare. A Triple Point version of the just described scenario is when the right-turn guy is in a police car, that's right, a police officer. He definitely knows the law, he's a cop. You do have the green light, and unless he has his emergency lights and siren on, you have the right-of-way.

If it is a cop, you shouldn't delay-start or soft-start. After all, the cop could mistake your hesitation as a sign that you're texting or high on something and he might pull you over and issue a Game Penalty; increase your local government's revenue. Also, if the right-turn guy is a cop, it's a safe bet that no one behind you is going to run the yellow or red light, so you'll snare a few more White Rabbits than normal. You can only score Triple Points when a police car is part of the play. Like I say, it's a rare occurrence. Most people don't have the balls for it, anyway.

A little off point, but I know you've seen those pickup trucks that have those metal testicles dangling from the back. What's that all about? Could anything be more tacky and inappropriate? Apparently, somebody's over compensating for something, a short story I imagine.

I suppose it could be that the truck owner wants you to know he's driving a "man's" truck. If that's the case, shouldn't women have metal breasts on the front of their vehicles so we'll know it's a "woman's" vehicle? Maybe the steel balls are a sign that the driver sees himself as a superman. Wouldn't a man-of-steel have balls-of-steel? Just another random thought.

I hate it when people play Make 'em Wait in a fast-food or bank drive-thru. You've seen these people. They take too long deciding what to order. They drive slowly to the pick-up window. Then they change their mind and order something else after they've already paid for their first order. When they get their food they take too long getting organized before finally pulling off. At banks they don't fill out their deposit slip until they're at the drive-thru window. Then they send it in and the teller has to send it back because they didn't endorse their check. Don't think I don't know what you're up to. I see you, Creeper.

TAKE MY CAR, PLEASE

A phenomenon that's becoming increasingly common is drivers that leave their vehicles "running unattended" in public places. I start my vehicle and let it run unattended when it's cold out and I need to defrost my windows. I sit in my warm house and wait for the engine to do most of the window scraping task. Some might say that's a waste of gas.

I'm employing the petroleum industry to scrape my windows. I'm helping the economy and I don't have to get into a freezing car. It's nice and warm when I climb in. It's my winter sanctuary on the road.

Cars left running unattended account for a large portion of the one-million-plus vehicles stolen every year in the U.S. And yes, I know my car could be stolen. But I have two keys. It's locked while it's warming up. And yes, I know a thief could break a window. I've been lucky so far.

It's not much different than someone with an Auto-Start feature on their vehicle. They point their control out a warm window and presto, warm car.

Except I actually have to go out into the cold to start mine, and sometimes chipping through the ice on the car door is a challenge.

I suppose I could get an Auto-Start device installed. But then that's just something else that's going to break and cost me money to get fixed. Am I right? Every feature on your vehicle will sooner or later cost you hard-earned cash to repair, but I've drifted off point again.

I recently saw a Reality show about government-employed civilians (not police officers) who issue Parking tickets for a living. The crux of the show is the interaction between the ticket-givers and the drivers they ticket; a lot of fussin' going on. It seems that the ticket-givers are not very well liked. Hmm. Go figure.

In one encounter on the show, "a victim" comes running out of a coffee shop trying to stop the ticket-writer from ticketing his car that was illegally parked in a Fire Lane. The owner kept saying, "I left it running. You knew I was coming right back. I left it running." Apparently, (at least in this guy's mind) a vehicle is not illegally parked if it's left running. That explains so much.

I love it when I learn about a new unspoken traffic rule. It must be an extension of "a vehicle is not actually in the Fire Lane if you leave someone in it while you run into the store." I suppose, now that this "ticket show" has aired, you'll see more car thieves in coffee shops. Nothing worse than a jittery car thief.

I don't get the whole "leave your car running in a public place" thing, anyway. You see them in convenience and grocery store parking lots, or in front of coffee shops. Why not just donate your car? At least you'll get a tax write off. I've never found it difficult to start my vehicle after I come out of a store. I simply insert and turn the key. Maybe they believe it's a time-saving measure. If that's true, it's the Ultimate Goal run amuck.

In most states, leaving your car running unattended is an illegal and ticketable offense. Have I ever left my car running unattended other than defrosting it? Absolutely, I never claimed to be perfect. One particular time, now a rather infamous story among my friends, goes like this.

NO GOOD DEED GOES UNPUNISHED

Before I married my current wife I always tried to make good impressions by doing nice things for her (I still do nice things for her). One night, during that impressionable prenuptial period, while she was out of town on business, it snowed. So I decided I would *be nice* and shovel her driveway so when she got home later that day, she would find her driveway clear and be "very appreciative."

On her street, the houses and lawns on one side were level with the road, and the houses on her side were twelve feet or so above the surface of the road. Her front lawn and driveway sloped up to the top of that twelve-foot ridge at about a 35° angle. Not too steep, but slick and difficult when covered in snow.

The only flat surface on her side of the street was a four-foot wide city-government-easement with fire hydrants, streetlights, and "Speed Limit" and "No Parking" signs. Next to that, extending the flat surface a few more feet was a concrete sidewalk. Next to the sidewalk, the sloped front lawns and driveways began.

I'm an early riser. I get up most mornings by five, but on that particular morning I had set my alarm for four, giving me plenty of time to shovel her sidewalk and driveway before I had to be at work. It was cold, 15 degrees, so I stopped at a convenience store for some hot chocolate as a warm treat while I worked.

When I got to her place, I pulled up onto the easement and parked several feet from a No Parking sign. What can I say; I couldn't park in her driveway because I was going to shovel it. Besides, it was four-thirty; it was just me, my truck, and four inches of freshly fallen snow.

I got out and left my Explorer running unattended. I wanted it toasty to keep my hot chocolate warm. I decided that I should shovel her side-porch and then work my way down the driveway. I took my shovel out of the back of my truck, slammed the hatchback, climbed to the porch and started shoveling. While I was up on her porch I couldn't see my vehicle, my toasty oasis out in all that cold.

Shoveling the porch and the upper part of the driveway took about ten minutes. When I finished, I decided that a dose of hot chocolate was the next order of business. I started down the drive, rounded the corner of her house, and was shocked when I realized that my Explorer was "gone."

If you've never experienced "that moment," it's hard to describe. My eyes were wide with disbelief. Thoughts raced through my mind. *Oh My God, someone has stolen my truck. What am I going to do? How am I going to get to work? Oh My God, someone has stolen my truck.*

I ran to where my truck had been. I stood there stunned. I didn't own a cell phone at the time. I was out in the cold, and someone had stolen my truck. It was then I noticed the flattened No Parking sign. The thief hadn't bothered to back up and miss the sign. He'd jumped in my truck and plowed it down, probably in a panic due to the adrenaline-filled moment.

My eyes started following the tire tracks in the freshly fallen snow. They led through the easement, one track on either side of the fallen sign, then went up-slope into the neighbor's front lawn. Apparently the thief wasn't a very good driver. Why had he gone up into the neighbor's yard? I decided to follow the tracks. I had to do something.

The tracks, after running through the neighbor's yard for a long swipe, turned and began to follow the easement, paralleling the street for a while. Then they went into the street at a very shallow angle. They traveled the street for a hundred yards where they eventually crossed the centerline; then went another fifty yards in the oncoming traffic lane before exiting the street between two parked cars, barely missing both.

Once I got past the two parked cars I could see the tire tracks led through the front lawns of the houses on that side of the street. What the hell was the matter with this thief? I followed the trenches in the snow through five or six lawns and then I saw my truck. It had stopped inches from someone's front porch, engine still running. I ran up to my truck, opened the door and jumped in. No one had stolen my truck. I had left it in Drive.

Here's what I surmised happened. When I got to my girlfriend's house, I parked my vehicle on the easement, then, distracted by my hot chocolate (I'm a chocoholic) and my shoveling task, I had failed to put my truck in Park. It had stood motionless because it was just idling and perhaps held in place by the snow.

My Explorer was motionless when I got my shovel and slammed the hatchback. I believe that the door slam started my truck slowly rolling forward; that and the fact that it was still in Drive. Add that the street had a downhill slope, then couple that with a probable engine surge, and you see how it could pick up enough momentum to break the No Parking sign post.

The sign-impact had steered my vehicle up into the neighbor's yard. Their sloped lawn had steered it back down into the street where it traveled well over a hundred and fifty yards, went between two parked cars, barely missing both, up into someone's front lawn where it came to a halt inches from their porch. Thankfully, their lawn sloped up just enough to take all the momentum out of my driverless truck.

I backed my truck out of their yard, drove it, embarrassed, (thankfully no one was out to see my blunder) back to my girlfriend's house, put it in Park, turned off the engine, took the key, then finished the shoveling job. I still wonder what the people thought who lived in the house where my tire tracks ended. I would have loved to have heard that conversation. "Damn, Edith, I think the paper boy is getting lazier all the time."

Well, another long though sadly true story just to make a point. On the bright side, my hot chocolate was still warm and I ended up with a good story and a very appreciative girlfriend. It's never a good idea to leave your vehicle running unattended, strange things can and do happen.

UNFORTUNATE PEDESTRIAN SURPRISE

From one point of view, a critical moment can seem humorous, but from another angle, well, here's what happened. One afternoon as I was leaving work I witnessed a rather unfortunate moment for one individual.

The parking lot for the building where I worked was outlined by railroad tracks on one side and by two streets, a main road and a side street that sloped down, crossed the tracks, then dead-ended at the main road at a Stop sign. Straight across from the Stop sign was a small, brick storage building. As I was leaving work I noticed a delivery truck coming down the sloped side street headed for the Stop sign.

It had caught my attention because the boxy truck seemed to be picking up speed instead of slowing down. It quickly became obvious that it wasn't going to stop. Then I saw why. The driver was twenty feet behind the truck, frantically chasing the runaway vehicle. I began to look for other traffic but there wasn't much I could do other than watch the event unfold.

The delivery truck jerked violently as it crossed the rough railroad tracks. It wobbled out of control as it shot across the main road. Then, with a huge crunch, it embedded itself several feet into the right corner of the small building. Luckily, there was no traffic at the time and the storage building was empty, so no one got hurt. Well, maybe the driver's pride got hurt, and he probably got fired, but no one was injured. You never know what you might encounter on the road.

DO NOT TRY THIS AT HOME!

You've no doubt heard of the Darwin Awards. It's an award given to anyone who, by their own stupidity, ends up killing themselves, thus improving the gene pool by eliminating their stupid genes. We wouldn't want to pass along any stupid genes. You should visit www.darwinawards.com and read about some of their recipients, like the man who was protesting the Motorcycle Helmet Law by riding helmetless, flipped his bike, hit his head and died. A perfect example of natural selection at work.

Another of their recipients was a drunken college student who climbed over a power-station safety fence, then climbed up onto a high-voltage transformer because he wanted to pee on a wasp nest he spied up there. You know where this is going, right? But first, a bit of background on me.

Having succumbed to a "dare" in my youth, I once peed on an electric fence (see, I told you that you were smarter than me). The electrical connection was instantaneous. The moment my salt-laden urine stream touched the live wire, current flowed up the stream and through my genitals with an insulting jolt that made me clinch, curse, and worry that I'd done permanent damage to The Little General.

Of course, I just peed on an electric fence, not a high-voltage high-amperage transformer. I felt a few micro amps. (Do not take this dare. Believe me, a few micro amps flowing through your pride and joy is nothing you want to experience.) What the drunken college student felt was more akin to a white-hot lightning strike, more like a million amps; smoked sausage. Now I can't get that image out of my head; death by urination.

But let's move on. What I want to talk about in the next section are drivers that might not meet the criteria for a Darwin Award, but in my opinion, they've definitely "come up in the shallow end of the gene pool." Do not attempt any of this: I now present…The Moron Awards.

THE MORON AWARDS

Awards for Drivers that are "on the road"

to eliminating themselves (and us) from the gene pool.

M y first **Moron Award** has many recipients. It goes to all the morons who are in too big a hurry to make a correct left turn, so they "cut the corner." They start their turn too soon and, as a consequence, cross into your lane. Out on rural roads they cause head-on collisions because, driving by habit, they straighten out familiar curves (weren't no cars in that lane the other day). It's never a good idea to "cut corners." Stay in *your* lane, Moron.

My second **Moron Award** goes to dimwits that have their "brights on" at the wrong time. They fly up behind you on dark country roads, and suddenly your mirrors become blinding searchlights. They come down brightly lit streets with their high-beams blazing. They're the polar opposite of a Gray; anti-Grays, I suppose. Or Hot Pinks. Sparklers, maybe. Dumbasses. I knew I'd get there.

Moron Award number three goes to drivers who pass loading or unloading school buses. Really? You're in that big a hurry? If a school bus has its Stop sign extended, stop and wait. If it was *your child's* bus, you'd want vehicles to stop so *your child* would be safe. You can wait a minute. Chill out.

My final **Moron Award** (for the moment, anyway) goes to any moron that uses a turning lane to pass a Creeper. The light turns green and traffic starts to move, then a Jerk notices a vehicle-free turning lane, so he swings into that lane, passes a Creeper, then swings back into the straight lane so he can get one-more-car-ahead. I've seen Jerks use the shoulder to pass a Creeper. Again, really? What the hell's the matter with you? Give it a rest.

Without further ado, it's time to present...

THE MOST MORONIC MOVE IN A DRIVING SITUATION AWARD

The winner is - a teen driver in my area that ran a red light and killed someone. The stunt he pulled comes closest to the criteria of a Darwin Award. He was driving westbound at sunset and approaching an intersection. The sun was on the horizon directly behind the traffic signal, blinding him so he couldn't tell if the light was green or red. He decided arbitrarily that it must be green and he cruised right through a red light and T-boned another vehicle killing the driver. There's the Darwin Award disqualifier; he didn't kill himself, he killed someone else.

There was quite a stink around here about the "accident." Our local newspaper ran several letters-to-the-editor about the situation. Some opined that the boy should be charged with manslaughter. Several letter writers disagreed claiming the teen driver should not be held accountable because, poor dear, the sun was in his eyes.

He shouldn't be accountable? He was driving 3,000 pounds of life-changing carnage that he plowed through an intersection where he had no visual confirmation that he had the right-of-way. You can't get much more stupid or accountable than that. Definitely a Darwin Award candidate.

Driving tip: If you're approaching a traffic signal and you're being blinded by the sun, start slowing down until you can see, or stop if you can't tell. It's much better to stop at a green light, than to run a red light.

The family of the victim would not have been damaged forever if the teen driver had only followed that advice.

DIAMOND MINING

I love those Diamond Days when everything works in your favor. Like when you get all the green lights, or you make it to your destination without being stifled by a Creeper. Or you see the *dreaded blue lights* suddenly appear and your heart drops because *you were speeding just a little.* But then the cop passes you and pulls over the car in front of you. You smile as you slowly drive by because if that moron hadn't *snagged that ticket* it would have been yours and you know it. A day can't get much more Diamond than that.

Another Diamond moment is when you come up to a red light on a multi-lane road and all the lanes at the intersection are blocked, except one, your lane. It's a Diamond - you can't believe that you're about to get a "give me" front pole position. It was so nice of all those other drivers to leave a lane open just for you.

Then, as you start to slow down, another Diamond, the light turns green, and you, with all your forward momentum, let off the brake and *pass through* the open lane *and by* all the cars caught at the red light. You accelerate then check your rearview mirror and see that you have a large and commanding lead. You can grab another Diamond if you get-to-and-through the next light before it turns red. More still, if the group you left behind gets caught at that light.

You see that the next light is still green. You start focusing on the traffic signal, psychically trying to make it *stay green* until you get there and it does, another Diamond. Then, when it's apparent that you're going to *make it through*, you start chanting, "yellow, yellow, yellow" as you increase your psychic concentration on the stubborn green signal. Then it actually happens, the light changes to yellow just as you pass under it, another Diamond. Checking your rearview mirror you see that everyone else got caught. You smile as you sail off victorious. It was a Diamond bonanza.

Just for the record, I don't actually believe in psychic powers, but it doesn't stop me from trying to use them to make traffic signals bow to my will. Some days are just Diamond.

Sometimes, a surprise Diamond happens when you're stuck at a red light on a four-lane road and you're three or four cars back, and you've been behind Creepers all day. Vehicles are piling up behind you in both lanes. You need to change lanes because you have to turn soon. Then the Diamond happens. The light turns green and the only lane to start moving is yours. You can't believe it. There's a Tisket blocking the lane next to you.

The cars in front of you have taken off pretty quickly and you're coming up beside the blocking-Tisket. You glance over and see it's a Cell Assassin with his chin buried in his chest. White Rabbits start blowing their horns, but too late, you're already past the Cell Assassin. You quickly change lanes and you're free, open road in front of you. I love those moments.

DARK DIAMONDS

I don't know how much you've driven in the wee hours of the morning, but driving takes on a whole new tone in that weird predawn dimension, a very Diamond tone. Where I live there are places in the a.m. where the streets are vacant. It's then that Stop Signs and Traffic Signals have "new" Diamond Rules.

Of course you know about right turn on red, but at three a.m. I might make a left turn on red. I know it's illegal, but I can't see sitting there, *burning up gas*, waiting for the light to change. Again I'm being green.

Here are my thoughts on the matter. By definition, traffic signals are there to control traffic (multiple vehicles). One car does not constitute traffic. I don't endanger anyone while making a left turn on red because there's no one there to endanger. I come up to a red light, stop, look both ways and then proceed. I can't see the harm in that. Be forewarned, you can get a ticket using "a.m. Diamond Rules" as I can testify to.

Several years back I was coming home at two a.m. from an out of town trip. I'd been visiting my friend, Dean. The route home brought me through Paris, KY. I had chosen to drive through town, instead of around the bypass, because Paris a.m. streets are empty, like a ghost town, a straight shot, Diamond all the way. It was when I got to the far edge of town, where the bypass joins back up with the main road that I got into trouble.

The bypass connection on the south side of Paris is a bit strange; there are two traffic signals that change together but they're a hundred feet apart. As I was approaching the intersection both signals turned yellow so naturally I accelerated so I wouldn't get caught by the first one. There was no one anywhere. I was, as far as I could tell, the only car on the road. I'd been a little too far back to make the yellow and the light turned red just as I got to it, but I went through anyway; two a.m. Diamond Rules.

I traveled to the next light, stopped, and was just about to take off when (and to this day I have no idea where he came from) a Paris cop appeared behind me and turned on his dreaded blue lights.

Of course he gave me a ticket, and of course I had to wait the thirty minutes it took to "call in and check me out." It didn't matter to the cop that there were no other vehicles on the road. I ran the red light so he gave me a ticket. Be aware that Predawn Diamond Rules only exist in my imagination. The police have never heard of them.

A BLUE-WHITE DIAMOND

My favorite Diamond moment happened many years ago, but I'll never forget it. I was nineteen at the time. And it's not exactly a driving moment, but I was driving at the time, in the city, in a thunderstorm. Well, I wasn't actually moving. I was sitting in my car caught at a red light at a small intersection of two-lane roads. I had a front pole position. The traffic signal I was watching hung from the center of a wire that spanned diagonally across the intersection, a fairly common arrangement.

It *had* been pouring, but the rain had stopped. You could still hear thunder and see far off flashes in the sky. It happened just as I turned off my wipers. Lightning struck one of the telephone poles that supported the traffic signal.

This is where it got amazing. The startling flash was intensely bright and loud, and sparks showered down around me. Then, the next instant, centered on the wire supporting the traffic signal, "ball lightning" appeared next to the pole that had just been struck. It sat motionless for a moment, this eerie electric blue-white glowing globe about the size of a large beach ball, crackling and sparking, more like sizzling really. I was awe struck.

The traffic signal had gone completely dark; all of its lights were being drained of power by the strange electric sphere. Then the lightning ball, still centered on the wire, started slowly moving towards the signal.

All traffic had come to a stop. Everyone was transfixed. The sparking, sizzling globe took fifteen seconds or more to travel down the wire to the signal. When it touched the signal, the ball exploded with a bang, disappeared, and the traffic signal came back to life.

Still, for a moment everyone sat glancing around at each other as though to confirm what they had just witnessed. To this day it's one of my favorite moments. Ball lightning occurs very rarely. Once in a lifetime sort of thing. Right place, right time, an amazing Diamond.

PARKING LOTS

What the hell has happened to parking lots? They've become intricate mazes that are frustrating to navigate, full of come-hither dead-ends and concrete plant-filled traffic barriers. I miss the days when parking lots were rectangular and easy to navigate; when exits were simple to locate.

You can still find an easy to use parking lot if you find an old shopping center. But progress marches on. Old shopping centers come down and new "improved" malls go up. Surrounding these Modern Meccas of Commerce are those new-fangled parking mazes.

I'm not sure what happened in the school that teaches parking lot design, but apparently there was a turn for the worse. I did wonder the other day as I drove by The Marquis de Sade School of Parking Sciences, just what goes on in there.

PARKING 101

Professor Wormwood: "All right class, pay attention. Damian, sit down. Today we're going to take a look through the eyes of the victims, uh, I mean, parking patrons. Once the patrons are in the lot, your goal in parking lot design is to try to keep them there. You want to capture the exiting customers so they'll have to go back into the stores and spend more money. Their experience should go something like this:

"They leave a store, packages in hand, get in their car, then pull out of their parking space and follow the lane between the rows of parked cars out towards the edge of the parking lot, out towards the main road. They're used to this. Use their natural instincts against them. This lane of false-hope should invite them forward, all the perfect rows of cars and the beautiful landscaping beckoning them out towards the road home. They're content.

"But then they discover that their chosen 'way out' dead-ends just before the main road. Their only option is to turn right. They're now paralleling the main road but completely separated from it by a long concrete barrier filled with beautiful landscaping. Put this in your notes: As they make that first turn you'll want them to see the prize, the main road; to see the cars on the other side, the 'free cars.' So the landscaping here should be low, flowers and groundcover, maybe throw in a few skinny trees spaced like prison bars. The road home is just a few feet away, so close yet so far.

"Now they're frustrated. They're looking for an opening in the concrete barrier, an exit, a way to escape. But no, now the parallel lane dead-ends as well, this time at a massive concrete barrier filled with huge hedges. They're forced to turn right again and head back towards the stores. That's the beauty of it.

"We borrowed this concept from Vegas casinos. No matter where you want to go in one of their massive complexes, you have to 'go through the casino' to get there. If you want to get out of the parking lot, you have to drive by the stores.

"It's here we hope the weak ones will give up. Maybe they'll see a '40% Off' sign or a 'Sale Ends Soon' banner, lose their train of thought, park, and shop some more. But for the strong ones, at this point, you'll want them to once again see the prize. It's an actual exit lane, but it's parallel to them, on the other side of a long concrete barrier filled with beautiful landscaping.

"Oh, that reminds me. Around any intersection or anywhere they'll need to turn, plant tall thick bushes and tall decorative grasses so they won't be able to see oncoming traffic.

"Okay, where was I? Oh, yeah. They're parallel to an exit lane that's on the other side of a long concrete barrier. To get around this obstacle they'll have to drive all the way back up to the stores, avoid the pedestrians, then turn left by the thick beautiful bushes. It's fun to watch.

"Once past that point, they'll have to make yet another left, if only those pesky pedestrians would get out of the way. This turn, through the pedestrians and incoming traffic, will put them on a section-exit-road that leads to a feeder-exit-road that leads to the main exit. Any questions? No, Damian, you can't take hostages."

INTERMISSION...

You know there isn't actually a Marquis de Sade School of Parking Sciences, right? It's just another figment of my imagination. Though, I can see it now. Sadists searching online for an enrollment application. "Sign up now and get a free thumbscrew."

I would, however, like for a parking lot design engineer to explain the use of tall view-blocking plants that crowd the intersections in these modern parking mazes. Parking lot design, you would think, would be about safety and functionality. It seems those points were missed in some of these mis-shapen nightmares.

ACT TWO

(Just kidding. There is no Act Two)

There is, however, **Parking Lot Etiquette:**

- Drive your 3,000 pounds of life-changing carnage at a reasonable speed (remember, pedestrians are out there with you).
- Use your turn signals (you know my thoughts on that).
- Use your cell phone *after* you park.
- Try not to hit the mall with your vehicle (it's the great big building, you can't miss it).
- Avoid crowded parking areas because that's where all the accidents occur. Park in the boonies.
- And remember Rule Three/sub-section(a): Everyone in the parking lot is a moron but you. The morons *are* out to get us.

BEWARE THE DARK ANGLE OF DEATH

With alarming frequency I see Dark Angles of Death roaming our parking lots. (It's spelled correctly, though amusingly, my "grammar check" wants me to use the word "Angel.")

A Dark Angle is a moron that cuts across parking lots at odd angles hoping to beat someone else to that "close spot." You'll see him weaving through rows of parked cars, wherever he can find an opening, crossing lane after lane, barely missing oncoming traffic and pedestrians. Don't do this. It's extremely dangerous.

Though, I'll have to admit that at four in the morning I have cut across *empty* parking lots at odd angles. Again, a.m. Diamond Rules; there's no one there to endanger. You can, however, even in the predawn hours, get a ticket for driving diagonally across a parking lot. It's considered Reckless Driving.

Parking lot Traffic Laws are a convoluted mix of publically-owned verses privately-owned control. But, in most places, in most parking lots, public and private, you can get a ticket. So, if at 3 a.m. you decide to be a Dark Angle and you see the dreaded blue lights suddenly appear, you were warned. It's the busy time of day Dark Angles you need to fear.

PULL-THROUGHS

I have my own view of parking, but I'm sure that doesn't surprise you. Most people pull forward into a parking space, then, when it's time to leave, they have to back out into moving traffic while trying to avoid pedestrians and other cars backing out of their spaces. A lot of parking lot mishaps occur because vehicles are backing out of their parking spaces. It's much harder to see when you're backing up.

When I park, I look for a pull-through, an open parking space that leads through to another open space on the other side. (Of course, I always watch for vehicles pulling into the space from the other side, or a Dark Angle cutting through.) That way, when it's time to leave, I'm facing out. I'm pulling forward into vehicle and pedestrian traffic. It's much safer. If you can't find a pull-through, back into an empty space. Better to back into a space you know is empty than to back out into moving traffic.

I am seeing an increasing number of drivers using this tactical advantage. Pull-throughs are considered illegal in some states, which I don't quite get. It's the safest way to park, facing out. I'll leave it up to you how you end up that way.

If they asked me how to improve parking lots (oddly, no one has), here's my suggestion: Arrange parked vehicles in single rows, instead of double rows, then every parking space would be a pull-through. You'd pull in going forward, and you'd exit going forward out the other side. I doubt this will ever happen because it's an inefficient use of space (you'd lose some parking spaces in favor of more driving lanes), but it would be *safer* and easier to use.

Finding a pull-through is often difficult. The rule is: the farther from the store, the more abundant the pull-throughs. Personally, I like to park farther from the store, anyway; there's less congestion. Often times I'm the only vehicle out in the boonies. Though, occasionally you find a Best-in-Show there.

BEST-IN-SHOW

You've seen these vehicles. It's usually somebody's "new car" parked catty-cornered across two parking spaces to avoid dings to their little Best-in-Show. Although, there is a *display* aspect to it as well. It's that, "Hey, Look at My Ride. See what I'm driving. I must be pretty special." I suppose they have a right to be proud of their cars. I've seen some nice rides out in the boonies. But I've parked right next to them anyway. Pulled up alongside, copying their exact angle across two parking spaces, like that's how you're supposed to park.

Although, I would never damage anyone's vehicle, Best-in-Show or otherwise. I always leave a comfortable gap so they or I can open our car door without inflicting damage.

To be honest, I've only parked catty-corner next to a Best-in-Show twice, and both times the cars were gone when I got back. I've always wondered what the drivers' reactions were to their perfect plans gone awry. I'm sure they had some choice words (Double Points). But I understand their concerns. I don't want door dings either, and I don't drive a Best-in-Show.

NOT IN THE THICK OF THE FRAY

Other benefits of boonies-parking are: I'm away from the "vehicular battle for the close spot," I'm never near a parking lot collision, and there are very few pedestrians out there to *get in my way*. They're all up by the store, threading their way through moving vehicles, sputtering when someone backs out and almost runs them over.

Plus I get a bit of exercise because, OMG, I get to walk a little further. I like to walk. There's the rub. Everybody wants the closest spot they can find so they don't have to walk an extra fifty yards. Sometimes, though, that close spot is the stuff of angry contention.

CLASH OF THE DARK ANGLES!

Coming soon to a parking lot near you.

One year, a few days before Christmas, I witnessed "a parking lot war of wills" I'll never forget. You know what Christmas parking is like. The boonies are even parked up. Panicked shoppers are scurrying about to get that last-minute item, and most everyone wants to park as close to the store as possible. That's the setup…

…here's what happened. I had parked and was walking towards the store when I came upon two cars *in contention* for a seasonally-rare close parking space. Coming from opposite directions, both drivers had their front ends partially in the empty space, neither allowing the other vehicle access.

These two morons were blocking the flow of traffic in the aisle and cars were piling up on either side. Horns were blowing. One moron had his window down screaming at the other moron to move; it was *his spot*, he'd seen it first.

I continued to the store entrance, stopped and turned around so I could watch the drama unfold. It's hard to find entertainment like that; morons on display. I stood for a while with a few other shoppers, everyone joking and voicing their opinion. I eventually lost interest and went inside to shop. I was in the store forty minutes, maybe more.

When I came out, I couldn't believe my eyes, neither car had moved. Both drivers were still holding out for that *close spot*. Neither driver was blowing his horn, neither was yelling. They were silently trying to out-wait the other, frozen in a parking lot war of wills like two horn-locked stags.

To me, these morons gave up at least an hour of their lives just so they could "get that parking spot, by God." Never give up a moment of your life to anger. Give it a rest. Park in the boonies and get a little more exercise. It'll help with your anger problem.

IT'S "MY SPOT" (CONTINUED)

A few years back my wife and I were out and about shopping for pet supplies. When we got to the pet store, we found a mid-lot space, parked, and were headed for the store when a car turned into the aisle then slowed to a stop right next to me. The driver rolled down his window and said, "I guess some people are special." I looked at him confused and said, "what?" "You took my parking space," he angrily answered. My wife, a little ahead of me, turned and asked what was going on. "This guy thinks I took his parking space," I answered. "You did," he spouted.

I don't even know where he came from. He wasn't in the aisle when I pulled into the parking space. If someone had been sitting there with their turn signal on I think I would have noticed. No one was in the aisle at all. I looked at him and said, "Life goes on. You'll get over it." This caused him to crack open his car door as though he wanted to get out and fight. I just stared and shook my head. He pulled his door closed and drove off muttering something under his breath.

I thought later he might have been one of the before-mentioned Dark Angles that battled for that rare Christmas space. I have no idea from where in

CONFESSIONS OF A TACTICAL DRIVER

the lot he spied that space. If another driver is in an aisle with their signal on, I let them have the space. The world is full of angry fruitcakes.

SPACE SAVERS

I've seen Dark Angles offer up their spouses or children as human sacrifices. "Nadine, jump out and go stand in that empty parking spot. Don't let nobody pull in there. Lay down on the ground if you have to." You've seen that, right?

I suppose it's much the same as saving a seat in a crowded movie theater, except the chances of getting crushed in a theater are considerably less. Don't stand in an empty parking space. You look like a fool and you could get hurt. Another Dark Angle could come careening down the aisle, whip into the spot and run you over. Parking spaces are for vehicles and are first-come first-serve.

Of course, the closet spots are in the Fire Lane next to the store. It never fails, there's always a moron's car parked in the Fire Lane. Apparently though, if a Space-Saving passenger is left sitting in the car while the moron is in the store, the vehicle is not in the way. Another unspoken traffic rule.

The Fire Lane is for emergency vehicles; don't park there. It's not hard to figure out. It's what those No-Parking Fire-Lane Do-Not-Block signs mean. It's not rocket surgery. I know; rocket science or brain surgery, but the other day I heard a college basketball analyst use that term and none of the other analysts seemed to notice, so it's become one of my new favorites. I suppose the flip side is Brain Science, but not nearly as funny as Rocket Surgery.

THE STALKER

One of my favorite parking lot characters is the Stalker. You'll see him circling a parking lot in his vehicle looking for shoppers exiting a store. When he spies one, he falls in behind his prey, slowly stalking them like a three-thousand pound oil-blooded predator, hoping to pounce on *their* spot, hoping it's a close spot, following along in the shadows.

If you notice that you have a Stalker, they're easy to mess with. Here's what to do. Once you get to your car, you'll want to store your purchases safely, so put some packages in the trunk and some in the backseat, painstakingly arranging each package for optimal travel. Then get in your car and start the engine.

Then get out of your car and pretend you're looking for something you've lost. Pat down your pockets, then open the back door and look around in there. Then reach in the front seat, turn off the engine and grab your keys so you can look in the trunk.

Finally, you get back into your car, slowly put on your seatbelt, restart your engine, check your mirrors, put your car in gear, back or pull out slowly, then surprisingly make eye contact with the Stalker and wave like, "Oh, sorry, I didn't see you," and drive off smiling. I've read studies that claim if people know you're waiting on a parking spot they occupy, they will intentionally take longer to pull out. It's the parking lot version of Make 'em Wait.

MY FAVORITE PARKING LOT MOMENT

This particular incident happened when I was married to my first wife. We were leaving a store where we hadn't purchased anything; no packages in hand. We had parked mid-lot and were headed back out to find our car. When we reached our vehicle there were no other shoppers around. We were pretty much alone as we stood on either side of the car ready to climb in and leave. My wife was driving so I was on the passenger side.

As I heard the doors unlock I noticed that my zipper was down. I looked across the car at my wife and said, "Damn, my zipper was down, the beast almost got out." She rolled her eyes and shot me one of those *you think you're funny but you're not* looks. Then she got in the car. I stood for a moment adjusting things and zipping up.

When I got in the car I was surprised to see that my wife was in the throes of some very funny joke. She had her hand covering her mouth trying to hold back a huge laugh. Tears were streaming down her face and her body convulsing. "What?" I said. I started giggling. You know how contagious laughter can be. "What?" She couldn't speak but she was pointing right at me. No, she was pointing past me.

I turn and see a woman sitting in the driver's seat of the car right next to me; her window down, her hand covering her mouth, her body convulsing as she tried to contain her amusement. My comment had really struck her funny bone. That memory still makes me smile and I'm sure she had a good story to tell.

That's enough on parking lots for now. But as long as we're here, I need to run a quick errand. Let's run into the grocery store. Besides, I want to stretch my legs.

THE GROCERY STORE

(Shopping Cart Driving)

S hopping Cart driving? If you've paid attention, you know as well as I that there *is* a Grocery Store Shopping Cart Driving Game. Why do you think those plastic-covered Kiddy Carts are shaped and painted like little Race Cars? Hmm. Grocery aisles are the last bastion of the "free for all" driving mentality. There are no rules. It's a jungle in there. And grocery shopping is all that's left of our hunter-gatherer heritage. Instead of a rock and a spear and a will to survive, we now have a grocery cart, double-coupons, and a will to survive.

Everyone's ancestors were hunters, or fishers, or gatherers of fruits and vegetables. Can you see yourself foraging for wild mushrooms, hoping to avoid the poisonous varieties? Or standing in a cold stream trying to spear a fish? How about building and setting a rabbit trap?

Those days are gone but the "competition instincts for the hunt" still linger in our genes. That's why on Black Friday you hear about *fights in the dress aisle* or the use of pepper spray to fend off the competition. *That's my iPhone, damn it.* If we're dreaming of a White Christmas, why does Christmas season start with Black Friday; well it actually starts on Thanksgiving now so I guess it should be Black Thursday.

Here's what I think. Now that Christmas season officially starts on Thanksgiving, they should change those pre-Thanksgiving ad campaigns to Black Thursday and Blue Friday, make it a two-day event: Throw Down! Black Thursday vs. Blue Friday! Raw! We need to get that black-and-blue Christmas Spirit in there. We'll get Mike Tyson to write a jingle. Heck, do away with the name Thanksgiving all together. Change it to Black Thursday. "Happy Black Thursday to you." Has a nice ring to it. Then we can add Intensive Care Saturday, all medical supplies 50% off.

Whatever happened to those meek After Thanksgiving Sales? When did it become necessary to "set up camp" in front of a store and "defend your position" so you can beat the other guy to that "special" item? But I've gotten off track. Got all fired-up again. My doctor says I'm doing better. (Did not.)

YOUR RIDE

The first step in the modern hunter-gatherer era is selecting the perfect cart. Perfect carts are rare and hard to pick from the cart corral at the front of the store. Some carts, of course, can be visually eliminated. You can see their plastic seats bent and bruised; their handles missing some of their covering; the obviously abused carts that should have been "put down" years ago.

You're looking for a thoroughbred cart, one that rolls quickly and stealthily through the often confusing maze of store displays. You want one that rides smoothly across the parking lot after the hunt. You don't want a lame cart with a wobbling wheel that snags and rattles every few feet, or a flat-spot cart with wheels that thump, thump, thump along.

You spy a decent cart and try to pull it from the embedded line only to find that it's stuck. The child-seatbelt buckle is hopelessly entangled in the metal ribs of another cart. If you could revert to your ancient hunter-gatherer-self you could pull your stag-horn knife from its leather sheath, slice the strap, and free the entangled cart. But no, you have to settle for the cart next to it, the one with the bent and bruised plastic seat. It'll have to do. Now for the "test drive."

You should push your cart along as you listen to its wheels and judge its steering. Avoid carts that pull to one side; much too hard to steer with one hand while you hunt for supplies in the crowded grocery aisles.

I have noticed that grocery stores now have ingenious test-drive areas that fool you into believing you have a good cart until it's too late. They cover the floor of the cart corral in rough-edged four-inch tiles so you can't tell if your cart is thumping across the tiles or if it has bad wheels. The distracting tiles go all the way up to the automatic doors that let you in but close when you get past them. Carts check in, but they don't checkout. Phase Two of the keep-'em-here parking lot strategy.

If I find I was duped and have a thumping, limping rattle-cart, I turn around, go back to the cart corral and wrangle another one. A little side note: If you can get a grip on the handleless automatic doors you can pull them apart and they will reopen. Or you can wait for the next incoming gatherer, then slip back into the cart corral and try again. If you're persistent, you will find a trusty rattle-free cart even if it is an "old paint."

Now that you have your cart, it's time to hunt and gather, to mingle with the masses, to compete with other hunter-gatherers. You need to know who you're up against.

MODERN HUNTER-GATHERER TRIBES

The Plow Tribe – A Plow walks behind his cart and uses the plastic-covered handle to steer the cart, much as a farmer would steer a plow, but that's not the source of the definition. Most gatherers use this method of steering. It's the correct and most streamlined method for negotiating the harrowing and crowded aisles, but very few gatherers are actually Plows.

A Plow is someone who, when they see an unattended cart blocking an aisle, uses his own cart as a battering ram to Plow the unattended cart out of the way. There is no Rule Two for Shopping Carts. It's not yours. It belongs to the store, and you're not going to damage it, you're traveling 2 mph.

I'm a member of the Plow Tribe. I don't plow too hard, I just push an unattended cart out of the way, forcefully, and try to wedge it behind a display. Often you never see the moron who abandoned their cart, but sometimes you do, and this knocking-of-carts apparently hurts their feelings. I love the look on their face as they see their cart rolling away. Some reach for their cart and snap, "Well, excuse me," or, "Hey, what do you think you're doing?" And I always reply, "I'm unblocking the aisle because some rude self-centered person left their cart in the way." That usually *shuts them up.*

Some still complain as I walk away shaking my head. But hey, life goes on, they'll get over it. I'm not going to reach out and gently move an abandoned cart. Don't be an ass, if you leave your cart alone while you shop elsewhere, don't leave it blocking an aisle. But I'm sure this is falling on deaf ears. Grocery stores are full of inconsiderate thoughtless idiots. Speaking of which…

The ICU$_2$ Tribe – The aisle-blocker I described in the Plow section is really an ICU$_2$ (**I**diotic **C**art **U**ser). Similar to an ICU on the road, the ICU$_2$'s main games are Slow Down and Make 'em Wait grocery store style. And although no one has ever confessed to being either an ICU or an ICU$_2$, I believe these people are halves of the same bun. They've simply exchanged their cars for carts. And leaving their carts in the way unattended is just one of their tricks.

Grocery aisles are just wide enough for two cart lanes. I would say one for each direction but there are no cart driving rules. Well, common courtesy, but you seldom see that anymore. However, I find most people pilot their grocery carts much the same as they drive their vehicles, staying to the right side of the aisle. Most people, that is, except for an ICU$_2$.

They position themselves in the center of the aisle so no one can pass them going either direction, then they stop and stare at the canned goods. They pretend to be lost in thought, oblivious. I will say, "Excuse me" one time if they don't quickly move to clear a path. If that doesn't work, my Plow heritage takes over. It doesn't take much of a nudge to wake them up. They usually let out an *exasperated sigh* like, *can't you see I'm shopping. Can't you wait a minute?* No, I can't.

Even in the grocery store I'm Ultimate Goal oriented. I *will wait* on an elderly or handicapped shopper, but if you're just standing in the way, I've got no respect for you. It's not your store. It's not your aisle. Have a little courtesy and stand to one side or the other, makes no difference to me.

Another ICU$_2$ trick is to use one of those round product displays that sporadically clog the aisles as a Traffic Dam. They position their cart beside a display, effectively damming the aisle, then wander off in search of supplies. If I leave my cart unattended for a moment, I always hitch-it *behind* one of those displays. At least then it's out of the way as much as it can be. This allows my fellow Plows to gather and hunt unimpeded.

The Wagoner Tribe - These gatherers pull their carts like a wagon. A Wagoner blocks an aisle much the same as an ICU$_2$ except, unlike an ICU$_2$, they seem to always be in a hurry; Jerks and White Rabbits. This cart pulling method takes up both cart lanes; the Wagoner in one lane and their cart behind them in the other. It's an abomination. If God had intended that you pull your cart, He would have put a handle on the front. Fall in behind your cart, dumbass, and leave room for others. More than one Wagoner in an aisle is considered a Wagon Train. Giddy-up and go, partner. Put the circles in the wagon.

The cart drivers I've described so far are solitary hunters (one cart, one hunter-gatherer) who make up the majority of the Gatherer population. However, there are a couple of multi-character categories that we need to discuss.

The Herd and the Trail Boss – This is when you see, coming down the aisle towards you, a cart loaded with groceries, surrounded by a herd of children. A true Herd has at least four children; one in the child seat and three scurrying about grabbing boxes of sugar-laden cereal and snagging brightly-colored toys that dangle like tasty carrots from those swinging wire arms. While the Trail Boss, usually the mom, tries to reign in the strays, screaming

"No, you can't have that," or "No, put that back," snatching at little arms full of candy, as *the tiny one* in the child seat stands up and reaches for the pretty glass jars on the top shelf (clean-up in aisle twelve).

As few as two children can be considered a herd if they're sufficiently hyper, ricocheting like pinballs through the aisles. One, if the child is completely out of control, crying and throwing a fit because they can't have a box of Mommy-Snapped Sugar Cookies. Technically, one screaming child is a Heard.

My favorite, however, is a Herd of Danglers. That's where two or more children dangle from the front and the sides of a cart, their little hands grasping the top edge of the basket with their little feet atop the lower wheel section, screaming, "Go faster. Go faster." Moms seldom give in and go faster. Mothers are serious shoppers who tend to tire quickly of the added Dangler weight. So they "pry" their children from the cart with "a look" (we all know that look) and "a word" (don't make me say it again) to roam freely in the untamed aisles.

But if it's Dad driving the cart, all bets are off. He might give in, speed up and give his kids the ride of their lives. For a short distance anyway. Until the real Trail Boss reins in her herd, bull and calves alike. But for a few seconds, it's that, "Hey, y'all, watch this" Darwin Award mentality as dad speeds down the aisle, children hanging on for dear life, eyes wide with excitement.

Though it's rare to witness one of these *thrill rides*, I'm always hopeful. I love those moments. I go on alert when I see a Herd of Danglers. I know that sooner or later there's going to be a miscalculation by some well-meaning dad and I'm going to witness some Danglers take out a towering display of Mommy-Snapped Sugar Cookies. It's on my bucket list.

The Hunting Party – A Hunting Party is usually "a couple;" a pair of significant others, but not always. For instance, you might see two or more Fire Fighters pack-hunting, prowling the aisles for supplies for those long shifts they pull. And though there's sometimes a couple in the Trail Boss scenario, they can never be considered a Hunting Party because they're not working in tandem. One is tending the herd, though an important task, it's still a distraction from the hunt. A true Hunting Party is a team. They work together to corner their prey. There are various incarnations of the Hunting Party:

A Gatherer and a Driver: This is a common team. One is the Driver and the other is the Gatherer. From my observations, the Gatherer usually chooses the path and decides when and where to gather. The Driver has to follow along, often by having to mind read, and stay close so the Gatherer has constant access to the cart. That's the Driver's job.

If you're the Driver, you should never drift off. Never get distracted by a display of doughnuts and fail to be there when the Gatherer turns to deposit their catch. You'll get that look. That *you're supposed to be "here"* look. Or *you're slowing down the process* look. *Do you see what time it is? Jeopardy starts in twenty minutes. Try and keep up.* I suppose in reality this is a twisted version of backseat driving where the Gatherer actually is, by proxy, driving the cart, leaving their hands free to grab that next Sale item.

A Union: Every decision about the hunt is shared by this type of Hunting Party. Lengthy debates about value and taste accompany every acquisition. You see them standing, discussing the nutritional information, blocking the aisle. Their goal is to make an informed decision; buy the best thing for their health and their wallet. Not a bad thing, but a bit slow for my tastes. (I'm a creature of habit. I know what I'm after.) You often see them pushing their cart side by side, elbow to elbow, Yin to Yang, joined at the hip for better or for worse. It's much the same as a lone hunter. It's really just one person in two bodies, a complete waste of one whole person. Divide and conquer.

A Gatherer and a Scout: When my wife and I shop together, she's a Driver/ Gatherer and I'm a Scout. She has the list and the cart, and I scout ahead, find items on the list, and meet back up at Produce Pass. Then I'm off again, hunting more items. This strategy is a true Ultimate Goal time saver.

It's great being a Scout. I'm carrying a hand-held basket so I'm mobile. I can move easily through crowded aisles. I can slip past a Traffic Dam like a UFO, gather and return to the Mother Cart, await further gathering instructions, and be home in time for Jeopardy without fail. But even being a Scout, sometimes, some aisles are almost impossible to navigate.

THE OBSTACLE COURSE

I'm beginning to believe that you can minor in Grocery Aisle Arrangement at The Marquis de Sade School of Parking Sciences. It seems that more and more stuff is cluttering grocery aisles; display after display, advertisement after advertisement.

Now they have those talking advertising screens at the end of every aisle, pointing out the pile of cans there, "It's easy and your family will love you for it. Spam, a true Black Thursday treat. Thanks, mom. You're the best." I despise those talking screens. Makes me not want to shop in stores that have them. Enough advertising already.

The aisles are Gauntlets; a mix of ICU_2's, Wagoners, and five or six of those little round product displays erratically scattered to confuse and trap. Even carrying a hand-held basket you can get caught and have to wait for a traffic jam to clear. It's Phase Three of the keep-'em-here parking lot strategy. Their thoughts are, if you *get caught* at a Traffic Dam, you might notice a product you'd otherwise miss if you could navigate the aisles unimpeded.

THE HUNTING APPAREL AND DRIVER CRITIQUE

Hands down, the most entertaining part of the grocery store experience or in any big-box store is the "other driver clothing critique." I give positive or negative points for personal attire.

Pajama Outfits are always awarded negative points; the worn house slippers scuffing the floor, the baggy green pajama bottoms tattered at the cuff, covered with cute little ducks, the mismatched pajama top ablaze with odd orange-colored flowers on a baby-blue background.

Apparently it's not fashionable to wear a matching pajama outfit. That would look too much like you were ready for bed, not dressed for the store. A female ensemble might include large pink hair curlers or the more fashionable gold curlers sprouting at weird angles.

The male participants usually wear those saggy-bottom pajama pants where the butt's all stretched out and hanging like a hammock. Stretched out like they used to store something back there, but not anymore. This is the one activity you can't do while driving a car, critique another driver's appearance. The grocery store is a people watching delight. It's a great place to go for an ego boost.

Thank God you don't dress like that, huh? You've got to admit that you give negative points when you see a Pajama Outfit. You might not actively think or say negative points, but you have an instant reaction whether you admit it or not.

It's rare to see a real jaw dropper, a Wal-Martian; that's someone wearing a particularly egregious outfit. When I do though, I never miss the opportunity to tag along at a safe distance for a few minutes and watch other people's reaction as they're shocked by the spectacle.

You've heard the expression, "written all over their face." They come around a corner and their eye catches a glimpse of that other worldly, sometimes wholly inappropriate outfit exposing far too much skin, and for a moment the observer is stunned. Sometimes their hand quickly moves to cover their mouth, keeping a gasp or a laugh at bay, their eyes wide with disbelief. You can see the gears turning in their head. *Why would anybody leave their home dressed like that? For that matter, why would anybody be in their home dressed like that?* The observer makes eye contact with other gatherers to confirm their amazement. Sometimes the reactions are priceless. Live long and prosper, Wal-Martians.

The Sunday *just came from church* Outfit. If anyone ever looked out of place in a grocery store it's someone dressed to the nines. Most modern gatherers wear jeans, T-shirts, and tennis shoes. When I see a group fresh from church, dressed like it's Easter Sunday, it's always a pleasant surprise.

I've seen some beautifully attired families. It's nice when people dress up (positive points). The reason this is not a Herd is that the children have a "good clothes" brake being applied by the mother. "Now stay close to me. Do you hear me, Timmy? I don't want you getting your 'good clothes' dirty."

There is a magical effect being *nicely dressed* has on most children. It's like they know they look good. Sort of reins in their rambunctious spirit, except for the three- or four-year-olds. You can see the desperation in their little eyes. "Please hurry, mommy. I'm going to bust if I don't get out of my good clothes."

The Slouch and the Crackasaurus. You've seen a Slouch. They drive with their elbows. They're hunched over their cart with their arms from the elbow forward stretched out along the top edge. I've never been able to decide if they're tired and need to rest, or if they're bored. The worst thing about this stance is when they become a Crackasaurus.

You've heard the term "Plumber's Crack." It's where men buy pants that fit under their belly instead of around their waist, and as a consequence, when they bend over or squat down, half of their butt is exposed. This is not something I want to see while gathering food. Well, I never want to see it, but especially not in a grocery store.

I coined the terms "Crackasaurus" and "Isoreacrackus" years ago when I worked with a guy that, even standing up straight, several inches of his crack was always on display. He had a huge beer belly and he bought Plumber's Pants. He was the butt of most jokes, of course.

Some of the guys I worked with (I didn't do this, but I thought it was funny) would sneak up behind him and insert coins or pencils in the exposed slot. It sort of irritated the Crackasaurus, figuratively I mean. But life went on, he got over it.

It never occurred to him to buy pants that fit. He would proudly proclaim, "I wear a size 32 waist." Yeah, when you were ten. Needless to say nobody ever picked up pencils of questionable origin. I don't know what happened to the coins. Think about that the next time you reach for some change.

The Full Diaper Penguin. This is the rarest cart driver. This style is apparently the "cool look" for the modern male teenager, and male teenagers are seldom hunter-gatherers. Unlike a Crackasaurus they buy their pants way too large, so when they walk they have to spread their legs at an awkward angle to keep their pants from falling off.

When you see one pushing a cart, they resemble a waddling penguin with a fully loaded diaper. It always cracks me up, no pun intended. All I'm saying is, if that look doesn't get you laid, you should reconsider your pant choice. But hey, I thought I was cool when I was a teenager. I mean, I was cool. I guess I'd be embarrassed for you to see my old photos.

A Herd of Zombies. I'm starting to see more Zombie Families. They're like the Shopping Dead. They wander the store in a cell-phone-induced-stupor. They've gone Zomular, none of them speaking, thumbs a twitching, mesmerized by their cell phones. The little Zombies seem to have a flocking mentality because they manage to follow the overall direction of the Mother Cart, though their little deadened eyes never leave their magic screens. It's as though their personalities and all their youthful exuberance have been "textinguished." Cell Assassins in the wild.

I read the other day that texting is now considered an addiction. An addiction? An obsession maybe, but not an addiction. I could be wrong, I suppose. Maybe there's a Secret Signal being broadcast by our government that's sucking all the Energy out of our young via their cell phones and turning it into Special Funds for their Covert Affairs.

That has to be it. It's a government plot. It's an electronic-drug administered visually to placate the masses. That's why Cell Assassins don't watch the road. They're getting their "fix." It's why they walk like Zombies through the mall. Oh My God, I need to get rid of my cell phone. Now I'm not sure I trust my answering machine either.

I want to shift gears and point out a serious problem in grocery stores; that's the purse thief or pickpocket. If you carry a purse, don't leave it sitting open in your cart. You're asking to have your credit cards, money, driver's license, and identity stolen. Don't make it easy for some lowlife to ruin your life. I recently had my email and Facebook accounts hacked and used in a failed attempt to extract money from my friends. Protect your identity.

THE CHECKOUT

The Checkout is the worst part of the modern Hunter-Gatherer experience. Most stores have cut back on their help. It's common now to find only one or two cashiers on duty. At least until the wait gets so long that gatherers start abandoning their carts to shop elsewhere. It's then you might see another cashier begrudgingly show up and open a lane.

And, for me, when the new lane opens, I'm usually trapped between those gum and candy displays. I've been waiting patiently for twenty minutes, and now all the people behind me stampede the new lane and start checking out. Then I realize I have an *extreme couponer* in front of me and it's going to take an extra ten minutes to swipe all their coupons. Nothing wrong with saving money, it just sucks to be behind a couponer when you want to get back on the road.

Then there's the "fifteen items or less" line. I always thought that meant carts with fifteen or fewer items could checkout there. Apparently there's new math involved. I regularly see morons with fifty items in that line. I've seen 'em roll through with two or more full carts. Then, when you start grumbling, they give you that "I'm sorry, I was in a hurry" look (typical red-light-running White Rabbit). The stores need to have cashiers with the gumption to tell those that abuse this checkout privilege to get in the proper line.

An ICU_2 trick is to checkout with more than one order. They have their handful of items that have to be rung up and paid for, and several of their friends' orders that have to be rung up and paid for separately. And it never fails; at least one of the multiple orders exceeds the money the friend gave them, so a phone call has to be made so the friend can decide what to put back. There needs to be a "multiple order" lane; two or more orders of fifteen items or less.

Then there's the Jerk. They come to the register already on their phone and talk the whole time they're checking out. They sluggishly unload the cart with their free hand. Then they stop unloading altogether because they need to concentrate on their phone conversation. It seems that a growing number of people are plain rude when it comes to cell phone use; they're amazingly self-centered. Apparently it's all "I, me, mine" now.

And the worst of the Jerks are the ones that talk extra loud because they want you to know they're on an important call. Their words are a swirl of business terms or there's a crisis they have to deal with. They're important people, at least in their mind.

It's much the same in restaurants when a couple in an adjacent booth is having a quiet conversation, then one of them takes a call and talks at the top of their voice the whole time they're on the phone. Yes, I can hear you now! I tried to come up with a term for these troublesome Jerks, a sonic level of Jerkdom, but the closest I could come is a Textrovert. I know it doesn't quite fit, but it has the right flavor.

Lastly, and I promise we'll leave, is the Coin-Operated ICU_2 who checks out using a bag of coins. They dump a pile of change on the grocery conveyor belt and start counting coins to come up with the twenty-four dollars and thirty-seven cents they need to cover their purchases. A word to you Coin-Operated ICU_2's; use one of those coin exchange machines and have your bag of coins converted into a credit slip before you get in line. I guess all I'm doing now is complaining. Let's take our stuff and get out of here.

BACK TO THE PARKING LOT

The trip back to the car is my favorite part of the hunter-gatherer experience. This is where I actually "ride" my cart. I take a running start, jump up on the back and take off. That's why steering and good wheels are important. I recommend that you <u>don't</u> try this. You could get hurt.

Another reason I park in the boonies is it makes my *cart ride* last longer. Most parking lots slope downhill away from the store, some gently, some a bit more extreme. The steeper the slope, the faster the ride. I'm not crazy. I'm not going to ride a cart down a really steep slope. I like a comfortable slope, no more than a 10% grade. I'm not looking to ride a bronco, but I do enjoy the ride.

It's exhilarating. What did you do today that was exhilarating? I suppose most would consider riding a grocery cart as something only a child would do. "It's time to put childish things away. I'll walk to my car, thank you very much." It's healthy to let loose, to ride a bike, or ride a sled down a snow-covered hill, or a loaded grocery cart back to your car. Life's about enjoying the moment, and letting your inner child out once in a while. To me, cart riding is fun. I accept the danger.

The "art of the ride" is predicting the exact moment to jump off before the cart gets going too fast. I've had a few unnerving experiences. That's why I wear good shoes, so I can stop a loaded cart. Sometimes, if the slope is too gentle, I might have to keep pushing with one foot, like on a skateboard, just to make it all the way back to my car. I've had people drive by while I'm loading groceries into my car and give me compliments on my ride, or ask me if it keeps me young. I think it might.

I suggest, however, that you *walk your cart back to your car* like you've always done. It's much safer and there's nothing wrong with walking. You are, after all, responsible for your own safety. It's the very essence of Rule One. Participate in your own health and well-being.

When you're finished with your cart, put it in one of those parking lot corrals. Don't leave it stranded in a parking space. Don't be an Ass. Just today, while leaving the grocery store I saw a car parked in a Handicapped space and the obviously-handicapped driver was putting his groceries into his vehicle. He then pushed his empty cart into an adjacent Handicapped parking space, got in his truck and left; which only goes to prove that a handicapped person can be just as big a Jerk as anyone else.

I sometimes refer to abandoned carts as Feral Carts, out wandering the parking lot alone. But abandoned carts are really more of a testament to the "it's just about me" mentality. "I'm finished with the cart now. Someone else will have to put it away for me. It doesn't matter to me that it's in the way. It doesn't matter to me if I inconvenience someone else." It has crossed my mind that these cart-abandoners are part of the ever-increasing depressed populace that are unhappy in their lives and want to demonstrate that fact by inconveniencing others. Maybe they're just lazy. Though I think it's the former.

Look at the time. We need to get moving. I almost forgot about Rush Hour Traffic.

RUSH HOUR TRAFFIC & BOTTLENECKS

T he joys of a Traffic Jam; cars moving inches at a time, Jerks jumping back and forth from lane to lane trying to get past one more Creeper, tempers flare, somebody cuts somebody off, ICUs and Cell Assassins slowing down an already slow process, everyone trying to get to work in the morning, or back home at night. Phew, it's enough to make you scream. Relax, take a deep breath. Don't let a traffic snarl ruin your day.

Here's what to do at Rush Hour: Get into the lane you need, resign yourself to the fact that traffic is going to creep along, turn on some music, keep your eyes on the road, and proceed cautiously until you get to wherever you're going. It'll help keep your blood pressure under control.

Don't be a White Rabbit. If you think it's a fifteen minute drive to work, give yourself thirty minutes to get there. You'll be more relaxed. You won't be in such a hurry, and not as likely to take chances and run a red light so you'll be "on time." Take the stress out of your life.

I say that, but sometimes it gets to me anyway. You want to get home and you realize that your lane seems to be the only one not moving. Cars are passing you on either side, and you can't see what's going on because you're caught behind one of those monster trucks that infest the roads now.

What's the deal with all those giant pickup trucks? They're damn near mobile homes. I thought transportation technology was headed toward fuel conservation. Nothing fuel efficient about those beasts.

I did get a good laugh the other day when I was trapped behind a dark-blue behemoth with the word Nissan emblazoned across the back. All I could see was a wall of truck. My lane wasn't moving and I wanted to get around the monster. I was getting frustrated. Finally, he changed lanes so I didn't have to. I could once again see; just a long line of traffic in front of me, but at least now I was behind a normal-size car.

As the traffic inched along I ended up beside the massive dark-blue vehicle and I could read the truck's name in bold letters on the driver's door. The driver was this mousey looking guy, and the name on his door was V8 Titan. I suddenly envisioned the driver in a bar using the pick-up line, "Hey, baby, want to see my V8 Titan." I'm surprised that dangling metal balls don't come standard on this truck.

HONEY BUNCH

A mistake most drivers make in Rush Hour traffic is not leaving much of a gap between themselves and the car in front of them when traffic is stopped. Cars bunched tightly together have to proceed elastically, slowly stretching out.

Lines of vehicles with comfortable gaps can proceed much as a train would, cars moving together as though attached to one another, still somewhat elastic but much more efficient at getting cars through a light. But people are creatures of habit and sitting bumper to bumper is the norm.

WHAT?

My favorite "stuck in a traffic jam story" happened late one night when I was coming home from playing a gig in Frankfort, KY (I played drums in a Blues band for years). It was two a.m., not a traditional time for traffic jams, but apparently there'd been a serious Fault and the police (pronounced *po'-lease* if you're a Hickamy) were routing traffic off the interstate at my exit which worked for me in one sense, but slowed me down because of all the vehicles jamming the exit ramp and the detour road; the road I needed to get home.

It was a forty-minute traffic jam torture from the interstate to the traffic signal where everyone, except me, was going to turn left to follow the detour. I was free once I got through that light.

It was nearing three a.m. and I have to admit I was tired. I did some lane changing trying to get to the traffic signal sooner rather than later. This struggle for my freedom finally put me sitting two or three cars back from the light, waiting for the green. The car in front of me was a station wagon. (You don't see station wagons anymore.)

As I sat there waiting I noticed something moving in the darkened, glass-encircled back of the station wagon. You know when you see something you don't expect, how it takes your eyes and your mind a moment to make sense of it. This was just such a moment.

I tried to focus. What was it that was moving in the back of the station wagon? Finally and stunningly, it made sense when I realized that the face of a full-grown male African lion was staring right at me from the back window of the station wagon. You could have knocked me over with a feather.

I kept trying to disbelieve my eyes. I glanced around at other drivers and found they, too, were in disbelief, shrugging their shoulders and shaking their heads. I could see that a cage was installed in the back of the station wagon. The lion circled the cage a couple of times, then laid down and disappeared from view.

When the light changed and traffic started moving I got a chance to see the side of the vehicle. The station wagon belonged to the Cincinnati Zoo. Apparently they were transporting the lion to some other location in the middle of the night. It's a moment I'll never forget.

RED ALERT

It never fails, it's Rush Hour and there's a bottleneck and a traffic jam. Finally your lane starts moving, and you almost make it to the light, but then the light turns yellow, and *you could make it* if only the guy in front of you *would go*. But no, he's a Creeper and he stops for the yellow light and you're caught behind him.

That's what happens, *you get caught.* "I would have been here sooner, but I got caught at a red light. If that dumbass in front of me would have just gone, I'd been on time."

ACT THREE

And for a little Rush Hour entertainment, it's always fun to see two Jerks side by side as the front two cars at a red light. They sometimes perform what I like to call The Inch War. You see them inching forward, itching to go, straining against the red light. First, one Jerk inches forward, then the other Jerk, not to be out done, inches a little past the first one. Then the first one retaliates and inches a little further still. With alternating steps they inch into the crosswalk, then a little past the crosswalk until one of them has to surrender before they inch into harm's way into cross-moving traffic. If you know what to look for, City Driving can be very entertaining.

But enough of City Driving, enough of getting caught at red lights. I've had it up to here with Stop signs. What do you say? Let's get out of town and onto the open road.

THE INTERSTATE

There's nothing quite like the freedom of the open road. Driving on the interstate is a whole new plane of existence as compared to city driving - no traffic signals, no stopping, just going and going and going. Free at last to just "go." Of course, there is the usual cast of characters: Players and Creepers and Jerks, oh my, and White Rabbits, and let's not forget Cell Assassins, all interweaving in the constant stream of traffic. Shortly we'll add a few new characters to the pool.

The great thing about the interstate is all those lanes. There's a lane for the slower traffic, all the Creepers and such, and one or more lanes for faster traffic, for me and you. That's the master plan, several lanes so everybody can travel unimpeded. But we all know that there's more than one obstacle on the interstate to slow down all that "going," to deny you unimpeded travel, to keep you from the Ultimate Goal.

If you think about the flow of traffic on the interstate as liquid, then semis are like whales and cars are like fish and sharks and turtles, all swimming next to each other, intermingling, whisking around and passing each other, all flowing independently together, until that flow encounters a Choke Stone.

CHOKE STONES

I've done some slot canyon river hiking in Utah, and in those narrow canyons, when a large stone fills the bottom of the canyon and slows the flow of water it's called a Choke Stone because it chokes the flow of water. There are several types of interstate Choke Stones.

The Sap (**The S**elf-**ap**pointed speed-guardian). The Sap rides in the fast lane because *he's going the posted speed limit* and *that's as fast as you can legally go*; therefore he *is going fast* in the *fast lane* and doesn't have to get over. If someone behind him wants to go faster, well then, they're breaking the law, and there will be none of that while he's on the road. He's a speed-guardian for us all. I often refer to Saps as Gomers, as in "Citizen's arrest, Citizen's arrest."

If you've never seen the episode of The Andy Griffith Show where Gomer makes a "citizen's arrest" when he sees Deputy Barney Fife make an illegal U-turn, you should watch it. It's extremely funny and you'll more clearly understand my calling these Saps, Gomer.

The law states that slower traffic is to stay in the right lane. It doesn't matter what speed you're traveling, if someone behind you is going faster than you, you *are* supposed to get over. But Saps seldom do. They're too enthralled in their own self-righteousness. It doesn't matter if the driver behind them is a Jerk or someone with a medical emergency, Saps are going the speed limit, by God, and they don't have to get over.

Don't be a Sap. What's it to you if I want to go faster than you? That's how the interstates work; faster vehicles are supposed to, by design, be able to get by slower traffic. That's why there's a fast lane and a slow lane. You are not in charge of the interstate. Get over, Gomer. I have little or no patience for Saps. I seldom wait for them to get over. I simply pass them on the right. I know it's illegal, but so is blocking the fast lane.

Dave, a friend of mine, has another theory about these Saps. He thinks that the Occupy Wall Street protest settled into the left lane on the interstate. He's not sure what they're protesting, but there seems to be an Occupy Left Lane movement, or lack of movement I suppose. And since possession is nine-tenths of the law, what-cha gonna do?

A PILE OF STONES

A **Crunch of Creepers.** On the interstate, a Creeper will set their cruise control for five-under the suggested speed limit. A **Creeper Dam** happens when several Creepers bunch up together and one Creeper attempts to pass the Crunch by getting in the fast lane and going one-mile-an-hour faster than the group.

A word of Creeper advice: Accelerate past the Crunch, get back over, drop back to your comfortable Creeper speed, and go your merry Creeper way. Don't tie up traffic with that one-mile-an-hour passing routine. Just give it some thought. As a point of interest, the other end of the spectrum from a Crunch of Creepers is a Pound of Players (might come up in Final Jeopardy; you never know).

SPLIT PERSONALITY

Another impediment on the interstate is drivers that have **Turtle-Hare Syndrome**. They fly by you like a Hare, get in front of you, then slow down. What the hell is that all about? If you're going to pass and get in front of me, I expect you to go. Don't pass me and then slow down. Then I have to pass you, and I was riding along, enjoying the drive, listening to my stereo, and not touching my cruise control.

ROUGHING IT

The ultimate Choke Stone is **Road Construction**, the bane of drivers everywhere. Road Construction slows you down and frustrates you like nothing else. If you're a White Rabbit, it's pure torture.

Usually, when you encounter road construction the speed limit drops by 20 to 25 mph. When you've been traveling at interstate speeds, a 25 mph drop in speed makes you feel like you're crawling. Speed withdrawal is a bitch. And there are all those concrete barriers as the road zigzags back and forth over rough pavement and you see those "Stay in Lane" signs. You know, then, you're in for a long haul.

There are drivers who treat those signs like the warnings on mattress tags, they ignore them. The best thing to do in Road Construction is relax, obey the signs, and don't try to speed. Road Crews are out there working. Do your best to keep them safe. You will eventually get past the slow down and, before you know it, be on your merry way once again.

MAKING TIME

Sometimes, however, interstate travel *is exactly* what it's supposed to be, unimpeded cruising. That's when interstates are great. Nothing like "making good time." Interstate trips are usually measured in hours rather than miles. It's not a five-hundred mile trip; it's a seven-hour drive if everything goes smoothly. "We did it in six hours. We made really good time."

DRAGON ASS

I like to set my cruise control for 5-over and enjoy the drive. Sometimes though, other drivers muck-up that enjoyment. One moron that particularly irritates me is a Dragon Ass. They fall in behind you and drive your exact speed. And that wouldn't bother me if they left a three-second gap. But a Dragon Ass stays a constant one or two car lengths behind.

It annoys me seeing them so close in my rearview mirror. A Dragon Ass hypnotically attaches to your rear-end because, apparently, they're unable to drive by themselves. I have a technique called "Wiping the Dragon's Ass" to rid me of these pests.

This is pretty easy. First, look ahead for a Creeper. Your plan is to wipe the Dragon Ass onto the Creeper so they can deal with him in *their* rearview mirror. Don't make your move too soon. You'll need to wait until you're a couple of hundred yards from your target Creeper.

When the distance looks about right, you quickly accelerate. Your sudden acceleration will catch the Dragon Ass off guard, but being hypnotically attached, he'll lethargically try to copy your move, but too late. You'll need a 15 to 20 mph increase to widen the gap enough to pull this off. When you catch the target Creeper, you change lanes, pass then duck in front of the Creeper so the Dragon Ass can no longer see your rear-end. They will then have the Creeper's rear-end to hypnotically attach to. You can reengage your cruise and be on your merry way.

Sometimes a Dragon Ass will pass the Creeper as well because, it would seem, they're spoiled for *your* rear-end. If you find that to be the case, you'll want to find a nice straightaway and put some serious distance between you and this interstate pest. This discourages most Dragon Asses. If you can't get rid of them, you might instead have a Radar Leech stuck to your rear-end.

A RADAR LEECH

A Radar Leech doesn't own a radar detector, but will attach themselves to someone they think has one. They drive the suggested speed limit until a car zips by, then they attach and follow along hoping to use the Zip Car as a Front End so they can make better time. They're hoping the Zip Car will smoke out any police hiding along the way.

The art of being a Radar Leech is staying close enough to see the Zip Car, but far enough back to see the police get the Zip Car before the police get you. Have I ever been a Radar Leech? Absolutely.

Being Ultimate Goal oriented I will attach to someone doing 10 to 15 over, for a while anyway. I won't follow someone going 20 or more over. I will jump onto a Whip.

A Whip is a group of cars (one Zip Car followed by several Radar Leeches) all zipping along together. I like to be the tip of the Whip, the last car. I often refer to this as "running with the big dogs." It's great having all those other cars out in front. What are the chances, with me being the last car, that I'll get a ticket? I haven't so far, knock on wood.

In the not so distant past, coming home on the Western Kentucky Parkway, with at least two hours in front of me, I was surprised by a wind shock as a car zipped past me doing at least 95. The suggested speed limit is 70. I was driving 75. It was late afternoon and I wanted to get home, so I jumped on the opportunity. This guy was either brave, stupid, or had a radar detector. He was flat-out moving.

The Western Kentucky Parkway is fairly straight and doesn't have much traffic. I left a two-football field gap between me and the Zip Car as I matched his speed. He *was* going 95. It wasn't long before he realized that I was being a Leech and he tried to lose me by accelerating. I stayed with him until he hit 110, then I surrendered and dropped back to my comfortable 75. I don't have a death wish. I never saw him again so I can only assume he survived his reckless abandon.

WHEN THE CAT'S AWAY

My favorite radar avoidance technique, to witness, that is, (nothing I'd ever do) is a Right Lane Camouflage Sneak About. This is where a wannabe Zip Car driver rides in the slow lane, zipping along until he's right on you (using you as a radar shield or as radar camouflage so to speak), then at the last second, switches lanes, zips around you, then darts back into the slow lane.

Sneak Abouts must believe that they'll only be tagged in the fast lane; that the slow lane is somehow immune to radar, particularly if they hide behind slower cars. They're a ton of fun to watch, hiding behind Creepers, peeking out like timid little mice scanning for the cat, scurrying into the open, then darting behind another Creeper. You got to love their logic. Be brave little mouse people, ride in the fast lane.

DRIVING SPEED RELATIVITY

Two problems with "driving speed" are that it's relative in comparison and it's addictive. In the previously described Parkway/Radar Leech story I was zipping along at 75, happy as a clam, then I accelerated to 110, chickened out, dropped back to 75 and it felt like I was crawling. Relative to 110 mph I *was* crawling. It's strange when 75 suddenly feels like 55.

For me, when I get to 10-or-more over, and realize I no longer have a Zip Car for cover, my speed addiction makes it hard to slow back down. I know I should slow down to my usual 5-over thing, but I can't do it. If I slow down, it feels like I'm *not making good time.* When it gets too bad and I'm traveling with my wife, I take an exit and let her take over driving. That way the speed relativity sensor in my head is reset to normal.

COMPETITION ON THE INTERSTATE

You should always keep Rule Three in mind. Always be on the lookout for Morons. A prime example of this, especially when there are three or more lanes, is when two Jerks are competing to be *the winner* in *the race* they're having on the interstate.

You'll be cruising at 5-over in the center lane of three when suddenly, in your rearview mirror, you see two cars coming up behind you, weaving in and out of traffic, each one trying to outdo the other. Suddenly, the front Jerk

CONFESSIONS OF A TACTICAL DRIVER

speeds by you on the left, and the rear Jerk, seeing a gap, passes you on the right. It's most often the Jerk in the right lane that will drive the most erratically to gain that all-important front spot, but both Jerks are dangerous. I refer to this type of competition as a Jerk Off.

The best thing you can do is stay out of their way. Hopefully they'll only kill themselves. Jerks have a need for speed and a need to be in front. That's why when two Jerks bump into each other on crowded highways this kind of stuff happens. It's a Rule One situation, protect yourself. I don't consider this to be an example of Road Rage because it's more about the race than the rage. It's that "ain't nobody gonna git in front of me" Moron Award mentality.

ROAD RAGE

It's never good to do anything in anger. Your poorest judgments are made when you're angry. Driving is dangerous enough without introducing anger to the road. Though it happens every day; somebody cuts somebody else off and tempers flare. I'm not saying I've never driven angry, I have. However, there is no slight to your ego that's worth dying for. If someone cuts you off, back off and let them go. But just like it's hard for some drivers to slow down, it's hard for some drivers to recognize and let go of anger. "By God, I'll show them." And a dangerous time was had by all.

The next two stories didn't happen to me personally, but I think they're worth telling. The first is about Road Rage, and the second is about Revenge.

ROAD RAGE ON THE INTERSTATE

The Road Rage incident happened to a friend of mine, Ray, while on vacation with his wife and his mother. According to Ray, for no apparent reason another driver started intentionally messing with him. Ray came up behind a slower car on the interstate, changed lanes to pass, but the slower car changed lanes as well, blocking Ray's attempt. Ray switched back to pass on the right, but no matter what Ray tried, the other driver kept him trapped behind him. Of course, Ray got angry. Wouldn't you? What if a Jerk decided to keep you blocked in?

Ray got right on the Jerk's ass and "it was on," which had his wife and mother in a panic. They wanted him to back off and let the Jerk go, so Ray relented and did what his passengers asked. He slowed down. Except when he did, the Jerk slowed down and matched Ray's speed, always keeping Ray directly behind him. Ray finally had enough.

Ray turned on his "high beams" making sure that they were always in the Jerk's eyes. This apparently went on for quite a while; Ray now being the aggressor, riding inches from the offending car. Ray's mother and wife were pleading for him to stop. Finally, the Jerk surrendered, got over, and let Ray pass.

I'd like to ask the Jerk why he thought it was okay to bring anger to the road and endanger other lives. I don't know who you are and never will, but you deserve a Moron Award. Though, by now you've probably already received a Darwin Award and are no longer with us. May you rest in peace.

I've had other drivers pass me, blow their horn, then the driver or a passenger, or both, flip me off, and I had no clue as to why. I'd never seen these people in my life. Who knows what perceived slight I caused to their egos? Maybe I unintentionally cut them off. Maybe they didn't like the fact that I'm a Hickamy. Maybe their ex was from Kentucky. But even if Ray unknowingly offended the other driver, for him to intentionally try to anger Ray by keeping him blocked in is moronic. It's always best to let the anger go.

AND NOW FOR REVENGE

I know you've had the following happen to you. You're on the interstate going too slow for some Jerk in a semi and he gets right on your ass doing 75. You know that view in your rearview mirror, that "wall of semi" inches from your butt, that huge image completely filling the reality behind you. Good, keep that in mind. This story is secondhand, but it's worth telling nonetheless.

The guy who told me this tale had a friend that knew a female law enforcement officer who had a co-worker that started carpooling with her to and from their job every day. He, too, was in law enforcement. Their daily commute was about an hour each way and, at first, the male officer volunteered to do some of the driving. It was the female officer's vehicle. But after a couple of months he had given up offering to drive and was instead catching a few winks during their daily commutes. One day, being a bit put off by this sleeping turn of events she decided to get revenge and pull a practical joke on her snoozing partner.

The opportunity presented itself when she saw, in front of her, a tractor-unit (of a tractor and trailer) in tow. The tractor-unit was being towed rear-end first, so the front of the vehicle was facing towards her. The closer she got to the Creeper tow truck and the tractor-unit-in-tow, the larger the "wall of semi" grew until it completely filled the view from her windshield.

When she was just a few feet away she let out a blood curdling scream which startled her partner awake. When he opened his eyes, all he saw was the huge face of a semi truck bearing down on him. He screamed, lost control and wet himself. The way I understand it, he has once again chosen to help with the driving. True story as far as I know. Gives me a whole new respect for female officers.

NOTE WORTHY

The best part of a long drive, especially if I'm making a trip alone, is that I can let loose and be myself. I'm cocooned in my own special world. I've got my snacks and my soft drink. The temperature control is at my command. I can listen to any music I want, as loud as I want, and I can sing along as loud as I want.

You do that, right? Sing while you drive? It's even better than singing in the shower. You're surrounded by all those speakers. You've never sounded better, at least to your ears. Heck, you could be the next winner of a singing reality show.

Though I get a kick out of the vocally-discordant few who want to share their musical taste and talent. They drive along with their windows down, music blaring, their heads bobbing this way and that, while they soulfully and loudly butcher some classic song. It's hard to keep a straight face sometimes when I hear caterwauling erupt from a nearby vehicle. I mean, Oh My God, it's like some of them must gargle with drain cleaner, their vocal cords spewing a cacophonous squeal reminiscent of animals in severe distress.

I'm glad you like to sing. Really, I am. But, in the future, you might consider keeping your marvelous talent contained to the interior of your car. You might want to put some glass in that bleating hole. That's all I'm saying, keep your windows rolled up; keep your tone-deaf sanctuary...soundproof; for all our sakes. Just something to consider.

That's what you're vehicle's interior is supposed to do. It's supposed to keep you and your talent securely contained, making you feel comfortable and in control. The exterior of your vehicle is all about image. The interior is your home away from home, your sanctuary that shields you from the weather, noise, and problems of the world. The more expensive a vehicle, the more secure and comfortable it feels: heated leather seats, built-in GPS, satellite radio, top of the line speaker system, DVD players, and on and on.

I don't drive an expensive car, but I'm happy with my vehicle. It has two very important features: a great steering wheel and dashboard for playing the drums. As I mentioned earlier I'm a drummer. You can't play air-guitar while driving but you can tap out a funky beat on the steering wheel, using the dash for those accent cymbal crashes.

I see lots of steering wheel and dashboard drummers. You know how everyone is a wannabe musician. I always wanted to play the guitar. Anyone, however, can let loose and play the steering wheel. Unlike a vocally-distressed windowless singer, the great thing about playing drums in the privacy of your car is no one can tell if you're actually keeping time.

I've played in lots of Dance bands, and on stage, we, the band, always watched for dancers who had no sense of rhythm at all, the truly clueless ones, or as we referred to them, the Rhythmically Challenged. It kept us entertained.

If you've been to any dance event anywhere, you've seen these people. They have no idea where the beat is. Their arms and legs flail about to a rhythm heard only in *their* head. And I guess ignorance of the beat is bliss because they're always the ones having the most fun. So to all you wannabe musicians, sing with your windows up, keep playing the drums on your steering wheel, and if you're one of the rhythmically challenged, when you're at a party, dance like no one's watching.

I suppose I should get back to the interstate. Sometimes I get to writing, get caught up in the moment and head off in some strange direction.

THE STREAM OF TRAFFIC

Speaking of getting caught up in the moment, remember when, way back at the beginning of this book, I used the phrase, "caught up in traffic like a bug in a stream." On my many trips to Florida, I've used the Atlanta bypass. If you use that bypass thinking you're going to drive the suggested speed limit, you've got another think coming. When you get on a large city bypass you'd better be ready to go. The semis and the locals will flat ass run you over. There is no slow lane. Well, there is a slow lane but no one's driving slowly in it.

You jump in the stream and get up to speed only to find traffic piling up behind you. You're already going 5-over, but the wall-of-semi in your rearview mirror urges you on, faster and faster, until you're racing like a local - 10, 15,

20 mph over, zipping along in a pod of semis, and a school of frantic sharks, all going 90, and the tension builds. You notice your shoulders hunched; your grip on the wheel tight and uncomfortable; your breathing shallow and tense. It's easy to get caught up in frantic traffic. Everybody is going fast, why shouldn't you?

You don't have to, regardless of the peer pressure to speed along. If you're not comfortable, get in the slow lane and go the suggested speed limit. I do it all the time. In heavy traffic, with Morons and Jerks frantically zipping about, I get in the slow lane, set my cruise for 2-under, and cruise on home. Nobody drives 2-under, so I rarely have to touch my cruise control. I'm the Creeper Choke Stone everyone has to get around.

It's great. I'm not tense and caught up in traffic like a bug in a stream. I don't care what the Jerks and White Rabbits think. Occasionally, I encounter someone going 5-under and have to pass them, but that's rare.

THE REALITY OF DRIVING IN A POD OF SEMIS AND A SCHOOL OF SHARKS

If at all possible when I'm on the interstate I like to be alone on the road. I know that's not possible all the time, but if you pay attention you'll notice that cars and trucks seem to travel in groups, and that there's usually gaps between the groups. I like to stay in those gaps. It's the safest and the most relaxing place to be, away from all the traffic.

If you consider the fact that a loaded semi weighs up to 80,000 pounds, and those monster Pickups and SUVs weigh 6,000 pounds and the average car weighs 3,000 pounds, that's a lot of bone-crunching metal on the road beside you. It's nothing to find yourself in a pod of five or six semis. That's a half-a-million pounds of life-changing perhaps life-ending carnage to contend with should something go wrong, like your vehicle having a tire blow out. Or a semi right next to you having a tire blow.

I once had a semi truck tire explode right next to my closed window while driving at high speed. The tire blew with such force that the window glass rattled in my door. I thought I'd been shot. Scared the hell out of me. I didn't lose control, but I swerved a little.

Let's say you're in a group of ten or twelve SUVs. That's 60,000 pounds of SUV shrapnel you'll need to avoid should something go wrong. That's why I like the gaps. There's just me to contend with should problems arise. My buddy, Ray, recently had a back wheel come off his vehicle while going 75 mph. His car, the previous week, had been in for a brake job and apparently the lug nuts hadn't been correctly tightened. So you never know.

[Speaking of lug nuts, that reminds me of a story that happened to a friend of mine, Danny. He was driving by our local mental hospital one day when he had a flat tire. He pulled to the side of the road and proceeded to change the flat. While he was working, a patient from the hospital wandered up to the fence surrounding the hospital grounds and started watching Danny work.

Danny removed the hubcap, sat it on the ground next to him, and was placing the lug nuts in the hubcap as he removed them. When he jerked the flat tire from his car, he accidently knocked the hubcap over and all the lug nuts spilled out and disappeared down into a storm drain. Danny stood there not quite believing what had just happened. Flustered, he sat down on the curb wondering what he was going to do. It was then that the mental patient spoke up.

"If it was me," he started, "I'd take one lug nut from each of the other wheels and use them until I could get new ones."

Danny looked up, surprised, and said, "That's a great idea."

"Yeah," replied the patient. "I'm in here because I'm crazy, not stupid.]

Now where was I?

Of course, the down side to staying in the open gaps on the interstate is you can easily be tagged for exceeding the suggested speed limit. I suppose there is safety in numbers in Radar detection matters, but I'll deal with that problem on my own. I'd rather be tagged and see the dreaded blue lights than end up with a "toe tag."

It's funny the things you remember. After reading that last sentence, it reminded me of something Danny used to say. "I'd rather have a bottle in front of me than have a frontal lobotomy." I always thought that was clever.

WHY IS IT "YA CAN'T FIND A COP WHEN YA NEED ONE?"

'm going to take a bit of a detour from the interstate and talk about the police. As you know, I interviewed some Ambulance Drivers for this book and
those conversations were a lot of fun, and I learned a great deal. I wanted to
interview some Traffic Enforcement Officers. I wanted to "personalize their
view" of the current American driving environment.

I made phone calls. I sent emails. I got names from friends. I tried for two
months to get an interview with a Traffic Enforcement Officer, but to no avail.
And it wasn't that I was being turned down, I got no response at all - no phone
calls saying they weren't interested - no return emails - nothing. I'm not sure
what I did to piss 'em off.

I was just about to give up and go in another direction, book wise, when,
at last, through a friend, I was able to get a list of questions to a police officer.
He persuaded an "unnamed active traffic enforcement officer" to answer a few
of my questions by email, for which I am very grateful.

155

His answers were police-like, very formal and proper. I didn't get a feeling about who this guy was as a person, but his answers were interesting nonetheless. I'll share my questions along with his responses. I liked the very cloak and dagger "active traffic enforcement officer" title given to the unnamed officer. I feel like a double-naught spy.

Question 1: What's the most dangerous trend you see on American roads?

Answer: It's a lack of focus, or Driver Inattention that's a huge danger to all drivers. As technology continues to advance we not only become more reliant on it, we also become more distracted by it. Whether it's your GPS, cell phone, radio, a "quick snack" or texting; they all take your attention away from the job at hand...getting there safely. So, put it down, turn it off, use hands-free devices, wait until you're stopped, whatever it takes...don't let your 3-second lack-of-focus affect your life or someone else's life forever.

[Isn't that what I've been saying all along?...pay attention.]

Question 2: What would you change, if anything, about Traffic Laws and Enforcement?

Answer: Personally, I would change the law regarding the use of helmets for motorcycle operators and passengers. For years, motorcycle riders were required by Kentucky State Law to wear safety helmets, but a few years ago the law was changed. And, while I know that many riders feel the use of a helmet decreases the "full experience" of riding a motorcycle, they can't argue that the helmet provides them more safety.

I think we contradict ourselves, as a society, when we require everyone in a car to wear a seat belt, but allow others to ride motorcycles without head protection. Luckily, many riders still wear helmets. Unfortunately, those who don't are commonly the ones with the least experience and are thus more likely to have an accident and die.

[I haven't talked about motorcycles so far in this book. I'll admit that I'm not a motorcycle enthusiast. Not that I haven't ridden motorcycles before, I have. And I get the attraction – that "crotch rocket" rush of adrenaline, the exhilaration of cruising through open air. Motorcycles are cool, some are amazing, they're just not my thing.

I try to keep an eye out for motorcycles because of the Whoop Ass factor. As a motorcycle enthusiast you have to be aware that you, as the rider, are not much more than a piece of raw meat dangling amongst the sharks. No matter how big and mean you are, you're no match for 3,000 pounds or more of metal vehicle crunching into you. In a head to car contest, a huge can of Whoop Ass is going to be opened on…you. A collision with you and anything (a car, a tree, the road, a building) is going to be damn tough on you. I have to agree with The Shadow, you should be wearing a helmet. "The Shadow" is my undercover name for the active traffic enforcement officer.

I'm going to combine the last two questions because The Shadow's responses were overlapping.]

Question 3: What's the funniest thing that's happened to you as a Traffic Enforcement Officer?

Question 4: Is there actually an end of the month traffic ticket quota?

Answer: One of the more comical things I've heard an officer say when asked if he or she issued a citation to meet their ticket-quota is, "No, I don't have a quota. I can write as many as I want". Though I can see how the person getting the citation may not see that as being funny. I think it speaks to the concept that officers are sometimes seen as robots that are governed by rules and not reason.

> While I can't speak for every law enforcement entity, I think the "end of the month traffic ticket quota" can be chalked up as an urban legend, or at least be considered an outdated philosophy. It is true that law enforcement agencies from time to time "target" certain types of offenses (i.e. seatbelt use, texting while driving, child restraint system use, DUIs, etc.) and that they encourage officers to increase the issuance of citations in those areas. However, law enforcement agencies don't normally openly require officers to issue a certain number of citations.

First, before I go any farther, I want to thank my Contact Officer and his friend The Shadow for participating in my Q & A. They didn't have to take time from their busy schedules, and weren't compensated for their effort. Thank you, again.

Though I think that The Shadow didn't really understand the power he had when I asked about the end of the month ticket quotas. He should have simply said, "Yes, there are end of the month ticket quotas." That would have made you check your speed and your calendar every time you got in your car.

The sentence that grabbed my attention was, "I think it speaks to the concept that officers are sometimes seen as robots that are governed by rules and not reason." I'm sure it's tough being a police officer. Very few people are happy to speak to the police, especially when caught breaking the law. I don't envy their job. They deal with tough and dangerous situations. You should try not to be one of the problems they have to sort out.

CAUGHT RED HANDED

How about the urban legend that "red cars" are the most likely to get ticketed? A question I didn't pose to my police posse (Officer Contact and The Shadow) was, "Do you have a favorite kind of car or driver that you enjoy giving a ticket to?" I did pose that question in some of my earlier attempts to get other interviews. Maybe that's what pissed them off.

But ask most anyone about the red-car/ticket thing and they'll agree, because that's what we've always heard. Red cars get more tickets because they stand out. And there is a kernel of truth in that. New, young drivers want to own fast, flashy cars. They buy Candy Apple Red sports cars and they drive fast because they believe themselves to be indestructible. And they get speeding tickets, in red cars.

However, I'm going out on a limb here and say that I believe "driving speed" has more to do with getting a ticket than car color. I know; how can I think that speed is the only factor when we're sure police departments everywhere are filling their red car quotas? Actually, they ticket red cars all year long, except December, red being a Christmas color and all. Just kidding. Radar is colorblind. It only sees your speed.

There's the real problem, Radar. Wouldn't it be great if you could drive a Stealth Car? You've seen Stealth Bombers with their angular specially-coated sides that absorb and deflect radar. Surely someone can build a slick angular sports car painted chalkboard-gray that cruises undetected down the high-way. List it at 1.3 million dollars. We wouldn't want everybody to have one.

Though, in retrospect, I probably shouldn't have said anything about a stealth car. Now someone is sure to try it. "I don't know how you caught me, officer. I was supposed to be invisible. I painted my car with chalkboard paint. I saw it in a book."

Now some shocking news for you red-car conspirators. According to an article I read at forbes.com, using comparative statistics, the most ticketed car on the road is a Mercedes-Benz SL Class sports car. (That only seems fair, huh?) This shocking news comes from a one-year study by Quality Planning, a San Francisco based company that collects data for insurance companies.

According to their research, Mercedes-Benz SL Class drivers are four times more likely to get a ticket than the average driver. Ya think? Mercedes-Benz SL Class sports cars are designed to be driven fast. They have 400 HP V8 engines. Of course they're going to get speeding tickets. It's a racecar. And I'm sure they hug the road like warm butter.

Then there's simply "the rush" of piloting a vehicle with that much smooth power. Could you resist if it was your foot on the gas pedal? I doubt I could. And I can't afford to get a ticket. That's why I drive my car; that and the one-hundred-thousand-dollar-plus price tag of a Mercedes-Benz. Hmm, this again suggests that speed, not car color is the deciding factor in getting a speeding ticket.

The least ticketed vehicles are SUVs and minivans. The thinking here is that these are multiple-passenger vehicles carrying children and families, which necessitates the drivers be more cautious, therefore receiving fewer tickets. Someone should do a study to see if Candy Apple Red minivans get more tickets. When I build my stealth car the outside is going to be a hologram of a minivan with a soccer mom at the wheel and a passel of children in the back. She'll be wearing a charcoal-gray sweater. Shields up, Mr. Spock.

Well, enough talk of cops and tickets. Let's get back out on the interstate to where some of that ticketing takes place. One quick side note: If you are pulled over by the police, you only have to answer questions pertinent to why you were pulled over. Always be aware of fraud and protect your personal information. The police *will* want to see proof of insurance and your driver's license. I usually hate my driver's license picture. I always look like one of the FBI's Most Wanted. Though, I did manage to smile for my last picture.

THE EXPENSIVE CAR DIVISION

Weren't we just talking about high-end cars? See? When an expensive car comes flying down the road, whips past you and you think, *I hope you get a ticket*, you now know they will. I've just demonstrated that they're Radar bait. Let them troll for speed traps. But don't believe that because one sports car gets pulled over that the way is clear for you. The police, like wolves, sometimes hunt in packs.

If someone wants to go faster than you, let them. What's it to you anyway? Why introduce anger to the road. I always get over and let faster cars get by me, expensive or otherwise. However, I clear a path much more slowly if they ride right on my butt.

But expensive cars are more than just fast, they're also Status Symbols. They have that "look at me" factor. Look how rich I am, look how powerful I am, look how fast I can go. In a social experiment conducted in Germany in 1986 titled "Social Status and Aggression," it was shown that there is a measurable effect that Social Status has on Aggressive Driving.

They found that the higher the driver's status (based on the class and expense of the vehicle being driven), the more aggressively they drove. The drivers of the most expensive vehicles had the lowest tolerance for the habits of other drivers. They were quicker to anger, quicker horn blowers and headlight flashers.

If low tolerance is an indication of wealth and social status, then I'm supposed to be rich. I have little tolerance for all the morons on the road. Maybe I was rich in a previous life.

Conversely, as the social status of the vehicles decreased, the tolerance of the drivers in dealing with road frustration increased. Lower social status drivers were slower to anger, slower to blow their horn and flash their lights. Apparently, the lower on the totem pole of life you are, the more forgiving you are on the road.

THE THREE-SECOND GAP

A three-second gap is a Rule One thing. It's the recommended safety cushion between your car and the car in front of you. What this means is that for whatever speed you're traveling, the gap between you and the car in front of you should take three seconds to cover if the car in front of you suddenly stops, thus giving you a three second opportunity to react. Three seconds can be a lifetime in an emergency situation.

Let's take a look at some numbers (don't worry, this is simple) so we can get a feel for this gap. On the next page you'll find a chart that shows what the three-second gap between vehicles should be for the listed mph. For those of you wanting to calculate a three-second gap for any given speed, the short formula is (mph x 4.4 = a three-second gap in feet for that mph).

Example: a three-second gap for 25 mph would be: 25 x 4.4 = 110 feet.

MPH	Three-Second Gap
25 mph	110 feet
35 mph	154 feet
50 mph	220 feet
75 mph	330 feet
100 mph	440 feet

At 25 mph your car will travel 110 feet in three seconds; that's 36.6 yards. So the gap you're supposed to leave when traveling 25 mph is a third of a football field. You'll definitely be out of field goal range here. You'd cover the whole field (100 yards) in eight seconds at 25 mph.

At 50 mph you're traveling 73.3 feet-per-second, that's three-quarters of a football field in three seconds. You will be able to kick your field goal from here. It's fourth down and a field goal will tie it, thirteen seconds on the clock. At 50 mph you'd cover the field in 4 seconds.

At 75 mph you'll cover the entire field plus one end zone in three seconds. So you've scored a touchdown and won the game. One football field is a three-second gap at 75 mph.

At 100 mph you'll cover 100 yards in two seconds. But at this speed, you're likely to go to "sudden death." Unless you're driving a high-end sports car built to handle the speed. Some of them top out at 200 mph. It takes one second to cover a football field at 200 mph.

The easiest way to determine a three-second gap is to spot something in front of you alongside the road, say a lamp post, wait until the car in front of you passes that lamp post, then start counting, one-one-thousand, two-one-thousand, three-one-thousand. At three-one-thousand you should pass the lamp post. I try this occasionally and I usually have a one-and-a-half to two-second gap in front of me.

Now, all that being said, how many drivers do you see leaving gaps even close to the ones described? Nobody, right? Well, not nobody, but very few. If you're on a busy interstate, gaps between vehicles are sometimes scary close, as close as five feet. Let's look at that math.

DON'T BLINK

At a conservative interstate speed of 65 mph, five feet is a one-twentieth-of-a-second gap. If you're following five feet behind somebody at 65 mph, you're giving yourself .05 seconds to react to an emergency. It takes longer to blink. At 65 mph things can happen quicker than the blink of an eye. Those close gaps on busy, high-speed road systems are why multiple-vehicle collisions happen so frequently. Do not follow too closely.

However, there is one problem with leaving a three-second gap and that's the Jerk. I always leave a comfortable gap, but inevitably, some Jerk, wanting to get ahead of one more car, will jump into my comfortable gap. So I have to slow down so I won't hit the Jerk.

It's been my experience that a gap of more than one car length is always going to be filled. Often times, gaps of less than one car length will be filled. You've seen those Jerks, forcing their way in front of other drivers. You know how you want to play the Game as soon as a Jerk makes the scene; mess with him; keep him from getting in front of you. It's hard to leave a safety gap, but you should always try.

DON'T LOOK DOWN

Now, let's consider some modern distractions. If you look at your cell phone or your GPS for five seconds at 45 mph, you've traveled 110 yards, more than the length of a football field, without looking at the road. At 75 mph, a five-second lapse in judgment will move you almost two football fields blindly down the road. The safest thing you can do is keep your eyes on the road, three-second gap or otherwise.

CAR TROUBLE

Second only to having the dreaded blue lights appear in your rearview mirror is the feeling you get when you realize that your vehicle is developing mechanical problems; an engine failure, or you're running out of gas. Personally, I've never run out of gas. When I get down to a quarter-tank, I fill up. But there are people who must think the "E" on their gas gauge means they have "Enough" to go for a while more. They're the ones you see hiking down a road with a little red gas can in hand.

A moment I particularly dread is having a tire blow. You're suddenly very aware that something bad has happened. Your adrenaline kicks in as you feel a difference in the steering wheel. Your ability to safely steer has changed.

If a front tire suddenly goes flat, your car will want to pull sharply to the flat-tire side, so you have to keep a firm grip on the steering wheel. If a back tire goes flat, depending on the balance of your vehicle, one of your front tires will lift up and lose contact with the road. Steering becomes very precarious at that point.

Steering is a function dependent on both front tires gripping the road. With one front tire not touching you might not be able to steer at all. It feels like your front end is floating. The steering wheel becomes very loose in your hands, very disconcerting and dangerous.

I once had a right back tire go slowly flat while on the Mountain Parkway. The balance of my SUV was such that the flat tire, even though it had little air pressure, still slightly supported my vehicle. However, because my right back tire had lost pressure, my front left tire had lifted slightly and I started noticing moments where the front of my vehicle felt like it was sliding. I would let off the gas in a sudden panic to get the steering back under control, then it would seem to be fine again.

I drove at least thirty miles wondering why my steering felt so weird. Even my passenger, Dave, felt it and would grab the door handle in a minor panic every time it happened, very unnerving. We both contributed the sensation to the fact that it was a very windy day.

When I took my exit I pulled into a parking lot to check things out. It was then I discovered I had a flat tire. I was extremely lucky that I hadn't lost control. Anytime your steering seems questionable, pull over and check it out.

The most important thing you can do for your own safety is to make sure your vehicle is well maintained. Well maintained vehicles seldom break down. An article published by the American Automobile Association entitled "What to do when your vehicle breaks down" has some useful information; though you should see their list of recommended emergency items. I thought as I read the list, *Yeah, I should have that in my car, but where will I store a snow shovel and a bag of cat litter?*

Anytime you have mechanical problems pull off the road as far as possible, or if you can make it to an exit you should try. Accept "help" only from police officers or from whomever you called to come and rescue you. If a stranger stops to offer help, tell them through your locked-door rolled-up window to call 911, or that you've already contacted the police. There are a lot of weirdos on the road. Protect yourself first. (Suddenly, "Riders on the Storm" by The Doors is squirmin' like a toad around in my brain. Don't you hate it when a song squirms around in your brain, Clarice?)

A DOUGHNUT OR LUG NUT

There's a direct correlation to the condition of a vehicle and how fast you should drive it. Old worn out cars should be driven more slowly than new tight and tuned vehicles. It's been a while since I brought up any cutesy nick-names for other drivers so I thought I'd take this opportunity to throw in a Doughnut; though a Lug Nut works here equally as well.

A Doughnut is a moron driving at highway speeds on one of those little doughnut spare tires. It's one thing to drive cautiously on a spare until you can get a flat fixed or buy a new tire; but to drive at highway speeds on anything but four good tires is moronic. And I've seen cars where you know that's the tire they're using as a semi-permanent thing. I once saw a car with two dough-nut tires (Hickamy all the way).

You can expand the definition of Doughnut or Lug Nut to include drivers in any of the following vehicles:

- One Headlight vehicles. On dark roads you're not sure if a motorcycle is coming at you or if it's a car with one headlight.
- Overloaded vehicles. (Come listen to a story about a man name Jed.) Someone's moving and they have all their belongings precariously tied in the back of their pickup like some modern art sculpture sprouting out at odd angles.
- And I know you've seen a chest of drawers or a lawnmower hanging out of a trunk tied with kite string.
- Or a car with every inch of space filled with clothing and household goods and mattresses tied to the top.
- Or the home improvement enthusiast who has eight sheets of plywood and a load of two-by-fours strapped to the top of their compact car.

All these vehicles should be driven cautiously. If you end up behind one of these Lug Nuts, keep your distance. Having a mattress or a lawnmower hit your vehicle at interstate speeds can be extremely dangerous.

IF THE SHOE FITS

Well, I guess I'll exit the interstate with one last story. This actually happened on an entrance ramp, so that might seem a little backwards, but I am a little backwards, a proud Hickamy. "Hey, Ma, watch me walk in my new-fangled shoes." (I actually used to embarrass my mother with that very line while on family vacations as a preteen.)

Anyway, I turned onto an interstate entrance ramp and as I was picking up speed, I noticed a car with bicycles strapped to the roof pulled off on the right shoulder of the ramp about three-quarters of the way down. No one was outside the parked vehicle so I got as far left on the ramp as I could but continued to accelerate. It seemed safe enough.

As I got closer, I realized that lying next to the car, in the center of the ramp, was a shiny new sports shoe glistening in the sun, apparently owned by the driver or one of his passengers. I eyed the car cautiously because now I could see the driver's door was slightly ajar. I assumed that he was waiting for me to pass so he could retrieve the shoe. Nearing merge speed I centered my car in the lane so I would pass harmlessly over the shoe.

Just as I was about to pass the parked vehicle, the driver threw open his door causing me to react and swerve. Because of the swerve I suddenly felt a thump-thump as I ran over the rather nice shoe. Looking in my rearview mirror I see it tumbling along the pavement and the driver getting out to retrieve the flattened shoe. Everyone in my vehicle busted out laughing. What a moron.

If you're parked alongside any road (or an entrance ramp), never open your door without looking to see if it's safe. If the shoe-guy had opened his door a fraction of a second later I would have removed it with my car. He could have gotten seriously hurt. As I drove off I could see him examining his shoe and looking numbly in my direction. I suppose knowing when to safely open his car door was a driving skill he did not possess.

DRIVING SKILLS

L et's talk a little about driving skills. Most people think of themselves as good or great drivers. But safely driving a vehicle is a combination of knowledge of the vehicle and of driving experience. Just because you've driven a low-profile car doesn't mean you can safely operate a top-heavy van; whole different center of gravity, whole different thing. Skills come from practice and experience.

I'm going to recommend a website sponsored by Ford called "Driving Skills For Life" at drivingskillsforlife.com. It's a site for new drivers, teenagers really, but I found it full of great information; everything from safety tips to steering tips very entertainingly and professionally presented. I consider myself a knowledgeable driver and I learned a few things from their site.

Did you know that the air pressure imprinted on your tires is not the correct driving air pressure for your vehicle? Me, neither. The place to find the correct tire pressure for your vehicle is on the door jamb of the driver's door or on the driver's door itself. The psi number on the tire is the maximum pressure for that tire. I also learned that with every ten degree rise or fall in outside air temperature, the pressure in your tires correspondingly rises or falls one degree.

The contact-friction-area of a correctly inflated tire is approximately a five-inch square of rubber. All four tires combined total less than one square foot of rubber holding you on the road. Acceleration, braking, and steering all depend on the friction of that one square foot of rubber. Without friction you're slip sliding away. Your life depends on your tire's contact with the road.

Most people slow down on snow and ice, but they don't reduce speed on rain-slick roads. Feels safe, huh? Until you need to suddenly stop. Then the thin layer of lubricating water between your tires and the road reduces friction so you can't stop, then you rear-end somebody. Snow, ice, rain, wet leaves, dry pavement, and gravel, all have different friction factors. That's why driving slowly is always a good idea until you get a feel for the road. Understanding road conditions is a driving skill.

Knowing where your car is on the road is another valuable skill. When I taught my son and daughter to drive, I used a little trick that they claim made them better drivers. Learning to do this will help you get a feel for where your car is on the road.

Find an empty parking lot where you have room to safely operate, then lay a piece of notebook paper on the ground. When you can run over the piece of paper with either front tire, you'll know exactly where your vehicle is on the road. This comes in handy in emergency situations, or anytime you need to miss potholes or debris in the road, or if you're following a narrow lane.

I enjoy this notebook paper skill because I use it to play a game I call "Road Kill." I recommend that you don't try this game. Don't worry; it's not about killing anything.

Road Kill is about flattening litter, usually drink cups or soda cans, left behind by the depressed populace who won't dispose of their trash properly, and who choose, despondently, to toss it out on the highway. I'll comment on that a little later. However, if I do see a soda can in the road, I make a quick decision about the safety aspect of an attempt to flatten it. I only play Road Kill in empty parking lots or on roads free of people and other vehicles at the time. If I'm not going to endanger myself or others I will attempt "the smash."

For me, there is a perverse sense of accomplishment to the act. It's like, "Look at that. I know exactly where my car is on the road." I might even compare it to a golfing hole-in-one. I give myself ten points for a driver-side tire smash, and twenty points for the more difficult passenger-side tire smash. I give partial points for a partial smash.

Again, I recommend that you don't play Road Kill. It can be hazardous to your tires and your safety. Use the notebook paper in the parking lot trick to learn where your car is on the road. Once you have that perspective, you will feel safer and less crowded. Oh, when you're finished running over the notebook paper, pick it up and take it with you.

MY TOP TWO DRIVING SKILLS STORIES

I suppose the best bit of driving I've ever done happened way back when. I don't remember how old I was, probably in my twenties. And I was doing something I wasn't supposed to be doing. I was driving down a shoulder to get to a right turn. I really need to illustrate this one.

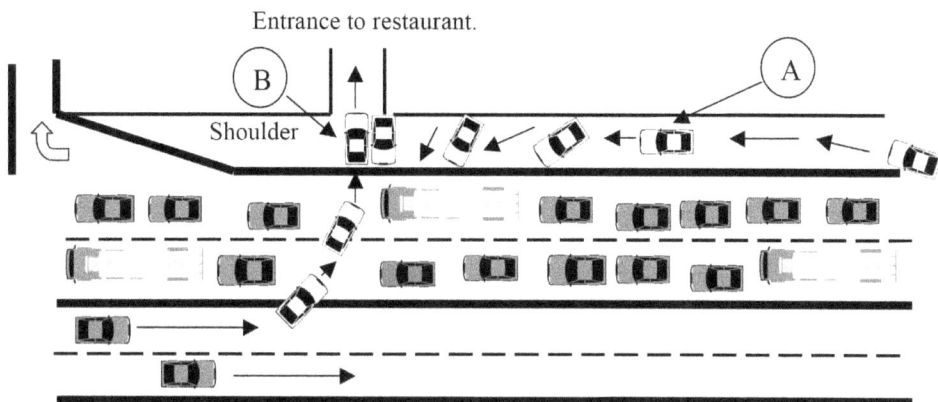

Entrance to restaurant.

I was in white car A trying to get to a right turn at the next intersection so I decided to drive down the shoulder past a line of stopped vehicles. I wanted to get a jump on all of the Creepers. Of course, this was a moronic thing to do for the reasons demonstrated here.

What I couldn't see was that the stopped traffic was letting white car B turn left into a restaurant parking lot. As I was speeding down the shoulder I suddenly see car B in my path. If he had just gone on there would have been no problem, we would have missed each other.

What happened was: He saw me. He panicked. He screeched to a halt directly in my path. Impact was imminent, but I didn't give up. I slammed on my brakes and turned my steering wheel, which caused me to start sliding sideways. I came to rest parallel to and only inches from car B. And I do mean inches; three or four at best, but I never touched the other car.

I'd taken a sure collision and turned it into a bit of miraculous driving and a long moment of embarrassment as I waited for traffic to clear before I could again move. It's not a good idea to drive down a shoulder, dangerous things can happen.

In retrospect, it was some damn fine driving. Although I can't say it was a learned driving skill. My instincts took over and I did the right thing to prevent a collision. Could I do that again? Maybe. I hope to never find out. I guess to put a good point on my dumb driving stunt, never give up trying to avoid a collision. And to the guy in car B, if you can avoid a collision by moving out of the way, do it. Never give up. I no longer drive down shoulders hoping to save time.

LET'S BACK UP FOR A MOMENT

My other driving skill story is not as dramatic as the first, but it describes a useful skill nonetheless. On one of our many hiking trips out west, we, Ray and I, wanted to again see The Barracks near Mt. Carmel, Utah. Part of The Parunuweap Canyon, The Barracks (in the upper part of the canyon) is an amazing slot canyon with thousand-foot high vertical sandstone walls. The Barracks, in places, is just a few feet wide. To add to the excitement, the East Fork of the Virgin River tumbles shin-deep through The Barracks.

In times past, you could follow the river from Mt. Carmel, Utah through The Barracks to Labyrinth Falls, then through the lower Parunuweap Canyon in Zion National Park and come out in Springdale, Utah; about a sixteen mile hike. That route is no longer available because to exit The Parunuweap (a Paiute Indian word meaning Roaring Water Canyon) you have to cross privately owned land that is closed to the public. Plus, you have to hike through the lower canyon in Zion National Park which is also closed having been designated a National Research Area.

When you could pass through there, we made that hike once. We hiked at a very casual pace, exploring side canyons as we went, taking about three days to reach Springdale, camping at night on sand banks along the river in the Utah wilderness. It was a ton of fun and an exhilarating adventure. Because of the higher elevation, the Utah night sky is intense. It's an amazing visual treat. You can clearly see The Milky Way.

Even though you can no longer go all the way through to Springdale, you can still hike The Barracks; a hike down, hike back situation. Although there is a strenuous exit over the Checkerboard Mesa in Zion if you're so inclined.

On this particular trip Ray and I discovered that a good portion of where you once had to hike was now a rough dirt road that followed the river down through the canyon almost to the entrance of The Barracks. It required an all-wheel drive vehicle with high ground clearance. We didn't have that. We had a nice, family SUV. We decided to see how far we could drive anyway.

At first the road was fairly easy to navigate, following alongside the river, but then the road started crossing through the river over large boulders. We made several of the river crossings, but eventually came to a crossing that was impassable because the boulders were just too large. We came to a stop, considering our options.

We were at the end of our forward journey. We needed to turn around and head back, but there was no turning around. In front of us, the river blocked our way, and on either side, the curvy canyon road was lined with thick bushes that had been scraping the sides of our vehicle for a half-mile or so. The only option was to back out. This is where one of my driving skills came into play.

I put the SUV in reverse and proceeded to drive backwards as comfortably as anyone going forward on the curvy, bush-lined dirt road. I simply watched my side mirrors to see the turns I had to make and the obstacles I needed to miss. I must have snaked a third of a mile backwards before I came to a wide spot where I could finally turn around.

I learned how to drive backwards using my side mirrors when I drove a van that had no windows in the back doors. Driving backwards is much the same as driving forward. If you want the rear of your car to go right, you turn your steering wheel to the right. If you want your rear to go left, you turn the steering wheel left. Find an empty parking lot, put down a piece of notebook paper, and when you can run over it with either back tire, you'll have the skill.

"NOT" DRIVING SKILLS

There are things drivers do regularly that are not driving skills. Knee Driving, for instance, is not a driving skill. You've probably done this; your hands are busy putting ketchup on your fries so you use your knee to momentarily steer your vehicle. If the correct hand positions on the steering wheel are at "ten and two," then the correct knee position would have to be at "six," right? Trick question, there is no correct knee driving position. Don't drive with your knee. Of course, I suppose the new hand position is either "ten" or "two" depending on whether a left- or right-handed Cell Assassin is driving.

Unless you're using a clutch, driving with both feet on the pedals is also not a driving skill. One foot on the gas and one on the brake is a bad idea. It's why people end up plowing into convenience stores. I suppose I understand the two-footed logic a little bit. It's like being ready for any driving emergency. "I can go if I want to, or I can stop if I want to; no waiting. I've got two perfectly good feet. My left foot is just sitting here bored, might as well put it to good use." Use it as a place to store your left shoe. Drive with your right foot.

Here's the single foot logic: Stopping and Accelerating are two mutually independent functions. You don't want to brake if you're accelerating, and you don't want to accelerate if you're braking. If you only use one foot for both operations, the two functions can't happen simultaneously, which is a good thing, a safe thing. (When I broke my right heel I had to drive using my left foot for several months. When asked if I found left-footed driving difficult, I'd reply, "No, I just drive on the other side of the road.")

It's irritating being behind someone that drives with two feet. Their brake lights are constantly flashing on then off, off then on, all the while they're driving down the road "not-stopping." Maybe there should be a tiny left ankle belt on the front of the driver's seat to hold that pesky left foot in place.

The other day I was behind a car merrily not-stopping and his brake lights were driving me crazy. It was one of the worst cases of not-stopping I'd ever seen. As I followed along behind this irritating brake light display, the thought occurred to me that maybe the driver was sending me an SOS. That hiding in his back floorboard was an escaped convict brandishing a stolen pistol. That, perhaps, he was being forced to be a getaway driver, the wheelman so to speak, and this brake tapping was the driver's way to "let me know" so I could call for help. Or maybe he was trying to tell me that Timmy was in the well. It was a toss-up.

Then it hit me. He was keeping time on his brake pedal with his left foot to a song he was listening to. The more I watched the irritating display of not-stopping, the more I became convinced I was right. The flashing brake lights did seem to have an odd rhythmic pattern, though not perfectly so. Probably a rhythmically challenged driver. Play the floorboard next time, moron.

Look ahead. Steering by watching just a few feet in front of your bumper is also not a driving skill. You should always look well ahead, three or more cars lengths, so you can see what's coming, see the nuances of the road. I always find it disconcerting to be driving next to a near-target driver. They're all over the road, constantly correcting, particularly on a curve. They bounce back and forth between the edges of the lane as if they're trying to miss invisible obstacles scattered across the road. The farther you watch ahead on a curve, the smoother you'll negotiate the curve.

DRIVING SKILLS COME WITH EXPERIENCE

Driving skills come with practice and time spent behind the wheel. That's why so many young drivers are involved in serious and fatal crash-es. With youth comes the erroneous feeling of being indestructible. It also comes with the notion that nothing is ever going to go wrong. "I know what I'm doing." "I'm in control." "I passed my driver's test for crying out loud." "Mom!"

I've tried to avoid age as a factor in my discussions so far because there are morons sixteen to sixty, and older, on the road. But for a moment I want to ad-dress new drivers. When you first get your driver's license it's liberating. And when you find that driving isn't all that difficult you get comfortable with the process and start to take driving for granted. You try stupid stuff because you think you're bulletproof.

You are not indestructible or bulletproof. In fact you're really quite fragile. It doesn't take much of a collision to damage your body for life. That's why I keep saying that you're driving 3,000 pounds of life-changing carnage. The key phrase is "life-changing." Are you happy with your body being intact and functional? Every time you get in a vehicle and head out, all that could change in the blink of an eye.

The reason that driving is dangerous is that as you accelerate you add Kinetic Energy to your body; energy that has to be dissipated slowly if you like your body as is. You might feel like you're sitting quietly in the driver's seat, but if your car is going 60 mph, your body is traveling 60 mph. It just doesn't feel like that because you're encased in a glass and steel bone-crunching cage with pretty dials, leather seats, and a pumping stereo.

Kinetic Energy increases with the square of the speed. In other words, if you double your speed, you've added four times the kinetic energy to your body. If you triple your speed, you've added nine times as much energy to your body. All that energy has to be dissipated when you stop; either gently as you brake, or violently in a collision. That's the origin of the phrase, "Speed Kills."

Some memories stay with you a lifetime. Most people know someone that died in high school, a fellow student that was suddenly forever missing from math class. In my case, it was four fellow students.

I can't say I knew these four guys very well. I didn't. We moved in different circles. But I knew who they were. I'd see them every day in the hallways. The reason they died was because of youthful over-confidence; that "I'm indestructible" feeling that plagues your youth. It was a weekend summer night when these four guys died. They were out partying in one of the group's convertible. It was a warm night and they had the top down.

The problem was that they were drinking alcohol and speeding, and they weren't wearing seatbelts. The mix of over-confidence, alcohol, and excessive speed caused the driver to lose control on a curve. The car skidded sideways, then started flipping, flinging the four guys out onto the road. They spent their excessive kinetic energy sliding skin to pavement for fifty feet or more down the road, one of them face to pavement. All four had closed casket funerals. Knowing when not to drive is a driving skill.

For a new driver, every added passenger in the car increases the risk of a fatal accident two-fold. Hanging with a group of friends while driving is fun, but it's a distraction for the driver and therefore hazardous for all. You know what I mean, the driver wants to stay in the conversation so he turns his head to say something over everyone else, takes his eyes off the road, then Bam! hits something. Just a note to everyone everywhere: If you're the driver, you don't need to look at your passengers to talk to them. They can hear you. Keep your eyes on the road.

DRIVING ACCIDENT SCAMS

L et's take a minute to discuss a serious problem: Driving Accident Scams brought to you by criminals who want to steal money from you and your insurance company. "Staged Driving Accidents" (Scams) costs each of us hundreds of dollars yearly in higher insurance premiums. I don't know about you, but I'm spending more than I want to now. So, if we're all a little more vigilant, maybe we can prevent some of these Scams and reduce that financial burden a little. Here's some of what to be on the lookout for:

The Cuts-n-Crunch (sounds like some demented cereal) - This scam is usually perpetrated using two accomplice vehicles. The first Villain Vehicle speeds past you, then **Cuts** in front of you. An accomplice Villain Vehicle then comes up beside you so you can't change lanes. Then the Villain Driver in the front vehicle slams on his brakes and you **Crunch** or rear-end him.

The Villain Driver will claim that he had to brake to avoid hitting something in the road, so it's your Fault because you were following too closely. This is easy. Never follow any vehicle too closely. If someone cuts in front of you, slow down and keep a comfortable gap so you won't fall victim to this scam.

The Courteous Crunch – Here, while you're trying to make a left turn from a parking lot or a side street across the flow of traffic, a Villain Driver, in the flow of traffic, disguised as a **Courteous Driver,** will make it seem as though he's slowing down to let you make your turn. He might even flash his headlights as though he's signaling you, or he might wave you out. Except when you pull out, he speeds up and crashes into you.

The Villain Driver will claim he never signaled for you to pull out. Courteous drivers are the bane of drivers everywhere. Just follow the rules. Make your left turn when it's clear. Never pull out in front of cars that are coming right at you. See Rule One.

The Flicker Crunch – This is similar to The Courteous Crunch. Here, the Villain Driver in the flow of traffic has his "turn signal on" as though he's going to turn right onto the street your turning left from, which, you believe, means it's safe for you to pull out because he's turning. He wants you to believe that you and he are not going to cross paths. As you pull out he speeds up and crashes into you.

The Villain Driver will claim that he didn't have his signal on. So, again, it's your Fault. I never pull out in front of a driver that has his signal on. I wait until I can see that the vehicle is, in fact, turning. And how many times have you seen someone driving along simply unaware that their signal is on? Participate in your own health and well-being.

Trumped-Up Claims – This is where you had a slight fender-bender, hardly a scratch. But when a claim is filed against your insurance by the other driver, much more vehicle damage is reported. The Villain Driver in this case took a sledge hammer to his vehicle to enhance the monetary value of the claim before an insurance adjuster had a chance to look at it.

Ghost Passengers – This is where more people than were actually in the Villain Vehicle at the time of the crash file injury claims. Though, usually, Villain Vehicles are filled with accomplices so they can maximize "the scam."

Here's a list of things you should do if you are involved in an accident:

1. Never just exchange contact and insurance information. Always call 911 so a police report is filed. Get a copy of the police report and the officer's name.

2. Report the claim to your insurance company. Don't accept or offer a cash settlement on site.

3. Always carry a pen and paper in your car and, if possible (don't put yourself in danger), try to get "contact information" from all the passengers in the other vehicles. Get the other car's license plate number.

4. Be careful of what personal information you give, keeping in mind the scourge of identity theft.

5. Use your cell phone or camera to take pictures of all the damage to both vehicles. Get pictures of all the people in the other vehicle if possible.

6. Never confront the other driver, even if you think you were involved in a staged accident. You never know what a criminal will do.

7. Look for witnesses, but be aware that often times, "witnesses" are working for the Villains.

From the research I've done, staged accidents cost the insurance industry about $20 billion a year. They generously pass that financial burden along to me and you as increased premiums. All I can tell you is to keep your eyes on the road, be aware of the vehicles around you, don't tailgate, and wait until it's clear before pulling out into traffic.

RANDOM THOUGHTS

Littering – It's my belief that the litter covering America's roads and streets is left there by "depressed" individuals. Their life sucks. Their world, to them, is trashed, so they want your world to be trashed as well. They're demonstrating their dissatisfaction with their life choices. They're stuck in dead-end jobs. They have a house full of ungrateful children. They're in festering and loveless relationships. Litterers are unhappy people.

I police my street and neighborhood. If I see litter, I stop and pick it up. If I'm caught at a red light I jump out and grab litter to dispose of later. I'm not going to leave trash as an eyesore for me or for others. I keep sanitizing wipes in my car so I can clean my hands. My life is not trash.

I live in a middle class neighborhood, nothing fancy, but it's nice, and I want it litter-free. Though, I'm one of the few willing to pick up someone else's trash. For most it's "I didn't throw it down. Why should I pick it up?" You pick it up to demostrate that your world is not trash; as revenge against those who do litter. You're taking away their advertisement of self-loathing. If everyone would pick up one piece of trash every day, our streets would soon be litter-free.

If you're one of the growing population of depressed litterers, do something to make your life better, not something to demonstrate your unhappiness. You need not be a prisoner of your poor choices. Work to improve your life and your immediate environment. Get out and pick up some litter. Take a class. Get a hobby. Get some exercise. Help someone in need. "Sorry your life sucks. Please don't litter."

The most egregious litterers, hands down, are cigarette smokers. You've seen the thick coat of discarded butts that line our streets and highways, it's disgusting. It's because smokers don't want to deal with the debris from their addiction. Smokers don't smoke because they want to; they smoke because they have to. They're drug addicts. Smoking is about as far from the Rule One concept as you can get. You are not participating in your own health and well-being if you smoke.

The problem is smokers have trained themselves to believe that they're not littering. "It's just one little cigarette butt." The truth is a pile of butts is a reminder of the depth of their addiction, so they flick each one away, no harm, no foul odor, gone from their reality before it hits the ground. I can't foresee that ever changing. It's a lifelong addiction. I don't pick up cigarette butts. They're too nasty for me.

The local government in my area ran a TV campaign that featured, of all people, The Cigarette Fairy. I laughed even as I typed it. The Cigarette Fairy, a young woman with multicolored striped leggings, tennis shoes, a frilly tutu, wearing a tiara, appeared on local TV to remind smokers not to throw their cigarettes butts on the ground, that it is indeed litter. The Cigarette Fairy changed absolutely nothing. They're drug addicts, not children.

Smokers are a predictable bunch. It's why when the government needs income they slap a tax on cigarettes. They know nicotine addicts might complain but they're not going to stop smoking. They're a "cash cow" for the government, and a huge burden on our health system. If you don't smoke, don't start. Smoking doesn't make you look cool, it makes you stink. You've walked by smokers; they smell so bad it takes your breath away.

One final litter note: Did you know that the slogan, "Don't Mess with Texas," comes from an anti-littering campaign? I thought it meant that Texans were all a bunch of bad asses. But that's not what I read on that bathroom stall in Oklahoma. Just kidding, Texas. Good for you for having an anti-littering campaign. Maybe you need a Litter Fairy. Find a tiny Texas woman, dress her up like a Rodeo Queen and let her lasso litterers as they drive by. Snatch 'em right out of their car. Just something to think about.

An Off Sides Penalty - If I were allowed to issue traffic citations, I would give them to drivers that commit Off Sides penalties. This happens when you're approaching a side road with a Stop sign. You have the right-of-way, but seconds before you pass the side road a car comes flying up to the Stop sign but doesn't stop until they're well past the Stop sign and a little bit into your lane. They're "off sides." You flinch and jerk the steering wheel because you're not sure if they're actually going to stop or not. It's more Jerk and White Rabbit activity. (Sounds like a Cajun recipe.)

Conversely, you're approaching a street where you want to make a left turn but at the last second a vehicle comes careening up to the Stop sign to make a left turn across your path but they don't stop until they're well into their left turn and in your way. So you have to steer around them to make your turn. I don't care how far they pull out, I always turn in front of them. Stop where you are supposed to (the front of your vehicle is supposed to be even with the Stop sign) and then look to go.

A Self-Absorbed Penalty - Another citation I would write is for Jerks that park anywhere they want. They park in front of store doorways, or sideways across two parking spots, or in the middle of a lane because they're just going to be a minute. Again Jerked White Rabbit. Why be an ass? You are not special. Park where you're supposed to and pick up the trash around your car.

A "What's Up?" Penalty - This citation is for those who, when they see someone they know in another vehicle on the road or in a parking lot, pull up next to them in their vehicle to chat, thus blocking traffic in both directions.

Driverless Vehicles - Technology is coming that will drive our cars for us. In fact, it already exists. You'll just get in your car, punch in your destination and your car will drive you there while you snooze or read a book. The notion that sensing cables would have to be embedded in roadways is old hat and erroneous. Nothing would have to be done to our existing road system. Driverless cars will be a reality within ten years.

The only impediment apparently, according to the manufacturers of these vehicles, is making it legal for driverless vehicles to share the road with me and you. I disagree. I think the biggest obstacle is going to be gaining the trust of the public. Would you let a computerized vehicle drive you around? Would you feel safe cruising down the interstate at 70 mph while your car makes driving decisions for you? I don't think I would. I want personal control of my 3,000 pounds of life-changing carnage.

Apparently long range goals are to have future vehicles be in constant contact: with other vehicles around them; with the traffic signal systems helping to control traffic; with the internet and Big Brother; with global positioning satellites; with your bank so your car can pay tolls and pay at the pump for you. I don't know if I want my car having access to my bank account. What if the machines rise up against us? I already don't trust my cell phone and answering machine. They are out to get us.

So you better drive while you can. If it's proven that driverless vehicles are safer and more predictable than human drivers, driving privileges will eventually become a thing of the past. But don't worry, there's still time to get in that road trip you've been wanting to take.

Hypermilers - Hypermiling is the use of driving techniques that maximize fuel economy. You've seen gas prices. Saving on fuel costs is a good idea, and getting your miles-per-gallon as high as possible is great, but there are good hypermiling techniques and there are bad hypermiling techniques. Some of the good (legal) techniques are as follows:

- Slow down – speeding is a waste of fuel.
- Accelerate and brake smoothly – fast acceleration is a waste of fuel.
- Don't let your car idle – if you have to sit and wait for more than thirty seconds shut off your engine.
- Keep your tires properly inflated. Replace old worn tires.
- Keep your vehicle well maintained – a Rule One application as well.
- Travel light – the lighter your vehicle the better its fuel economy.
- Close your windows at high speeds – helps reduce drag (wind resistance).

- Drive a vehicle with a standard transmission – Yeah, right. Can't text if you do that.
- Use your cruise control to eliminate inconsistent human speed control.
- Minimize the use of your vehicle's heater and air conditioner.

The reason for that last item is it reduces mechanical and electrical loads on your engine thus saving you fuel (and you thought I was kidding about my not using turn signals as a fuel saver. Okay, I guess I was kidding a little). Your GPS, your stereo, your turn signals and headlights, all put loads on your engine that reduce your gas mileage.

With the current trend towards saving energy (everything from using those low-energy compact fluorescent bulbs to setting your house thermostat lower in winter and higher in summer to dual-flush toilets), why is it that SUVs and Pickup Trucks seem to be getting bigger and brighter? I've noticed that some of these gas guzzling monsters now have four headlights. They look like giant four-eyed insects coming at you. It was bad enough when they could blind you with two headlights. Four headlights (more power consumption) is bad hypermiling karma.

Some **Bad Hypermiling Techniques** (violations of Rule One) are as follows:

- <u>Tailgating larger vehicles to reduce drag</u>, such as riding on a semi's bumper (drafting) to save fuel is a life risking situation. Your choices here are to save fuel or save your life. Which one of those would I choose? Hmm. I'll take "Save My Life" for a thousand, Alex. Never follow another vehicle too closely.

- <u>Shutting off your engine while at highway speeds and coasting to save fuel</u>. You can lose control of your vehicle's powered systems (like steering and braking) if you shut off your engine. See previous choices.
- <u>Coasting through Stop signs</u>. I get this. By not completely stopping you maintain some forward momentum which saves a little fuel. It's illegal. They're not called Stop signs for nothing. Though I'll have to admit to a few rolling stops. They had nothing to do with fuel economy, however.
- <u>Over inflating your tires</u>. Over inflated tires have small contact friction areas with the road. Correctly inflated tires have large contact friction areas necessary for control. Control is important in not dying. Follow your vehicle's recommendations for tire pressure.

All in all, I suppose I'm for saving fuel, energy, and money, but not at the expense of safety. Do I practice any hypermiling techniques? I do let off the gas and coast when I see an upcoming red light. (There's something you see a lot, vehicles racing up to a red light then having to brake quickly to stop in time. It's hard on brake pads and fuel economy. Personally, I hate sitting at a red light. The last thing I want to do is get there quicker so I have to wait longer.) I'm not too good at slow acceleration, though I am good at slow deceleration. And I love my cruise control. So, yeah, I do practice some fuel-saving techniques.

X's & O's – Ask someone what they think of their "new car" and they always have the same response, "I love my new car." It is your sanctuary. Car interiors are designed to embrace you, to relax you, to make you feel good about yourself, and now (just like your spouse) talk to you and tell you where to turn. Of course, you love your new car.

And it doesn't have to be a brand new car, it can just be new to you. You know, when you upgrade and you have features you never had before like heated leather seats; "Oh my God, Erma, it's like havin' a warm cushy seat in heaven."

How about a built-in GPS system? I love my GPS. How did I ever get anywhere before? Although, those GPS voices can be annoying. I've set mine on a British woman's voice, so every time she tells me she's "Recalculating," I feel like I'm in England. If they added some new voices you wouldn't hear me complain.

Marilyn Monroe's voice would work. Have it sound like when she sang Happy Birthday to JFK, that silky, sexy tone that said, "I want you, Mr. President. Right here, right now, Mr. President." "Turn right in one hundred and fifty feet, Mr. President." That would be great for all us guys. Have her sigh every time she says, "Recalculating."

George Clooney's voice, I'm sure, would have some feminine appeal. "Turn Right in one hundred and fifty feet, and what are you doing later? Want to come back to my place? Recalculating."

I feel that there should be a nice Hickamy voice choice. "Tern ryte in a hunard n fifty feet. Recalculate-un." My ex-father-in-law, Willard, who lived in backwoods Florida, would have been perfect for the Hickamy voice. He had a slow drawl that sounded thick even to a southern boy like me.

One time while on vacation in Florida, Willard took me in his pickup truck on a driving tour of Ponce De Leon, a small town in the panhandle. As we drove through town, he pointed to a round structure in a town park and said, "See there. That's a brand new gazelle. They just built that." What they had just built was a new gazebo. I didn't correct him. It's what made Willard such a memorable guy. I just replied, "That's nice, Willard." I knew what he meant. Though, I'll admit that I laughed at my sister-in-law on that same vacation when, while discussing childbirth, she talked about "the um-biblical cord."

Your sound system is another part of the car love fest. If you love music, there's nothing better than a great sounding car stereo system. The reason that car systems sound so good is that they're designed for that specific space. Home systems are general in design and their sound depends on the room and where you sit in the room. Sound Engineers know exactly where you're going to sit in your car, so the speakers are placed for your maximum enjoyment. From Classical to Rock to Rap, everything sounds great in your car.

Some vehicles have backseat video screens with DVD and game players to keep children occupied. (Are we there yet?) There's satellite radio. And satellites that track your vehicle; that know when you've been in an accident and can dispatch help; or unlock your vehicle should you lock yourself out. Fiat recently introduced an in-car coffee maker (put in a flapjack grill and we'll talk). There are cars that parallel park themselves. Though I'm proud of the fact that I can parallel park on the right or the left; another of my driving skills.

There's a never ending stream of "new and improved" technology to make us love our cars even more. All this so we'll love driving, even on long trips, even when we're alone in our cars. There's nothing quite like having your car and the road to yourself.

WITNESS PROTECTION

I've done a lot of driving in the southwestern part of the U.S. and out there you can literally be by yourself on the road. In the heavily traveled eastern part of the U. S. you might see road mileage signs that read 150 miles to some-place, seldom more than 200 miles. Out west it's nothing to see signs that read 500, 600, or 700 miles to wherever you're headed. You set your cruise, then sit back and enjoy the drive. Being alone in a car and alone on the road is some-times just the ticket, peaceful and relaxing. Sometimes, though, things happen where you wish you had a witness.

Why is it that you're always alone when you see a UFO? Not that I've seen a UFO, I haven't. But most of the stories I've heard start with, "I was alone in the woods, or alone on the road when this object came down from the sky, lights a blazing." Actually, I do have a questionable UFO story and a decent ghost story, but I'll save them for some other time. I do have an alone in the car story worth telling.

THAT'S A DEEP SUBJECT

This happened at two a.m. when I was driving back home after our Blues band had played a Frankfort nightclub. I-64 at that time of night has very little traffic; it was dark and empty. I was tired, so I set my cruise and headed for home. I turned on my radio to see what I could find. You know how when you're between towns, finding a strong radio signal can be difficult. This was one of those occasions.

I kept hitting the "seek" button, until I found a talk radio station that was conducting an interview with an author who had written a book about a whale. Well, actually it turned out that the whale had written the book. The author had "channeled the whale" so the whale could tell his story. I kept waiting for a punch line.

The whale had a new-age name like Zebulon. I kept thinking, *Zebulon the whale. I wonder if he got picked on in whale school.* Of course the whale didn't speak English. You couldn't have that. He spoke a whale language that the author had to translate so we humans could understand. The longer I listened, the more convoluted the whale tale became.

The author wasn't sure why he had been chosen to tell the whale's story. It had started as a dream where he had become one with the whale, diving together to the depths of the ocean so the author could see the plight of the ocean. Then, in a trance-like state, the author was able to understand and write the book. The station faded to static before I could find out if the author and the whale ever hooked up for a face-to-face or a face-to-fluke if you like.

You can probably tell that I'm not a big believer in Channeling, whales or anything else. There's a woman in my area who claims to be channeling a "two-thousand-year-old spirit" that curiously speaks perfect modern English. I believe there are people who can self-hypnotize into believing just about anything. The mind can do many mysterious and marvelous things.

MIND GAMES

Even with all the technology to soften the in-car hours, I spend a lot of driving time devoted to word play. (You might not want to read this section. The stuff I'm going to tell you is highly addictive. Once you see it you can't make it go away. Some doors you cannot close.) Here's how it works:

License plate words – In Kentucky, our car license plates have three numbers followed by three letters; such as 123-GRT. I always try to keep my mind active. So, as I drive, I look for an interesting license plate then try to figure out a word that uses the letters on that plate in the order that they appear.

GRT might be "great" or "gravity;" or a more difficult word like "aggregate" where the G is not the first letter of the word. If nothing comes to me, I reverse the letters, TRG, and try to find a word that fits that order, such as "target," or "outright." If I still can't visualize a word, I try to use the letters in any pattern, like TGR, "tiger," or RGT, "register."

This is not as easy as I make it sound. Some letter patterns are tough. Try it, you'll see what I mean. When I travel with other people we sometimes have contests to see who can come up with the best word. You'll have to make your own rules as to what defines "best."

A more difficult version of the license plate letter game is to use the letters, again in order, as initials, such as G.R.T. where each letter represents a word starting with that letter to make a phrase that makes sense, such as Grow Red Tomatoes. Or the reverse order, Try Red Grapes. I must be hungry.

If the driver with the GRT plate cuts me off I try and use the letters to insult the driver, such as "you Goofy Rotten Turd," or "you Greedy Road-hog

Twerp." Again, this is more difficult than I make it sound. But it keeps me thinking and amused, and it keeps me watching the vehicles around me.

Hidden words – When I see a sign (a billboard, a mileage sign, an exit sign, any sign, really) I play a word game that also involves initials. The best way to explain this is to use an illustration. Let's say I see a sign that reads:

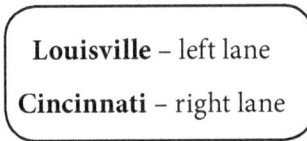

> **Louisville** – left lane
>
> **Cincinnati** – right lane

I take the first and last letters from Louisville, L & E, do the same with Cincinnati, C & I, combine them and try to form a word. L-E-C-I would become LICE or CEIL. If the hidden word somehow relates to the meaning of the sign you get Double Points. Take a look at this next example.

> **STOP**
>
> **AHEAD**

The letters to work with here are S, P, A, & D. From those four letters I can form the word PADS. It takes Brake PADS to "stop ahead," so the word relates to the meaning of the sign. Double Points. If I can't form a word from the first and last letters on a sign, I move one step in from the first and last to the next letter. In the last example one step in would give you T & O from STOP, and H & A from AHEAD. T, O, H, & A can form the word OATH as in, "Yes, officer, I swear I stopped at the Stop sign! Take a look at the next sign.

```
BRIDGE
FREEZES
BEFORE
ROADWAY
```

When I see a multiple line sign like the Bridge Freezes example, I'll either take all the first letters, or all the last letters. The first letters are B, F, B, & R: I can't do much with that. However, the last letters are E, S, E, & Y which can form the word EYES: as in watch for ice on the bridge. Double Points. It's difficult while driving to remember much more than four letters at a time. Six letters is my limit; after that I need to write them down which I won't do while I'm driving.

Words in other words – Being an SEC college basketball fan, my favorite "words in other words" is on the floor of the Colonial Life Arena, in Columbia, SC. Actually, it's the name Colonial Life Arena on the floor where I see the hidden words. I'll demonstrate:

COLONIAL LIFE ARENA
COLONI (ALL I FEAR) ENA

You can see the hidden message "All I Fear" right in the middle of the name. Is that a subliminal message? Isn't Colonial Life a "life and accident insurance company?" Isn't that how insurance is sold, by playing on your fears? You don't want to leave your family with nothing should you die. You want them to be well-off, comfortable. You'd better hurry and get insurance, before "what you fear" comes true, before it's too late.

You can take the remaining letters COLONI and ENA, and rearrange them to spell A LONE COIN, not that it means anything, just more of the word games I like to play. You can rearrange those same letters to spell EN COLONIA a Spanish phrase meaning "In Colony." All I fear is in what colony?

Maybe "All I Fear" is what the University of South Carolina Gamecocks want their opponents to think. All I fear is having to play the Gamecocks in the Colonial Life Arena. I'm sure it's all coincidence, but I see it anyway. Some doors you can't close.

Reverse the phrase No Pets and you have Step On. At 3:17 on a digital clock, you can turn the clock upside-down and it reads LIE. 0.7734 upside-down on a calculator says "hello." Some doors you can't close. I play these word games everywhere I go; in restaurants, stores, the mall, and while I'm driving. I look for hidden words in magazines and menus and the newspaper. It's addictive. It's hard not to see all the hidden words out there.

I suppose you could make a case that playing these word games while driving is a distraction, but I've never found it to be. It keeps my eyes on the road and the cars around me. I like mental exercises. I like solving puzzles and riddles, and looking for patterns in the ordinary. It keeps me sharp. I'm the sharpest tool in the shed. Although, I'm sure there are those who disagree with that last statement.

SHOTGUN
(Shoot 'em for he runs now)
(Do the Jerk baby)
(Now I have another song stuck in my head.)

Up to this point I've kept my focus on the driver, and that makes sense. This is a book about driving. Now let's talk about Riding Shotgun.

"I've got shotgun." How many times have you heard that phrase? That's because if you can't be the driver you still want to ride in the front seat. It's where the cool people ride, people in the know, the alphas. Though riding shotgun is like being vice president; you're not really in control but it's the second best seat in the car. There's a much better view of the world from the front seat. Some people get shotgun by default; parents for example. Seldom do you see a parent in the backseat.

The term "Shotgun" has its origins in the stagecoach days of the old west when the guy sitting next to the driver was a guard who held a shotgun to protect the stagecoach from bad guys. Bad guys like the infamous Charles Earl Bowles (aka Black Bart the Poet) who robbed twenty-eight Wells Fargo stagecoaches, occasionally leaving signed poems, over an eight-year stretch in the late nineteenth century. Doesn't sound like the shotgun guy was doing much of a job. Trump would have fired him immediately.

Riding Shotgun is great if you trust the driver. You don't particularly need to watch the road, so you're free to make music selections, to look at a map or GPS, to read, or text. You can even catch a few winks. If snacks are stored in the backseat, it's your job as Shotgun to carefully kneel in the front seat and grab the snacks so the driver doesn't have to pull over and stop. I'll have to confess that on several occasions I have been the snack getter.

It's a strange sensation when your rear-end is facing the oncoming road. I've often wondered what would happen in a collision. "Well, there are multiple lacerations to his butt. Which is to be expected. His butt hit the windshield at 70 mph. He was holding two cans of soda that we had to pry loose. The bad news is because of the extensive damage, we think we may have to make his butt crack go horizontally instead of vertically. He may have trouble going down slides in the future."

Riding Shotgun can be harrowing when you're in a car where the driver scares the bejeezus out of you. I hate riding with someone who follows other vehicles too closely, particularly at higher speed; it makes me nervous.

When you're riding Shotgun with a driver making poor driving choices you're very focused on the world around you; your right hand white-knuckling the door handle (I prefer to grip an Oh Shit! Handle), your left hand clenched to the edge of the seat or reaching out to brace against the dash, your eyes wide with anticipation, you're foot searching for that missing passenger-side brake pedal. An awful driver brings out the backseat driver in us all.

It's scary when you're not in control. Like when you accept a ride from a co-worker because your car's in the shop, and he wants to show off his muscle car so he puts the pedal to the metal and let's her roar, tires squealing, rear-end fishtailing, your heart in your throat as he speeds through traffic.

It bothers *me* when someone drives right on the outer edge of a shoulder-less road and I can feel the tires skimming the edge of the pavement. In my mind I see my impending doom. Or riding with someone who waits until the last second to slow down for a red light or for an upcoming turn. It's that, *Oh, No! They're going too fast to stop* feeling that stirs my adrenaline.

JUST CLOSE YOUR EYES

Once, on a family vacation out west we (me, my mom, my sister, and my grandmother) decided to visit Sequoia National Park in California. The drive up to the park followed a narrow two-lane road on the very edge of a cliff. Not only did it not have a shoulder, the two-foot wide edge of the road was crowded with a short guardrail that kept you from plunging to your death over the close and treacherous cliff. Sequoia National Park is, on average, seven thousand feet above sea level, so quite a ride up. I was driving. My mom was riding shotgun. Unfortunately for her that was the side the cliff was on.

I learned on that trip that she had a fear of heights. As we climbed higher and higher on the narrow road, she started leaning away from her window in an effort *not to see* the growing drop away. We were midway to the top when I noticed that she had a death grip on the door handle, her shoulders were scrunched and her face was sheet white, drained of blood in a grimace I thought only reserved for anticipated explosions.

The higher we climbed the farther she leaned over until she was almost lying sideways on the front seat. Almost, but not quite; her ability to reach the seat being limited by the fact that she was *not* going to let go of the door. Of course, we were all making fun of her, which lightened her mood somewhat. She did survive the trip to the top, though it was obvious she didn't think she would.

EXCUSE ME?

How about riding with someone who swears at other drivers as though no one else is in the car? My son and daughter both have loud things to say about other drivers. You can be riding shotgun and be in a conversation when suddenly they break in with, "Look where you're going, dumbass. Damn, where'd you get your license?" And then, "Sorry. You know I get that from you, right? (speaking to me) You taught me how to drive."

I did, in fact, teach both of them to drive, and I, too, speak ill of other drivers from the privacy of my car, but you can't teach that sort of attitude. It's ingrained from years of driving. I could be wrong. I suppose it could be inherited, so I might be at fault anyway. (A little joke for all you ladies: If a man speaks in a forest and there's no one there to hear him, is he still wrong?)

The only time I ever heard my mother swear was on a family vacation to Washington, DC. I was ten or twelve at the time (same group as before). I was riding shotgun because my grandmother had chosen not to enforce her shotgun privilege, and I had seniority on my younger sister. It was a mild summer morning and people were driving with their car windows down.

The road system in Washington, D.C. is a grid of odd intersecting angles and many one-way streets. My mom, a nervous small town driver not used to such a road layout, struggled to navigate the D.C. maze. We were looking for the Smithsonian (pre-GPS days) when my mom made a left turn onto a four-lane road and suddenly all the traffic, in all four lanes, was headed straight for us.

Two lanes of cars parted and began curving around us on either side as we straddled a centerline. The oncoming drivers were giving us that look; that evil eye reserved for moron out-of-towners. Finally, one man stuck his head out his window, blew his horn, shook his fist, and yelled, "Watch where you're going you stupid lady." My mom, flustered, returned the fist and yelled, "Go to hell, mister." To say the least, I was shocked. A curse word had just come from my good Catholic mother's mouth, mild as it was. Of course she was driving the wrong way down a one-way street and I imagine more than a little embarrassed. That was the only time I heard my mom swear.

The first adult I heard say the F word was my grandfather. I was ten. I'd been visiting my grandparents (they lived just a few houses down from us) and was about to leave. My grandfather thought I *had* left, but I was standing at the front door when I heard a sharp noise in the kitchen where my grandparents were, followed by my grandfather saying, "Fuck."

Immediately following the F word, I heard my grandmother in a hushed voice reprimand him. "Shh, Genie, he's still in the house." To which he replied, "Oh, mother, it's not going to be the only time he hears that word." I quietly opened the door and left. My grandmother hated for my grandfather to call her "mother." She was "not his mother," as she often pointed out.

My grandfather never had a driver's license, never drove a car, and would only ride shotgun with one particular friend of his, Pud (pronounced like the first syllable of pudding). Anyway, according to my grandfather, everyone else's driving made him nervous. Apparently my grandfather was a Gasper.

Pud would show up on Sunday afternoons in his Cadillac, then he and my grandfather would go for drives. My brother thinks that these Sunday drives were for collecting money owed to my grandfather; he ran a "bookie" business from his bedroom. He was quite a character. He also made bathtub beer during the Prohibition that he shared with a couple of Prohibition officers he'd befriended. At least that was the story I heard.

My grandfather *would* begrudgingly ride with my mother to church if he got to sit in the backseat. He was a funny guy. Got angry if you opened an umbrella in the house; a very superstitious man. I have some great stories about my grandfather. But let's move on.

CUPID

"New love" brings riding shotgun to a whole new level. You've seen vehicles where the driver and the only other passenger in the front seat are apparently glued to each other. Ah, but isn't that what new love is all about? You can't stand to be apart, not even the short distance across the front seat. They should make lovers' seatbelts; a two for one deal. Then you could strap-in with your loved one. Believe me, you will survive without physical contact with your significant other while you're in the car together. You might not survive not wearing a seatbelt.

MUD SLINGING

One of my favorite riding shotgun stories happened some years back in my friend Dean's pickup truck. It all started when I told him about a barn I'd seen that had been converted into a luxury home. I thought that he, being a photographer, might like to photograph it.

The barn was in the middle of nowhere on a pig farm in eastern Kentucky. I had gotten permission to photograph the barn/luxury home just a few weeks earlier while there doing electrical work for the owner. Dean and I were on our way to see it. It was early February and cold, in the thirties, but it was a sunny morning after a long night of cold soaking rain. The world looked new and clean and we were enjoying the ride.

When we got off the Mountain Parkway and found the entrance to the pig farm I was a bit confused at first. The driveway I remembered was a dirt road; this driveway was covered in a fresh layer of pea gravel. Still, it looked like the right place so we turned into the gravel driveway.

Everything was proceeding as planned until we came to a dip in the driveway, a twenty-five foot mud-filled washout topped with a thin layer of pea gravel. The mud looked slick and deep. A pair of tire tracks ran through the center of the goop; they were sagging and half-filled with brown water.

We sat for a moment wondering if we could make it through without getting stuck. We could see the barn/house several hundred yards ahead and considered walking, but it didn't appear that we could get past the mud on foot. We decided to back up and make a run at it.

Dean hit the gas and we headed straight for the washout. Gravel and mud sprayed out in sheets as the front tires dipped into the muck. Dean kept the pedal to the metal, but we started fishtailing and sliding. It quickly became apparent that we didn't have enough forward momentum. We slowed to a stop about halfway through. Dean put his truck in reverse and tried backing up, but to no avail. He tried forward then reverse, forward then reverse, tires screaming and smoking. He let off the gas.

We looked at each other and laughed because we knew that one of us was going to have to get out and push. This was well before cell phones so we couldn't call for help. Dean tried blowing his horn in hopes the farm owner might hear us and come lend a hand. No one responded. There was only one way out of this mess. Dean was driving, so the pushing job fell to me.

I opened the door and looked warily at the deep mud. I took off my shoes and socks, rolled up my pants then stepped into the ice-cold, just a fraction above freezing muck. Not only was the mud intensely cold, it was full of jagged pea gravel that scraped and dug into the tender flesh of my feet. It's called pea gravel because it's pea-sized, not because it's smooth like a pea. Those tiny bits of torture are sharp and angular when freshly cracked. My feet had just passed through a one-inch layer of the pointed, biting gravel.

It was like stepping into an icy red ant nest. I yelped then turned to Dean and said something profane. He only laughed. I sloshed painfully to the back of the truck and positioned myself in the center.

I signaled "go" and Dean hit the gas. Mud slung out beside me as the tires started spinning. I was able to move the truck a short distance but it was obvious that I alone did not have the force needed to get us out. (It would have been great to have had a shovel and cat litter like AAA suggests.) Dean decided that he needed to push as well.

His barefoot reaction to the stinging mud was very similar to mine. This time I laughed. Dean left the truck in gear and pushed against the open door frame as I pushed against the back. Slowly the truck began to move, then it started to gain traction. Dean jumped in and pulled up onto dry driveway. I waded out of the torturous mud and climbed back into the truck. We were a muddy mess. We drove up to the barn/house hoping that we might hose off there.

When we got to the house we found that no one was home; all that for nothing. Somehow I had gotten wires crossed with the home owner. We did find a hose and were able to clean up somewhat. We climbed back into Dean's truck and headed for the mud once again. This time Dean hit the washout going as fast as he dare go and we got across no problem. Live and learn. I still don't carry a shovel or cat litter. I just don't drive through mud if I'm in a vehicle that can't handle it.

HOLD ON TO YOUR HAT

I suppose my scariest riding shotgun story involves my older brother, Philip. Back in the seventies I played in several rock and dance bands. On one particular occasion, we had a gig in Louisville at a high school dance. I had ridden up with the bass player, Ricky, in his van with the instruments and equipment. Philip had driven up in his 290 HP black with gold stripes 1969 Gran Torino (bad ass car, sleek and powerful). It had a 351 V8 engine. The speedometer read from zero to 120. That range was good for most occasions, but not all. You've heard the phrase, "bury the needle."

Once we got to the high school, Philip helped us unload our equipment. While we were setting up I discovered we were missing a crucial part of the P.A. system, the amplifier/mixer or "the P.A. head." Without it we couldn't play the job. We were in a panic. It was seven o'clock and we had to play at nine. We had two hours to solve the problem.

A trip to Lexington and back would take two and a half hours if we pushed it, or three hours if we went the speed limit. That's when my brother spoke up and said, "Come on, I'll get you there." I said, "Okay." Desperate times call for desperate measures.

To be fair, we started on the eastern side of Louisville and our destination was the western side of Lexington, so point to point was mostly interstate. We made the round trip in one and a half hours; a half hour to spare, which was good because I needed to get my heart rate and adrenaline back under control.

The desperate journey was like being in hyperspace; all the vehicles we passed seemed to be crawling. Similar to my mother's story, I had a firm grip on the door handle. I also had my eyes glued to the road, though occasionally I would glance at the speedometer. There were times when the needle was past the 120 mark. I don't know how we didn't get pulled over. Luck of the draw, I suppose. No police were out that night.

I've often wondered what the people thought in the cars we blew by. We were flat-ass moving. I never want to go that fast again even if I'm the one driving. It's a miracle that we didn't get killed, though I trust my brother's driving. He did manage to get us there and back in plenty of time and in one piece.

YOU DIRTY COPPER, YOU GOT MY BROTHER

My brother tells a story about another night that he and his friend, Steve, were coming back from Richmond at one-thirty in the morning on the interstate. Again, he was driving his Gran Torino when they happened upon another black Torino cruising down the road, a 429 Cobra Jet. As soon as they were side by side the race was on. They stayed neck and neck as their speed increased; the early hour making the race possible; no other vehicles on the road.

How long the race lasted I can't say, but it ended as they came over a hill and saw a State Police car shooting radar. Philip said that they were well past the police car before the dreaded blue lights came on. Neither Torino let up. Philip knew that just ahead there was an exit. He took that exit. The Cobra Jet went on. A while later, almost in town, a State cop signaled my brother to pull over.

The policeman asked Philip where his friend was, to which my brother replied, "He's right here in the seat beside me." "No," the policeman responded, "the other Torino." My brother just shook his head and said he didn't know what the officer was talking about. The policeman didn't let up. "I clocked you and your buddy doing 140." My brother claimed that he and Steve had just come from a friend's house and that they hadn't been part of any race. Finally, the officer had to concede because he had lost sight of my brother's car and there was no second Torino. He glared at Philip and said, "I'm out on the road a lot. I will get you." It was a one time event. Philip never saw him again.

I suppose I'm proving my point that you never know what you might encounter. If you think that crazy stuff isn't happening on the road every day, think again.

PAM READING

I'm a little bit dyslexic. My biggest visual problem is with numbers. I have to concentrate so I don't read or write numbers backwards. On trips to Florida when I was a child, my mother would wonder why I kept saying I-57 instead of I-75. I seldom transpose letters, so words don't usually confound me, however I do have problems determining left from right.

If somebody tells me to turn right, I have to think about it. I have to concentrate on my hands, think about which one is my right hand (I'm right-handed) so I can decide which way is right. That's why I should never be put in charge of pam reading (map reading) and giving directions. I sometimes say right when I mean left, and verse vicesa.

Once, on a trip to locate a new hiking trail, Ray and I were driving the back roads of eastern Kentucky looking for the trailhead. I was riding shotgun and studying a fold-out paper map trying to figure out where we should turn. I had been giving Ray directions, but it seemed like we were lost. We saw a State Road sign and a mileage sign and we eventually figured out where we were. We were going the wrong direction.

I saw on the map that we could turn on an upcoming road that would head us back in the correct direction. I told Ray the road number and that it would be on the right. When we found the road it was on the left. That's when we discovered that I'd been saying right for left the whole time. What can I say? It seemed right to me.

Did you hear about the dyslexic, agnostic, insomniac who sat up all night wondering if there really is a Dog?

MUM'S THE WORD

I considered telling one more riding shotgun story of my youth, but then I thought better of it. What I did back then was stupid and a bit dangerous, and I knew if I published that story, someone would attempt it and I don't want to put that kind of information out there. Don't do stupid stuff. Try and rid yourself of that Darwin Award "Hey, watch this" bulletproof mentality. You are extremely fragile. Your body can easily be broken.

MORON'S THE WORD

I recently read a disturbing report about morons who lay on the centerline of busy roads for thrills. What? What the hell's the matter with you? Don't lie in the middle of the road. What if you get killed? Think about what that would do to the person that accidently ran over you. How would you feel if you ran over and killed someone? Maybe you won't be killed, just maimed for life. Don't try anything stupid on the road, in or out of the car. Pay attention. As we've discussed all through this book, there's a lot to watch for. Well, I guess we need to start heading back. We're getting very near the end.

ONE FINAL CONFESSION

I might as well get right to it, I'm a watermelon thief. Shocking, I know, but it only happened once. I only stole one watermelon. But it's not the watermelon I stole that's the most interesting. It's the circumstance of a watermelon that one of my friends stole that's worth the telling. It's a "once in a lifetime" moment. I've had more than my fair share of those moments.

In high school I ran with three other "like souls" (Rick, Ricky, and Danny) and we four did a lot of stuff together. We went to school together, partied together, drank, got high, listened to and played music together, and went on camping trips together. It was the 70's and we were in our teenage prime.

On this particular occasion we had decided to go camping on Freak Creek. That wasn't the creek's actual name; it was a title we had given it. If you were cool in the 70's you called yourself "a Freak." I'm not sure of its origins but it meant you were "in the know" about "cool stuff." We *were* cool, two of us played in the same rock band; I mean, how cool is that? Right? We thought we were cool, anyway.

To get to Freak Creek, you have to take a certain State Road out of Lexington and follow it almost to the Kentucky River. The last several miles of that road, before it crosses the river, is nothing more than a narrow, shoulderless two-lane road on the edge of a thirty-foot drop overlooking a creek that the road follows to the river. Freak Creek joins up with and flows into the roadside creek not too far from the river.

To get to where we camped, we took a side road off of the main road, parked at the head of Freak Creek, then hiked several miles down the shallow stream. We always set up camp far enough back from the roadside creek so we couldn't see the road and the road couldn't see us. But it was simple enough to walk to where you could see the traffic above you on the road.

We set up camp, then went exploring, looking for fossils and whatnot. (To this day, I enjoy creek hiking. I have a nice fossil collection.) As night fell we wandered back to our camp, built a fire, roasted some hotdogs, then sat back to enjoy a night out under the stars.

It was then that Rick surprised us with a quart of whiskey that he'd taken from his father's liquor cabinet. We all high-fived deciding that we should drink it. We were staying put for the night, anyway. (I suppose the whiskey thing is a "bonus confession," just a bit of plot development. Remember, this story is about a stolen watermelon.) I'd never had whiskey. I'd had beer, but this was going to be a new experience for me.

We sat around the campfire, passing the bottle and taking "shots," grimacing at the taste, and reacting to the burn after each gulp. Slowly, as the alcohol entered our bloodstreams, we got that "I'm cool, let's party" sort of feeling. Before long we were laughing and talking about how buzzed we were.

As the night wore on, we hit the bottle from time to time. We weren't inca-pacitated by any means, we were drinking soda and snacking, but we did have a bit of alcohol-fueled enthusiasm. I can't remember who came up with the idea, but we decided to hike down to the roadside creek and climb up the thirty-foot embankment to the road. Do a little midnight moonlight exploring, if you will. Flashlights in hand we headed down Freak Creek looking for adventure.

The embankment that led up to the road was steep, 70° or so, but easy to climb. It had lots of footholds and rough rock edges to grab if you were young and agile. We climbed up to the road. The part I haven't told you is that a few hundred yards up from where we stood was the only wide spot in the road, and in that wide spot was a country store; one of those small wooden struc-tures where they sold fruit and groceries and soft drinks. I think it was called Cliffside Grocery because it was built into the vertical cliff that lined that side of the road. There was a streetlight in front of the store. It was well-lit and easy to see from where we stood. We decided to wander up to the store.

As we approached the grocery it was obvious that it was closed. Out front, however, in a large cardboard box on a pallet, was a bunch of unguarded water-melons. There was a car parked to the side of the store which meant the owner was probably sleeping inside. We decided that if we were very quiet we could grab one of those watermelons to take back to camp. Hot summer night, alcohol-fueled enthusiasm, it sounded like a good plan. I volunteered to get a watermelon.

My friends stayed in the shadows on lookout. I stuck my flashlight in my pocket and made my way quickly and quietly to the box of watermelons. My heart was racing as I scooped up a large green melon. Holding it with both arms against my chest I hurried back to my partners in crime. We stood

216

silently waiting for the hammer to drop, waiting for the store owner to appear, gun in hand, to vanquish the watermelon thief. Nothing happened.

After we were sure all was quiet, my friends decided that they, too, wanted a watermelon. Why we needed four watermelons, I don't know. One by one they carefully went and *lifted* a melon. Soon we were standing in the shadows, each of us burdened with a large watermelon. I whispered that we should go, but Rick whispered *no*, that he'd spied several glass jugs of apple cider sitting unguarded next to the store's front door. I whispered *no*, that it was too risky. He whispered that he was going to try for the cider anyway.

That's when Danny and I decided to head back. We felt we had tempted fate enough, that too much activity would surely get noticed. Ricky said he'd stay with Rick while he went for the apple cider. Danny and I started down the road.

We hurried along to the climb down spot. I turned to see if the two Ricks were on their way back as well. They were still standing in the shadows watching the store. It was then that I noticed, in the distance, that a car was coming. I could see its headlights following the curves of road, headed right for us.

"There's a car coming," I screamed. Hurriedly the two Ricks gathered up their stolen merchandise and started running our way. Danny and I, in a panic, climbed over the guardrail and scooted down the embankment to hide. Seconds seemed like minutes. The car was closer still. Where were Rick and Ricky? I decided to stand up and look.

What I didn't know until that very second was that Rick, in an effort to carry his watermelon and his jug of apple cider had lost control of his watermelon. It had hit the ground and was rolling precariously down the road picking up speed as it headed for where Danny and I were hiding.

What I saw when I peered out from under the guardrail was an out of control watermelon doing at least 25 mph, rolling and bouncing wildly, seconds from my head. I quickly ducked. The watermelon shot under the guardrail, grazed my shoulder, then tumbled down the steep embankment. I looked at Danny in stunned amazement.

After the car passed, Danny and I climbed back up to the road. It was then we saw Ricky and Rick casually walking towards us; one carrying a watermelon, the other carrying a jug of apple cider. They had also climbed over the guardrail and hidden. Later, back at camp, we talked about how lucky I'd been not to have gotten knocked down that steep, rocky embankment, taken out by a watermelon. We came up with an epitaph for my tombstone: "He lived a short but fruitful life."

What does any of this have to do with driving? One person I left out of the story was the driver of the car. He didn't know we were out there up to no good. Worse things could have happened other than me almost getting hit by a runaway watermelon. Rick could have dropped the glass jug instead of the watermelon. The car could have hit the broken glass, blown a tire, and crashed over the embankment. Several bad things could have happened.

The other person I left out of the story was the store owner. I still feel guilty for stealing his watermelon. I went back there years later to make restitution but the store was completely gone; just an empty wide spot in the road.

Remember, the world is still full of crazy teenagers. Pay attention and hide your watermelons.

THE DRIVING GAME RULES

B efore we get out of here I'd like to revisit The Ultimate Goal, then do a countdown from Rule Four down to Rule One. You're thinking, "There's a Rule Four? I don't remember any Rule Four."

You've been such good company that I thought you deserved a "Bonus Rule." How about that? Just like one of those infomercials; a surprise gift "if you order right now." What is Rule Four? You'll have to keep reading if you want to know. It's on the next page. You already peeked, didn't you? Spoiled the surprise. Eyes right here, mister.

The Ultimate Goal: Every time you get in your car you must safely get to wherever you are going as fast as possible with the least amount of resistance and the fewest amount of stops. This is, apparently, the way most people drive. I'm guilty of it; you want to get there; I get it. You will get there. Relax, enjoy the drive, take the tension out of your life, it's good for the soul. All right, all right, Rule Four.

Rule Four – Keep your eyes on the road; it's why blind people don't drive. If you only remember one of the four rules, this is the one. Rule Four partners well with the other three Rules. But speaking of blind guys, I guess I have time for one more story. I cannot confirm that this incident actually took place; it's probably an Urban Myth.

A car was swerving erratically down the highway, crossing the centerline, surging then braking. It was very *suspect driving* which caught the eye of a traffic cop who, of course, turned on the dreaded blue lights and went after the erratic car. When he finally got the vehicle pulled over and went to interrogate the driver, here's what he found:

The owner of the vehicle was riding shotgun because he was drunk and didn't want to drive; sound judgment on his part up to that point. The Yin to that Yang was that his chosen designated driver was his blind friend. The drunken guy was the eyes for the blind guy, telling him what to do, when to go straight and when to turn. I agree that this story does have that Urban Myth feeling. I mean, what blind guy would agree to drive a vehicle? Recently, however, in the news, a similar situation was reported where the drunken guy's designated driver was a nine-year-old boy.

I was discussing the above story with a few guys at work and they related some of their confessions of youth. Many tales of late nights being "plasterized" (their word, not mine) and not remembering how they got home. They knew they had driven home drunk but had no recollection of it the next morning. One guy's story was about how once he was "so high on mescaline and pot" that when he wanted to pull into traffic, he had to look one way then the other, over and over, because he couldn't remember anything clearly from one second to the next. So, you never know who you're going to "run into" on the road; which brings us to Rule Three.

Rule Three – Everyone on the road is a Moron but you. That almost doesn't need to be said. Of course everyone else is a moron. The roads are full of Morons. There's just a few of us good drivers out there. Believing Rule Three will make you constantly aware that The Morons Are Out To Get Us, making you ready to swerve when a Moron crosses the centerline. Oh, I just thought of a joke: Why did the Moron cross the road? Who the fuck knows, he's a Moron! "Everyone on the road is a Moron but you" could be said to have roots in Rule One. Pay attention.

Rule Two – Your vehicle cannot collide with any other object. That means you can't hit vehicles, trees, people, buildings, or animals. There are people who take joy in running over live animals. If you're one of those people, you're sick, get help. Rule Two also means that you can't, by doing something stupid on the road, cause another driver to break Rule Two. Don't bring anger to the road. Don't "get even" by forcing someone else into a dangerous situation. Everyone wants to get there alive.

You're driving 3,000 pounds of life-changing carnage. You might believe that you're safe and sound in your car, but in reality, you're surrounded by a cage of bone-crunching metal. Keep that in mind. Every time you drive somewhere, it could be the last thing you ever do. There's a seemingly never ending supply of vehicular contact every day. People die in some of those vehicular contacts, don't add to the total.

Rule One - Participate in your own health and well-being. This is a good everyday life sort of rule. Your health is your life. If you don't believe me, visit an accident survivor and ask how their life has changed now that they're para-lyzed from the waist down because they weren't paying attention to the road for whatever reason. Go see a smoker in an oncology ward and see how they're do-ing now that they have lung cancer. I'm sure you've seen that new anti-smoking campaign: Every cigarette you smoke takes you one step closer to cancer.

If you don't believe your "physical health" defines your "quality your life," talk to someone who's ill or injured. Your health is the definition of your life. Think about that while you're driving. Think about what you eat and drink. Think about what you put into your body. You only get one body, take care of it while you're driving and otherwise.

A sad thing I see in America now is all the "fat families." More and more I see people "not participating in their own health and well-being." Remember the Hunter-Gatherer tribes I mentioned earlier. No matter who you are, your body is inherited from your hunter-gatherer ancestors. They were, by neces-sity, active people, and as a consequence, to be healthy, you need to be active.

Every function of your body improves with movement and exercise. Everything from blood pressure to depression can be improved with exercise. The human body is not designed to be stationary. It's designed to move. Use it or lose it is absolutely correct.

And Energy begets Energy. If you burn energy by exercising, your hunter-gatherer body will produce extra energy when you're not active. That's why people who exercise seem to always be in a good mood. You feel better when you exercise. Exercise helps fight the effect aging has on the brain. People who exercise stay sharper longer.

Park your vehicle and get out and walk. Walking is the perfect exercise for the human body. If you walk, you're following your hunter-gatherer ancestry. Find someplace safe and walk for twenty to thirty minutes a day. You can "walk in place" in your home for thirty minutes. Walkers have a lower risk of heart attack, stroke, and diabetes. Walkers sleep better at night. Walking is free. Get out and walk.

Get some exercise DVDs, move. Of course, don't try anything you're not capable of; use your common sense, but figure out how to get some exercise. Dance, it's great exercise and tons of fun. I've been known to shake a tail feather. I came to dancing late in life. Don't make that mistake.

Mostly, I'm a hiker and a walker. I've been hiking most every weekend for 25 years. It has served me well. I'm a little overweight, but overall, I'm healthy. I don't have cholesterol or blood pressure problems. I take very few pharmaceuticals. I do take them when needed. Modern medicine is useful. Though, I'm against the trend that everyone should be on pharmaceuticals all the time. Back to me participating in my own health and well-being.

I've done a lot of slot canyon hiking in Utah. Slot canyons are sometimes a thousand feet high but extremely narrow at the bottom, anywhere from a few feet to fifty feet wide; sometimes filled with flowing water, and with no escape should a flash flood come roaring down on you.

One of my favorite slot canyon hikes is The Narrows in Zion National Park in Utah. It's a beautiful slot canyon carved by the Virgin River flowing between its walls. Most people enter The Narrows from Zion's main canyon and follow the river upstream. You're walking against a swift but usually shin-deep river most of the time. There are places where the water is chest deep, but there are sand banks along the way as well. The scenery is amazing.

One particular year when Ray and I were in Zion doing some back-country hiking, the weather pattern was such that every afternoon it rained; unusual for a Utah summer. We wanted to hike The Narrows but consider-ing the daily afternoon downpours we decided we should get there early, 6:00 a.m., hike until about 11:00 a.m., turn around and come back before it clouded up. That's exactly what we did. Slot canyon hiking is an exhilarating adventure.

On our way downstream out of the canyon, we encountered a Boy Scout Troop from Salt Lake City hiking up into the canyon. We talked to the Scout Leaders for a moment, pointed to the then clouding sky and explained that maybe they should go back. They said they were fine and went on anyway. Not much later, we ran into two men hiking up into the canyon and we explained the same thing to them. They said they knew what they were doing and they went on.

When we got back to the entrance of The Narrows, Park Rangers were there getting everyone out of the river because it was raining upstream on a watershed that feeds the river. We told the Rangers about the Boy Scout Troop and the two men still in the canyon. The Rangers explained that those people were "on their own." It was a choice they'd made and they would have to deal with it.

The next day at breakfast we heard that the two men had died in a flash flood and that the Boy Scout Troop had survived because, by chance, they'd been exploring a side canyon and were spared the flash flood that roared down

The Narrows. They were, however, trapped and had to spend the night in the wilderness.

You don't drown in a flash flood in a slot canyon; you're beaten to death by debris and sharp rocks. It was the Boy Scouts that found the beaten bodies of the two men the next day. Not a good way to spend a morning in the wilds of Utah.

The point is neither the Boy Scout Troop nor the two men participated in their own health and well-being. They made decisions contrary to that concept. And it wasn't that they should have listened to me and Ray. The sky was clouding up. They were in a slot canyon prone to flash floods. It should have been obvious. Sadly, two people died. Luckily, the Boy Scout Troop survived; a roll of the dice.

Every time you text while driving you're making the same decision that those two men made, you're rolling the dice. You aren't participating in your own health and well-being. Every time you take your eyes off the road you're instead participating in your own destruction and you're putting others in danger. It's clouding up, you're going to die. All I'm asking is that you pay attention. You may have a death wish, but I don't. Remember Rule Four for my sake and yours.

THE HIKE

I love to hike. It's good for the body and the mind. It's mentally and physically refreshing after a long week at work. Here in Kentucky we have miles of hiking trails through beautiful forests, and hundreds of creeks to explore. My friends and I do some pretty strenuous hiking. We climb steep slopes (75° or so) just for the view. We follow deer trails through untamed forests, climbing over fallen trees, wading through stinging nettle just to get to a creek we want to explore. We skirt six-inch wide ledges over forty-foot drops just to get around a corner. It's all exhilarating.

When I stand atop a spine ridge in the Red River Gorge I'm never more relaxed. The scenic panoramas from those narrow ridges can't be captured by camera, though we always try. When I'm exploring a creek in the winter, and it's covered in ice, I'm always amazed by the ice's intricacies. Sometimes the ice is huge and powerful; sometimes it's impossibly delicate in detail.

One of my favorite hiking memories happened on a winter hike when Ray and I came upon a large circular depression in a creek. The water there was covered with a thin layer of ice, maybe a quarter of an inch thick. We decided to test the ice with a baseball-sized rock. I tossed the rock high into the air and when it hit the frozen surface, the ice shattered into a thousand pieces that stayed in place like a jigsaw puzzle, rocking gently as the circular waves from the impact spread out.

What was amazing was the sound the ice made. The edges of the pieces were musically bumping into one another. It's hard to describe. It was like a thousand bits of tuned glass clinking together in a breeze. We kept tossing in rocks repeating the magical sound over and over. An amazing Diamond moment.

I particularly love the winter hikes; no snakes, no bugs, and you don't get hot. Most people think that you get cold on a winter hike. That's not the case at all. The first time I took my daughter on a winter hike, she came wrapped up like she was about to explore the North Pole. I told her that she was going to burn up. She disagreed. Not fifteen minutes into the hike she removed her gloves, her hat, and opened her coat; she was burning up. She knows how to dress for winter hikes now. The human body in motion heats up. You don't need as much clothing as you might think. Several layers work best so you can adjust your heat loss.

Sometimes, in the summer, on a creek hike, if we find a long stretch of flat water, we take a break and have a rock skipping contest. We pick a target, a log or a rock sticking up out of the water, then skip rocks across the water and try to hit the target. I'm not bragging, but I'm a deadly accurate rock skipper. I usually hit the target at least once, usually more. It's great fun, good for the body and the mind, and a great way to spend time with friends.

Also, in summer, I like to see what the insects are up to. If you've never watched a spider build its web, you've missed a marvelous feat of engineering. I'm still amazed that spider silk is, pound for pound, many times stronger than steel. Scientists are trying to synthesize spider silk to take advantage of its strength. The world around you is amazing. It should capture you with child-like awe.

The universe is amazing. When you see our sun and you're not amazed, you don't really understand the sun. It's ninety-three million miles away, yet so bright that you can't look directly at it, and even at that distance it warms our earth. The sun is so large that one million earths could fit inside it. And our sun is a small star (865,000 miles in diameter). There are stars much larger. Like Betelgeuse (600,000,000 miles in diameter) in the Orion constellation. If you could take a road trip to our sun and drove 75 mph, it would take you 141 years to get there. Probably 150 years if you count bathroom breaks, and stops for food and gas.

If you're not astounded by a starlit night sky, you really don't understand the vastness of space and the wonders displayed there. If every day you don't do something mentally or physically exhilarating, you're missing the point of being alive.

Don't take life for granted. Be careful who you open your life to; some doors you can't close. Enjoy every moment. Enjoy your family and friends. Be careful who you shut out of your life; some doors you can't reopen. Dance like no one is watching, and remember Rule Four - Keep your eyes on the road; it's why blind people don't drive.

And if you do want to enjoy a drive, take The Road Untraveled. Go somewhere you've never been. Put a little adventure in your life.

Well, it looks like I've finally run out of things to say. Thanks for listening, and thanks for letting me be mice elf.

The end?

DYSLEXICS UNTIE

One last joke: Two Cell Assassins were simultaneously taking an online "Test your IQ" quiz. Each had his cell phone in hand, thumbing through the questions.

The first question was: Old MacDonald had a _____?

One of the Cell Assassins thought for a moment then looked at the other and asked, "Say, man, what did Old MacDonald have?"

The other one looked sort of stunned. "He had a farm, moron."

"Oh, yeah, that's what I thought, a farm. Just checkin'." Again he seemed lost in thought. Then he asked, "Say, man, how do you spell farm?"

"I can't believe you're so stupid. It's E – I – E – I – O."

And one last bumper sticker:

Textinction ...

A systematic thinning of the human herd via cell phones.

(Now that's enough.) Is not, I want to keep writing. (I said that's enough, stop.) Well, aren't we a bit testy? I think maybe you need to be recombobulated. (That's not a word.) Is, too. (Mom!)

"Say ten Hail Mary's and go in peace."

GLOSSARY!

3,000 pounds of life-changing carnage – the average car.

Auto Projection – When another driver "projects" their personality onto you in an effort to make driving decisions for you; such as how fast you should drive, when you should pull into traffic, etc. They usually use their horn to show their dissatisfaction with *your choice* to drive how you want.

Backseat Driver - A title given to any passenger who believes that you, as the driver, need help driving. They can see that your driving skills are woefully inadequate and it's up to them to *help you drive.*

Best-in-Show – A car parked cattycorner across two parking spaces so that no one can ding or scratch the beautiful "Ride."

Blind Man's Bluff – An accident caused by someone riding in your blind spot and you not checking your blind spot before changing lanes.

Boonies – The outer regions of a parking lot. It's often where you'll find a Best-in-Show.

Cell Assassin – Any driver using their cell phone while driving. These Morons are most likely to kill themselves or kill you in a car accident.

Cellicide – This is when a Cell Assassin kills themselves in an accident.

Choke Stones – Creepers on the interstate that impede (Choke) the flow of traffic.

Coin-Operated ICU$_2$ – An **I**diotic **C**art **U**ser in a grocery store. These are the people in the checkout line using a bag of coins to pay for their purchases.

Crackasaurus – Any person, usually a man, wearing plumber's pants. Plumber's pants fit under the belly, instead of around the waist, so when the Crackasaurus bends over their Butt Crack is exposed.

Creeper – Any driver going slower than the posted Speed Limit.

Creeper Parade – A Creeper leading a line of vehicles down an acceleration ramp.

Crunch of Creepers – Term used to describe a group of Creepers. On the interstate, when a group of Creepers are blocking all the lanes it's called a **Creeper Dam.**

Dark Angle of Death – A driver that dangerously cuts across Parking Lots at odd angles instead of driving in the lanes between the rows of parked cars, hoping to "save time" or get that "close spot."

Diamond – A Diamond is when something good happens to you while driving, like hitting all the green lights, or getting the front spot at the red light. Some days are Diamond, and some days are Stone when nothing goes your way.

Dragon Ass – A driver on the interstate that hypnotically attaches to your rear-end, drives exactly your speed, and stays a constant one or two car lengths behind you.

Dreaded Blue Lights – The lights you see in your rearview mirror when you're being pulled over by the police.

Drifter – In a multiple turning lane situation, it's a driver that drifts from one turning lane into another without looking to see if the way is clear.

Drive-By Waving – A driving game where you drive-by an unsuspecting pedestrian, blow your horn, wave like you know them, and yell something like, "It was great seeing you the other night." The payoff is their expression. You always get that pitiful little *do I know you wave* and that scrunched face of unsolved mystery.

Driving Game – Any driving situation where one driver intentionally messes with another driver.

Driving Phobic – A driver that's constantly afraid that they're going to be killed while driving.

Driving Phobic Phobia – The fear of being on the road with a Driving Phobic.

Driving Rules:

    Rule One – Participate in your own health and well-being.

    Rule Two – Your vehicle cannot collide with any other object.

    Rule Three – Everyone on the road is a Moron but you.

        Rule Three/sub-section(a) - Everyone in the parking lot is a Moron but you.

Double-Stitch Injury-Lawyer Bowtie – Fictional traffic interchange that puts Traffic Circles at each end of a Double Crossover Diamond.

Doughnut – A moron driving on one or more of those little Doughnut Spare Tires at highway speeds.

Drone Mode – A condition caused by driving long distances where you "zone out" and don't remember driving the last one hundred miles or so. You get lost in your thoughts and ignore the road signs because, well, you have one hundred miles to go, no need to pay attention right now, then suddenly, where'd the time go, you're almost home. You were in Drone Mode.

Faults – A correct term for some "accidents." An accident is a tire suddenly going flat causing you to lose control and hit another car. Accidents are caused by circumstances beyond your control. Faults, on the other hand, are caused by Morons not paying attention.

Flickers – Drivers that drive for miles unaware that their turn signal is on.

Floridiot – A driver from Florida that "cuts you off" in traffic.

Full Diaper Penguin – A description of the modern male teenager wearing those extremely large pants, with what looks like a full load in their diaper, so they have to waddle like a penguin with their legs spread at an uncomfortable angle just to keep their pants from falling off.

Gaspers – A Backseat Driver that Gasps every time you turn in front of oncoming traffic.

Gatherer and a Driver – A grocery store shopping team where the Driver pushes the cart while the Gatherer chooses the cart direction. An extreme version of Backseat Driving.

Gatherer and a Scout – A grocery store shopping team where one person is a Driver/Gatherer with "the list" and the cart, and the other person Scouts ahead with a hand-held basket, gathering supplies and bringing them to the cart.

Grays – Morons that drive without headlights during those gray pre-dawn and post-sunset hours, or on gray rainy days.

Herd and the Trail Boss – A mother (Trail Boss) pushing a grocery cart, herding three or more children through a grocery store.

Herd of Danglers – A group of children dangling from the sides of a grocery cart.

Herd of Zombies – Children and teens wandering through a store hypnotized by their cell phones. Sometimes referred to as **The Shopping Dead**.

Hickamy (Hick-a-my) - Anyone from the south.

HYD! – Masked message, but OMG don't spend too much time thinking about it.

ICU – Intentional Creeper Underground – Drivers that drive slower than the Speed Limit with the intention of irritating other drivers.

ICU$_2$ – Idiotic Cart Users – ICU members with a grocery cart.

Isoreacrackus – See Crackasaurus definition.

Jerk – A driver with a need-for-speed and a need-to-always-be-in-front; a driver that sits inches from your bumper because, to him, everyone's a Creeper.

Jerk Off – A competition between two Jerks on the interstate where one Jerk tries to outdo the other Jerk.

Left Turn Jumper – A driver that takes your right-of-way when he makes a left turn.

Lug Nut – General term that describes any Moron on the road.

Make 'em Wait – The most popular Driving Game on the road.

Mangle – A driver that tries to beat a train at a railroad crossing.

Moron – A driver that's unaware of vehicles around them: a distracted driver.

Moron Awards – Driving Awards dedicated to the mistakes made by some drivers.

Newbies – A new driver; a person that just received their driver's license.

Oh, Shit! Handle – Small handle just above the car door on the ceiling that you can grab when things look dangerous.

Players – Drivers that are aware of the other vehicles around them.

Plow Tribe – Anyone in a grocery store willing to use their grocery cart as a Plow to move unattended carts out of the way.

Pound of Players – Term used to describe a group of Players.

Radar Leech – A driver on the interstate that falls in behind a Zip Car who, the Leech believes, has a Radar Detector and is likely to sniff out Speed Traps.

Right Lane Camouflage Sneak About – A radar avoidance ploy used by some drivers on the interstate.

Rise of the Cell Assassins – The modern driving environment where you constantly need to be on the lookout for Cell Assassins; a boon for Accident Attorneys.

Roadkill Game – A driving game that involves smashing litter, such as soda cans, with your tires.

Sap (**S**elf-**Ap**pointed speed guardian) - A driver in the fast lane going the exact posted speed limit, who won't get over because that's as fast as you can legally go, therefore, in his mind, he *is* going fast in the fast lane.

Suggested Speed Limit – A satirical phrasing of Posted Speed Limit because that's how most drivers treat Speed Limit Signs, as mere suggestions.

Slouch – A grocery cart driver that uses their elbows to steer their carts.

Stalker – A driver that follows a pedestrian leaving a store through a parking lot hoping to get their parking space when they leave.

Texas Turd – A driver from Texas that "cuts you off" in traffic.

Textinction – A systematic thinning of the human herd via cell phones.

The Marquis de Sade School of Parking Sciences – A fictional school devoted to designing Parking Lots that are nearly impossible to navigate. In other words, Modern Parking Lots.

Textrovert – Someone who loudly talks on their cell phone.

Tisket – A distracted Driver.

Tuttle-Hare Syndrome – The condition of a driver that speeds past you, gets in front of you, and then slows down.

Ultimate Goal – A driving philosophy that states: Every time you get in your car you must safely get to wherever you're going as fast as possible with the least amount of resistance and the fewest amount of stops.

Wiping the Dragon's Ass – A driving technique to rid yourself of a Dragon Ass.

Whip – A Zip Car followed by several Radar Leeches on the interstate.

White Lie (a secret) – The fact that there are really four Driving Rules, not just the three stated at the beginning of the book and in the Glossary.

White Rabbit – A driver that's in a hurry because they're late for an important date.

Zip Car – A car exceeding the suggested speed limit.

Zomular – The condition of some cell phone-addicted users who wander around in a cell phone induced stupor. They've gone Zomular.

BONUS SECTION
An analysis of Forrest Fenn's Treasure Hunt
© 3/17/2013 C. G. Knight LLC

Phase One
(in which Doris gets her oats)
The Forest for the Trees!

Phase Two
(The Real Deal)
Cut to the Chase!

Phase Three
(The Third Ω)
???

For those of you interested in Forrest Fenn's Treasure Chest hunt, I'm including my personal notes on the matter. I am not offering a solution. I don't know the solution, but I'm working on it.

If you want the solution, you'll have to wait for me to solve it, or you'll have to figure it out on your own. I'm just showing you how to start looking and what you're actually up against. It is not as simple as you've been led to believe. And it could be worth a great deal more than you think.

Please note that this analysis reads like I came to all this quickly. That's not the case. I'm more than a year into the solution process. And, no matter how convoluted or circuitous my logic might seem, read the analysis to the end. It does prove out, and there are "surprises" along the way.

I recently read an online post that asked the question, "Why hasn't anyone been able to solve Forrest Fenn's poem and find the hidden Treasure?" I know the answer to that question, and I've earned the right to tell the story.

THE FOREST FOR THE TREES!

If you're intrigued by Forrest Fenn's Treasure Chest story, his book "The Thrill of the Chase," and his 9-clue treasure-hunt poem, I may know a little something about that. I read Mr. Fenn's poem and became interested in The Chase, but the poem, being vague, seemed to point nowhere at all. I thought if it was solvable, you needed a starting point.

On The Today Show when Mr. Fenn was asked to give a 10th clue, the first words out of his mouth were, "Well, I'm not going to put an X on the map for you." Then his clue was, "The treasure is hidden higher than 5,000 feet above sea level." I thought the "elevation clue" was as vague as the poem. Then it hit me: he gave two clues; one about a relationship to sea level; the other about an X. *He's* not going to put an X on the map. You have to figure out an X yourself. (In hindsight, I think it's clever that when giving a 10th clue Forrest mentioned an X. The Roman numeral for 10 is X.)

I pulled out my Road Atlas and studied a map of New Mexico. I tried connecting New Mexico's square corners into an X, but that lead nowhere. So I pulled out my U.S. map and looked for anything obvious.

It was then I noticed the adjacent state of Arizona, and its state capital, Phoenix. One line of the 9-clue poem says "if you've been wise and found the blaze." "Blaze" could easily be a clue for Phoenix - the mythical bird with fiery plumage – and Phoenix has an X in its name. Then my eye was drawn to Austin, capital of Texas. This seemed obvious; Austin starts with Au, the elemental symbol for gold. "I give you title to the gold." And Texas has an X as well. (Side note: Au comes from the Latin for gold, Aurum.)

It seemed I had two state capitals that fit the poem, but what to do with them? I decided they must somehow help draw an X over New Mexico. Beginning with Phoenix, I took a yardstick and started projecting lines that crossed through New Mexico to other state capitals. It was when I hit Indianapolis that it struck me, "If you are brave and in the wood." "Brave" as in "Indian Brave" could be a clue for Indianapolis. (Another Clue? Forrest is known to have said, "It is more than 300 miles west of Toledo." There are five cities named Toledo in the U.S., two of which are in states that sandwich the state of Indiana - Ohio and Illinois. Forrest apparently said something about needing a sandwich.) So I had:

Gold = <u>Au</u>stin

Blaze = Phoenix ("The Thrill of the Chase" was bound by Roswell Bookbinding in Phoenix.)

Brave = Indianapolis (Sandwiched by Toledo-bearing states.)

I drew a line from Indianapolis to Phoenix. It passed extremely close to Santa Fe, New Mexico. I felt I was on to something. Next, I began projecting lines from Austin to see if anything made sense. When I hit Carson City, Nevada I noticed that the line went through Grants, New Mexico. "I give you title to the gold" could easily mean, Mr. Fenn "grants" you title to the gold; two clues from one line. I connected Carson City to Austin and looked at the X. It marked a spot almost directly over Exit 96 on I40 near Grants, New Mexico. It's more accurate to say that the X is more like a "cross" than an X; it has one long leg. In fact it's very similar to the cross in the cemetery drawings on pages 37 and 41 in Mr. Fenn's book.

There are supposed to be 9 clues in the poem. There are <u>**9** capital **I's**</u> in <u>**6** verses</u>. Could that mean Exit **96** on I40? It made sense. I examined the four capital city names.

I had:

Carson City, Nevada (Carson City had a **gold coin**-producing U.S. mint from 1870 to 1893.)

Austin, Texas

Phoenix, Arizona

Indianapolis, Indiana

I looked at the four state capitals' initials, **C, A, P,** & **I.**

CAPI can form the word PACI.

According to Wikipedia...

1. Paci is a derivative of the Latin word Pax which means Peace.
2. It's an Esperanto verb meaning to be at Peace.
3. It's a prefix meaning Peace in such words as pacifier.

Which brings us to the line, "Just take the chest and go in peace."

I examined that line.

If you just take "**C**hest **A**nd go **I**n **P**eace," you can see the four cities' initials **C-A** (go) **I-P**"

C-A – **C**arson City and **A**ustin (one line of the X), and **I-P** – **I**ndianapolis and **P**hoenix (the other line of the X), separated by the word "Go." You have to admit, at a minimum, it's very curious. But what does it mean? Does it mean go there and you'll find the Chest? Or does it mean start there? Is the "Cross"

Point A and you have to find Point B? The first verse of Mr. Fenn's poem starts with A, and the second verse starts with B.

"Just take - **the** chest and go in peace." (Interesting side note: In "The Thrill of the Chase," if you hold the poem page up to a light, the pile of gold coins on the other side isolates the phrase, "the chest and go in peace.") I wondered about the word "the." It would seem that the instruction in this line of Mr. Fenn's poem is to include the word "the." The pile of gold coins, as seen through the page, seems to indicate this as well.

I thought perhaps the T from "the" might indicate another state capital, but I couldn't find anything that seemed to make sense. I tried combining the T with CAPI but I couldn't form a word from those letters. You can form CAP and IT. If you add AL you have CAPITAL. But that seemed to be going backwards. I already knew about state capitals. Perhaps, I thought, I had to find three more state capitals (TAL) to go with the first four (CAPI). So far I've found nothing that makes sense in that direction.

Then I combined THE with CAPI, ran them through my favorite online word unscrambler and found the word APHETIC. At first my eye saw the word APATHETIC which is apparently how Mr. Fenn feels about whether or not someone finds his hidden treasure before he dies. The word "Aphetic" has to do with the loss of an initial vowel in words such as Alone to simply Lone. I ignored this at first because it didn't seem to relate to this puzzle I felt I was unraveling. I only mention it now because it does come into play a little later on.

Next I looked at the four states' initials.

Nevad**a**...Texa**s**...Arizon**a**...Indian**a** (NTAI) I could find no connection in the poem for those letters, though NTAI can form the word **Tain** which is tinfoil used as backing for mirrors. There is a mirror image of Utah on the cover of Mr. Fenn's book hidden in the way the three photos overlap, and Mr. Fenn calls his book a "mirror" on page 4.

Then I looked at the last letters of each state, A-A-S-A. The first four lines of the 9-clue poem start with A-A-I-A. I had three A's and an S. That seemed to point out the third line, "I can keep my secrets where." If you put the S with the I you can spell IS, or SI which is Spanish for "Yes."

If you combine the CAPI from the four capital cities with the TAIN from their respective states you can spell I CAPTAIN. Aye, Captain? Aye also means Yes. Mr. Fenn does say he dreamed that he was Captain Kidd in the "Gold and More" section of his book.

Then I noticed that the state-capital-formed X was just a bit south of Santa Fe, New Mexico. I remembered that the Treasure is supposed to be hidden north of Santa Fe. So for a while I was stymied. I realized after a while, though, that just because the X or cross (which I believe to be the starting point) is south of Santa Fe, doesn't mean that it doesn't lead to a point north of Santa Fe. Then I decided to see if there were any other U.S. towns named Santa Fe. Lo and behold there's a Santa Fe, Texas near Houston. I believe this to be the "Santa Fe" referred to in "The Thrill of the Chase." (I'll have more evidence that this is true in Phase Two.)

Most of the continental U.S. is north of Santa Fe, Texas, which sits approximately on the 30th parallel. So if I'm correct, anything south of the 30th parallel is out of the running for the Treasure Hunt. A third of Texas, a small piece of Louisiana, and most of Florida is south of the 30th parallel. Austin, Texas, one of the four X points, makes it in by a hair.

Santa Fe, Texas, geographically speaking, is also very near the center of the U.S. If you extend a line north from Santa Fe, Texas, it divides the country into approximately equal east/west halves. This division pattern repeats itself time and again in this discussion.

Mr. Fenn did make the comment that, "Just because I said it was north of Santa Fe doesn't mean it's in New Mexico." Perhaps it's a clever clue. Everyone would think that he meant the Treasure Chest isn't in New Mexico. I think he meant that Santa Fe isn't in New Mexico. Nowhere in "The Thrill of the Chase" does it say north of Santa Fe, New Mexico.

But it's supposed to be hidden in the Rocky Mountains. The Rockies start right at Santa Fe, New Mexico and stretch for more than 3,000 miles into Canada. So how could my X be correct? It's south of the Rocky Mountains.

Perhaps, I thought, Forrest Fenn is cleverly misdirecting the public. He quotes his father on page 26 in his book as saying "you should always tell the truth, but you should not always tell ALL the truth." As I've demonstrated, his clues can have more than one truth. So I started examining the name Rocky Mountains. I decided to anagrammatize the letters of Rocky Mountains and look for any hidden messages.

ROCKY MOUNTAINS

There are hundreds of words you can create using these fourteen letters. Here are three combinations that stood out to me.

1. COUNTRYMAN IS OK. Mr. Fenn is definitely a countryman, and he seems okay, seems like a likeable guy. Perhaps OK stands for Oklahoma.

2. STAR UNION with the letters CKY leftover. That's how I formed the X or Cross. State capitals are Stars on a map. (CKY See KY?)

Though, the letter combination that grabbed my attention was…

3. CONMAN STORY with the letters KUI leftover. ("Conman story" is not what it implies. I'll explain a little later).

But what to do with the KUI? IU could mean Indiana University. Indiana's state capital is one of the four points that form the Cross. UK could be The University of Kentucky (See KY). Perhaps it's KU - Kansas University. KI is an abbreviation for "The book of Kings" in the Bible. There are lots of two-letter abbreviations you can make from KUI.

Then I started doodling with the letters, putting them together in various ways and I came up with the "I" turned sideways, "K", and the "U" turned sideways. You have to bear with me here, my computer drawing skills are not the greatest.

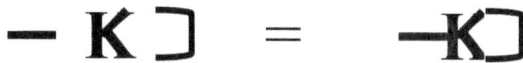

$$- \text{K} \rceil \quad = \quad \text{--K}\rceil$$

If you take the shoved together letters and rotate them so the "I" points downward you have an Egyptian Ankh.

☥

I know what you're thinking. What could an Egyptian Ankh have to do with Forrest Fenn's Treasure Chest? Good question. I'll get to that. Let's look at the possibilities. Mr. Fenn does claim to collect ancient Egyptian jewelry in the "Gold and More" section of his book, so there is that connection.

The thought occurred to me that you may have to look for pyramid shapes when you're treasure hunting, or for something that resembles an Ankh. The Ankh is a cross.

Then I looked at the letters A-N-K-H. I considered the possibility that these letters might be the initials of four new cities that form a new X, one that shows Point B, if the first X is indeed Point A. I could come up with nothing that made sense.

These letters can also form the names HANK and KHAN. Maybe some guy named Hank knows something. Maybe Ricardo Montalbán knows something, except he's deceased. He played Khan in Star Trek II – The Wrath of Khan. Mr. Fenn's book opens with four lines from a poem in a song called "Waiting For Ships That Never Come In" about life being a poker game and playing the cards you're dealt. (Mr. Fenn has several poems in his book.) The word "card" is right in the middle of Ricardo. Hmm. Just kidding. I don't think Hank or Khan know anything. A *telling* song title though, being that no one's ship has come in; no one has found the chest. Perhaps it's a warning that things aren't what they seem.

I looked at various two-letter combinations of A-N-K-H thinking that might tell me something. Then I decided to combined the ANKH with the original KUI that formed the Ankh and see what words might appear. The first word that jumped out at me was HAIKU with NK leftover. As in Carson

City, if you represent the common letters only once, in this case K, you have N HAIKU (In Haiku?)

A Haiku is a Japanese poem having three unrhymed lines of five, seven, and five syllables for a total of seventeen syllables. (Keep the number 17 in mind. Plus, three lines of two other poems do have importance in this discussion, but I'll get to that.) At first I thought this might be a clue to three unrhymed lines in Fenn's poem. I again examined the 9-clue poem. I didn't see three lines that stood out, but three words suddenly jumped to my attention – three words that start with the same letter - "where warm waters." "I can keep my secret <u>where</u>" – "Begin it <u>where warm waters</u> halt." Begin it, then, halt.

I studied those three words. WHERE WARM WATERS. I noticed that if you dropped the W's from WHERE and WARM you had HERE and ARM. Those two words, though starting with a consonant, related to the Aphetic term I mentioned earlier. WATERS was the exception, just as I felt Carson City was the exception to the rule in the Cross formation and had no clear clue in the poem. I had four cities with an exception to the rule. Now I had three words with an exception to the rule. It seemed like some sort of countdown.

Drop the W from WATERS and you have ATERS. Those letters can be anagrammed to spell STARE, or again STAR (how the X was formed) with a leftover E. I decided to move the E over to ARM and realized I could spell MARE. So I had STAR MARE HERE. Does Forrest have a mare named Star? There is a "lunar mare" having to do with plains on the moon once thought to be oceans. There is a Luna, New Mexico. (Luna, New Mexico is involved. I'll explain more in Phase Two.)

I took STAR MARE HERE and anagrammed those letters. There are several combinations that made sense:

1. EARTH REAMERS - Reamers are used to bore holes. Maybe you have to bore holes in the earth to find the Treasure Chest.

2. RARE EARTH MES - Rare Earth elements are on the Periodic Table. Perhaps there is a Rare Earth Message.

3. HEAR MERE STAR. Perhaps there's a small star in the night sky that gives a clue – a star somehow related to hearing; or maybe a small state capital that's somehow related to hearing.

Then I decided to see what happened if I substituted WHEN for WHERE. WHEN WARM WATERS. Drop the W's and you have HEN MARE STAR. If this Treasure Hunt is all about stars, the most logical letter combination is NAME HER STAR.

Then I thought if WHEN and WHERE, why not WHO and WHAT.

WHAT WARM WATERS = HAT MARE STAR = AM HEART STAR. Isn't Venus considered the morning (a.m.) star? Venus is associated with "love" aka "the heart."

WHO WARM WATERS = HO MARE STAR = AM HERO STAR or HAM ORE STAR. HAM-ORE STAR? HAMMER STAR, maybe? (Mr. Fenn states in his book that he uses words that aren't in the dictionary, and others that are, he bends a little. In his recent "Fish" interviews he confirms that statement.)

Then, if WHO, WHAT, WHERE, and, WHEN, why not WHY? WHY being the exception to the Aphetic rule stated earlier.

WHY WARM WATERS = HY MARE STAR = A RHYME STAR.

Could it be that these are all clues to other points on a map? Are these five of the nine clues hidden in the 9-clue poem?

1. HEAR MERE STAR or HERE MARE STAR. (Luna, New Mexico)
2. NAME HER STAR
3. AM HEART STAR (Venus)
4. HAM ORE STAR (Hammer Star) (Thor is mentioned on page 26 in the book.)
5. A RHYME STAR

Then, and this is where it gets really interesting, I took the five WH words, WHO, WHAT, WHERE, WHEN, and WHY and dropped the common WH from each word.

(Given those five words, I was suddenly reminded of the Whodunit board game "Clue.")

WHO…..WHAT…..WHERE…..WHEN…...WHY

O   AT   ERE   EN   Y, combined with ARM AT-

ERS from W**arm W**aters forms the following sentence…

O AT ERE EN Y ARM ATERS = START EYE NEAR AMORE. (Aye, Captain.)

If you separate "A Memoir" from the title of Mr. Fenn's book, those letters can be rearranged to spell "Mi Amore," which, in Spanish, translates to "My Love," which does come into play as I will explain momentarily.

But what did START EYE NEAR AMORE mean? Philadelphia, Pennsylvania is the City of Brotherly Love. Mr. Fenn does emphatically point out Philadelphia in his "My War for Me" section of his book. He talks about the Philadelphia saga, and flying down the east coast at night and blocking out the lights of Philadelphia with his thumb. And Philadelphia starts with PH like Phoenix which got me started with all this. But the instruction says to Start <u>Near</u> Amore.

So I looked at Philadelphia on Google maps. As I zoomed in and out I noticed that to the east of Philly, "not far, but too far to walk" is an area called New Egypt. It's located in Plumsted Township in Ocean County, New Jersey.

I thought this fit the Egyptian Ankh, the Lunar Mare as in Oceans on the moon, and the game Clue. Professor Plum is one of the characters in that game. It seemed to fit several clues, but I could find nothing in Mr. Fenn's book or in his poem to support this area, other than he collects Egyptian jewelry.

Also "not far, but too far to walk" from Philly is Washington, DC. I remembered from "Just take - **the c**hest **a**nd go **i**n **p**eace," the CAP IT. If you add AL you have CAPITAL. I thought if this all started with state capitals, maybe now I needed to include our nation's capital.

I went back to my U.S. map and, starting from Washington, DC, tried to find a line that crossed the U.S. that tied both coasts together. I was beginning to believe that this was becoming a national Treasure Hunt rather than a regional one (more on that in Phase Two). I tried passing the line through the original X, but that didn't seem to connect to anything. I tried passing the line through Indianapolis but that went nowhere as well. I abandoned the Washington, DC angle.

If not Washington, then perhaps the capital I needed was the state capital of Pennsylvania, Harrisburg. I tried going from Harrisburg through the original X, but that didn't seem to make sense. Then it hit me. The most obvious X on a U.S. map is the "four corners" area formed by Utah, Colorado, Arizona, and New Mexico. I passed the line through that X and hit Burbank, California. Burbank, not being a state capital, was an exception to the rule.

The "title" on page 119 in Mr. Fenn's book is "Father on the Banco." Banco can mean several things and one of them is Spanish for Bank (Burbank?). I felt I was on to something. I looked at those two cities.

Harrisburg......10 letters

Burbank..........7 letters

17 total letters (17 is important in this discussion)

I looked at the first and last letters of the two cities - H, G, B, and K. I couldn't spell a word with those letters and they didn't appear in any context in Mr. Fenn's 9-clue poem. Then I looked at the center letters of the two cities - IS from Harrisburg, and B from Burbank. That struck me as significant. It quite boldly says "Is B." The first verse of Mr. Fenn's poem starts with an A. The second verse starts with a B. But I wanted more proof that I was correct about this coast-to-coast connection.

I decided to look at page 7 of Mr. Fenn's book because of seven letters in Burbank. There was nothing pertaining to these two cities on page 7. Nothing on page 10 or page 17 either.

Then I thought about "the mirror" aspect. There's a mirror image of Utah in the way the photos overlap on the front cover of Mr. Fenn's book as I stated earlier, and Mr. Fenn talks about the book being "a mirror" on page 4. So, comparing the back of the book to the front to see where Page One actually was, I started counting backwards seven pages from the back of the book and

THE FOREST FOR THE TREES!

I came to another of Mr. Fenn's poem (page 142) – this one about his wife, his love, or as he might say, Mi Amore. The poem is entitled "Ode to Peggy Jean." Next to the poem is a photo of his lovely wife.

I examined "Ode to Peggy Jean" looking for the letters H, G, B, and K from **Harrisburg** and **Burbank**. I was stunned when I found them. The photo of his wife is tilted and the bottom corner of the photo is actually pointing at the three lines of the poem (clue from Haiku) where the letters are concealed. Even in the photo, three fingers of his wife's left hand seem to be pointing at the three lines.

There are four 4-line verses to "Ode to Peggy Jean." The letters in question are at the end of verse three. The first three lines of that verse end with the letter Y and the last line ends with the letter I. The lines are as follows:

Today I looked up in the s<u>k</u>y

   And saw my shadow floatin**g b**y.

It seemed so strange – I wondered w**h**y.

   And now it's gone, but where am I?

Corner of the photo of Peggy Jean, Mr. Fenn's wife.

Harrisburg and **Burbank.** I highlighted and underlined the **k, g, b,** and **h.** I was convinced that I was correct about the coast-to-coast connection. You can see that the k-g-b-h forms a straight line even in the poem. And the last line ends with an I. Is this coast-to-coast line an I (eye) across America? (While editing this analysis I noticed that these four poem lines start with T-A-I-A. You can spell AT "AI." Plus, the fourth poem line starts with A and ends with I. "AI" has a special meaning that I'll explain later.)

I then looked ten pages backwards (ten letters in Harrisburg) (page 139). The Treasure Chest is mentioned on that page in relation to frogs (important later), and the last line on that page is "Dancing With the Stars." That's what I've been talking about since the beginning of this analysis – Stars as in state capitals on the map. If you notice, the D, W, and S are capitalized in "Dancing With the Stars." The show's logo doesn't use any capital letters. So why in Forrest's book are there capital letters? I think that the W relates to Where Warm Waters and the S relates to the five Star clues that came from that phrase. I'm not sure what to do with the D just yet. Though, if you add the D to EARTH REAMERS, from earlier, you get EARTH DREAMERS. There are dreams to discuss.

Then I looked seventeen pages backwards (total number of letters in both cities names – page 132). Guess what I found there? – Mr. Fenn's 9-clue poem about where his Treasure Chest is hidden. I was convinced I was on the right track.

Keep in mind that all of this is strictly my opinion. At this point I don't know if I'm correct, and I don't know where the Treasure Chest is hidden. But here's what I believe to be the truth about Mr. Fenn's treasure hunt.

1. He says it's in a place special to him. The U.S.A. is special to Mr. Fenn. He fought for this country. His comrades-in-arms are from all over the U.S. In his section "My war for me," on page 92 he asks, "How do you thank guys like that?" I believe he's saying "thanks" by including them in the search for his treasure – including their hometowns and home states.

   If you take the ANKH from earlier in this discussion and add ST you can spell THANKS. If you take the CAP IT from earlier and add AL

255

you can spell CAPITAL. If you take the added ST with the added AL you can spell LAST or SALT. Mr. Fenn's family and friends are, I believe, to Mr. Fenn and in reality, the "salt of the earth." Perhaps SALT refers to Salt Lake City, capital of Utah. A mirror image of Utah is on the cover of his book.

Salt can be written as NaCl, the 11th and 17th elements on the periodic table. Again, the prime number 17, this time associated with the prime number 11. Page 11 backwards is page 137, the 33rd prime. "Dancing With the Stars" is again mentioned on page 137, as well as the phrase, "I'll tell you of my secret plan." If you combine SALT with NACL you can form SLANT CLA (see LA or AL?). Slant as in the Harrisburg/Burbank line, and LA as in Louisiana, or Los Angeles. AL could mean Alabama, or simply Al. Maybe Al knows Hank. There is a C, an AL, and a LA on the Periodic Table.

2. I believe he's thanking all the people in his life that have made a difference or been his "support system" throughout his life – all the people he's loved. That's why his father is tied to the word Banco or bank or Burbank. That's why his wife's poem points out the coast-to-coast connection. The line that runs from Harrisburg to Burbank slants and approximately cuts the U.S., again, into equal halves – an upper and lower half. I believe Mr. Fenn's daughters, Kelly and Zoe might play into that somehow. Though, there is another "two-part" connection I'll discuss in Phase Two.

3. I think you have to figure out the upper and lower halves of the U. S. map. He's given you a "Cross" and a "slanted line" and you have to draw the rest, possibly using the five "star" clues from earlier, giving you a beginning, a Point A, if you will. (Although, I think another map, that I'll discuss later, is involved.) Then, Mr. Fenn's 9-clue poem will lead you to the exact spot where the Treasure Chest "B" secreted, Matey. (Arrg - Talking like a pirate; a Captain Kidd reference. I get it. After all, he did hide a Treasure Chest.) And point B could easily be north of Santa Fe, NM.

If you go to Mr. Fenn's webpage and click on "View Excerpt," you get a brief section of his book. The first page of that "excerpt" starts with the line,

---

The following is an excerpt of

The Thrill of the Chase: A Memoir

By Forrest Fenn

Release Date: October 25, 2010

Somewhere in the mountains north of Santa Fe, New Mexico, a treasure is hidden. In his memoir, Forrest Fenn gives readers the clues needed to unlock the secret of the treasure's location.

(Then it gives some addresses for book orders and media inquiries.)

Nothing on that page is an excerpt from his book other than the title. Nowhere in the book does it say that the Treasure Chest is north of Santa Fe,

New Mexico. In the "Gold and More" section it simply says "north of Santa Fe." It does not name a state. The actual online "Excerpt" starts on page 2 with the cover of his book. You can make of that what you want. I don't think the first page was penned by Mr. Fenn.

Mr. Fenn's Facebook page opens with: "Author: Somewhere in the mountains north of Santa Fe, a magnificent treasure box is hidden. Will you find the treasure?"

Notice that it doesn't say Santa Fe, New Mexico. It does say "in the mountains north of…" Let's look at those letters.

"IN THE MOUNTAINS NORTH OF"

There are some interesting combinations using those letters.

1. **A FOOT IN THE US TINHORN NM** Maybe it's buried a foot deep somewhere in the U.S. NM is the abbreviation for New Mexico. I looked for Tinhorn, New Mexico. There isn't one, or anything that seemed to come close. MN is the abbreviation for Minnesota. There is no Tinhorn in that state either.

So I looked at TIN and HORN as separate items. This turned out to be very interesting. I added STAR to each word. I had TIN STAR and HORN STAR. TIN is SN on the periodic table. Substitute SN for TIN and you have SN STAR or N STARS. HORN STAR rhymes with PORN STAR. I immediately thought of SAX. Substitute SAX for HORN and you have SAX STAR or AX STARS. Pages 145 and 146 in Mr. Fenn's book feature the same sketch of someone holding an <u>AX</u> (I believe it to be Mr. Fenn's father, William Marvin Fenn) while staring at a <u>crescent moon</u> and <u>stars</u>. Page 145 is the first page of the Epilogue. The enlarged brown letter on that page is N (N Stars).

If you combine the N with the AX you have NAX, or perhaps N-AX. Could that mean ENACTS (N-AX)? Or, perhaps, IN (TWO) ACTS? Mr. Fenn does mention Shakespeare (a famous playwright) on pages 101, 102, and 103. Acts One, Two and Three? Though, I'm more inclined to believe that there are just Two Acts, or Two Halves. Pages 101 and 102 are the front and back of the same page – two sides of the same coin, I suppose. The number 10 can be written as the Roman numeral X. 101 and 102, X1 and X2? Perhaps the original state-capital-formed Cross is X3. X3 to X2 to X1. There are several countdowns in this tale as I will demonstrate later.

Combine the leftover NM with ENACTS and you can spell C MAN NEST. There is a <u>bird's nest</u> on the crescent moon in the before-mentioned sketch featured on pages 145 and 146 (again two sides of one page). If you combine Bird with Man you have C BIRDMAN NEST (the term "birdman" is part of this analysis). You can also spell SCANT MEN. There is the phrase TARRY SCANT in the 9-clue poem. If you combine TARRY with MEN you can spell TERNARY with a leftover M. "Ternary" means composed of three or arranged in threes. That does come into play later. 3M is a company that is listed on the DOW.

Mr. Fenn's 11th clue on The Today Show was about not digging in old outhouses. Outhouses are famous for having Crescent Moons on the door. After a little online research, I discovered that a Crescent Moon on an outhouse door meant it was for women. A Star on the door meant it was for men.

This next anagram I found to be the most interesting.

2. **FENN HINTS AI TRUTH MOON O** Considering letter manipulation, you easily see how AI could be AT. <u>AT "AI"</u> as in "Ode to Peggy Jean." Put another I on top of AI and you have AT. (Two I's) (Two eyes?) As I stated earlier, there are 9 capital I's in Mr. Fenn's 9-clue poem. I believe, however, the AI has a different meaning.

In "Gold and More," the section about the hidden Treasure Chest, the letters **A** and **I** are enlarged brown letters. (Each section of "The Thrill of the Chase" starts with an enlarged <u>brown</u> letter.) Equally as interesting is the fact that the first line of the 9-clue poem starts with the letter **A**, and the last line of the poem starts with the letter **I**. I believe that "AI" is "code" for the 9-clue poem and the treasure hunt. The first four "enlarged brown letters" in the book are <u>A</u> W<u>I</u>N. An AI win? "W" as in Where Warm Waters. "N" as in N Stars.

But what about MOON O? What could that mean? Before I get into that let's look at Forrest Fenn for a moment. Mr. Fenn is an avid collector of American Indian Art and Pottery. He used Indianapolis, Indiana as one point in his Cross on the U.S. map. (As an interesting side note, in Indianapolis, there's the <u>Eiteljorg Museum of American Indians and Western Art</u>. It houses one of the finest collections of Native contemporary art in the world. I'm sure Mr. Fenn is well aware of this fact.) Given all that, it made sense to me that he would somehow incorporate Native American culture into his treasure hunt.

First let's look at his by-line. On the front of his book at the bottom it says, BY FORREST FENN. If you represent all the letters in that line just once you have BYFORESTN. Those letters can be arranged to make the statement B FYRST ONE.

B FYRST ONE. Isn't that the deal? The First One to figure out the poem gets the Treasure Chest. Mr. Fenn does say that he uses words that are not in the dictionary. B does not spell BE, and FYRST does not spell FIRST but you can easily understand the message. BE FIRST ONE. For all you sticklers, the double letters leftover from his by-line are FERN.

Now back to MOON O. My belief that Mr. Fenn would include Native American culture led me to locate a list of American Indian tribes. As I scanned the alphabetical list of tribes and came to the O's, I saw the ONEIDA tribe. That struck me as a good possibility. ONEIDA starts with ONE as in Be First One.

Besides I had MOON plus O. If you separate the O from ONEIDA it leaves NEIDA. Those letters can be arranged to spell END AI - AI the apparent "code" for the poem and treasure hunt.

A short online search led to an Oneida language translator. I plugged in the word Moon and what came out was Wehni•talé.

Wehni•talé = Oneida for Moon.

WHEN I TALE

When, as in Who, What, When, Where, etc.

I, as in 9 capital I's in the 9-clue poem, and the line (I) that crosses the U.S.

Tale, as in??? That, I believe, is what you have to figure out.

Here's my theory. In the "Gold and More" section Mr. Fenn talks about his various collections. He goes into depth about his "multi-colored ball of string." He tells how the ball had gotten so big it wouldn't fit through his bedroom door. Then, one day when he came home from school, the ball of string was missing. It is, he claims, the one unsolved crime in his family. When he asked his mother about the missing ball of string, she didn't answer; she just kept nodding and looking out the window.

I think, somehow, the ball of string plays into the answer. I have no proof of that, but it makes sense being that he covers it in the "Gold and More" section, and it fits with the Who, What, Where thing, as well. I do have some peripheral evidence that this might be true.

His Mom was looking (or staring) out a window. (Remember STARE from waters.) The first four enlarged brown letters are A WIN. Add DOW and you have A WINDOW. DOW is a word meaning "having worth." Besides, I had 3M which is listed on the DOW.

If you take the added SALT with the added DOW you can spell LOADS with WT leftover. The twelfth line of the 9-clue poem is, "Just heavy loads and water high." Water has the WT. Remove the WT from WATER and you have EAR or ARE or ERA. (Ear High?) I'm not sure what to make of that just yet. Perhaps WT simply refers to the weight of the gold.

Curiously his mom is not directly connected to any clues or evidence like his wife and dad are. The word MOM does appear in the enlarged brown letters.

Page 45   M   "In Love with Yellowstone"

Page 47   O   "The Totem Café Caper"

Page 50   M   "My Brother being Skippy"

This MOM connection ties in his brother Skippy, as well as his sister June who is shown in the photos in those sections. This Tale and Treasure Hunt is about the people who have meant the most to Mr. Fenn.

Let's discuss the 10th clue: "The treasure is hidden higher than 5,000 feet above sea level."

If "The Thrill of the Chase" is indeed "a mirror" as Mr. Fenn states on page 4, then perhaps things are actually reversed. Maybe up is down, left is right, cold is hot, and north is south…maybe. Perhaps it's below 5,000 feet. Mr. Fenn said you had to think. Think can be written as HINT K. 5,000 can be written as 5K or FIVEK.

Though I'm paraphrasing Mr. Fenn (just as he did with Shakespeare on page 102 in his book) I decided to condense the 10th clue to the phrase; it's hidden Above Five-K feet. The next little bit you might find somewhat convoluted but it's interesting just the same.

ABOVEFIVEKFEET. I couldn't make much sense of that letter combination. K was part of the Ankh. Subtract the K from Ankh and you have ANH. I substituted the ANH for the K and had ABOVEFIVEANHFEET.

I came up with BEEHIVE FATE NOVA F. (The first poem in Mr. Fenn's book is about life being like a poker game. The third line of the poem is, "Fate deals you four cards and a joker." It is the first poem in the book. B FYRST ONE? Perhaps that's the poem you need to examine first.) (I will get to an earlier poem in Phase Two.)

A Beehive is on the State Seal and State Flag of Utah. Utah is on the dust cover of the book. A Super<u>nova</u> is the <u>Fate</u> of some Stars. I took SUPER plus the leftover F and spelled FE SPUR. There is a <u>Santa **Fe Spur** Trail</u> just south of Santa Fe, New Mexico. But I decided to take it a little farther. Fe is the symbol for IRON. IRON SPUR. One definition for "Spur" is branches or off-shoots from a main body. I decided to look for cities with Iron in their names. I found:

Iron City, Georgia

Iron City, Tennessee

Iron City, Utah (a ghost town) (more on this in Phase Two)

Then I looked for Iron Counties. I found:

Iron Co., Utah

Iron Co., Michigan

Iron Co., Missouri

The common denominator or main body is Utah having both an Iron City and an Iron County. So the lines branch out from Utah to Georgia, Tennessee, Michigan, and Missouri; in other words, all across this great nation of ours. The Treasure Chest is hidden somewhere in the whole of the U.S. Is it above or below 5,000 feet? You'll have to make that call. Perhaps it simply is in the mountains north of Santa Fe. But all of this is at least curious.

One more thing, I decided to look at the phrase "The Home of Brown." I used the "enlarged <u>Brown</u> letters" to demonstrate clues, but I didn't look at the phrase THE HOME OF BROWN.

The most interesting anagram is HER HEFT MOONBOW. "Heft" means having weight such as The Treasure Chest. "Moonbows" are nighttime rainbows caused by the spray of waterfalls in the moonlight. Mr. Fenn mentions the end of his rainbow as well as waterfalls in his book. There are only a couple of places in the U.S. where true Moonbows appear; several waterfalls in Yosemite National Park in California and at Cumberland Falls in Kentucky. I don't know what HER has to do with anything. It could be a hint. You'll have to figure that out for yourself. (As a side note: "Ball of string" can be rearranged to say "Bring to falls." Bring <u>Her</u> to Falls? Who is her? Maybe Al and Hank know.) (Remember "Name Her Star." Hmm.)

So to sum it all up:

1. Mr. Fenn is saying Thanks to his Comrades-in-arms, to his Wife, and his Daughters through his Treasure Chest hunt. He's including his family and friends in the solution.

2. If you think you have to look north of Santa Fe, New Mexico to find the Treasure Chest, I think your chances are slim. I believe you're being misdirected with the truth as I've demonstrated. Mr. Fenn is telling the truth, he's just not telling **all** the truth. The Treasure Chest could

be in a grove of trees near you. Another arrangement of BYFORESTN is Y - B - N - FOREST. Why be in forest. Is that a question or a statement? <u>WHY</u> as in Who What Where, and <u>Be In Forest</u> as in a place to be secreted, Matey.

Related to my belief that Mr. Fenn is "pointing the wrong way with the truth" is the earlier anagram "Countryman is OK." OK could stand for 0° Kelvin which is absolute zero. The second line in the sixth verse of his 9-clue poem is, "Your effort will be worth the cold." When you're searching for something someone has hidden, you might ask, "Am I warm or cold?" I believe Mr. Fenn is giving "Cold" clues. Mr. Fenn is OK (cold). You have to find the "Warm" and "Hot" clues as I've been demonstrating.

You'll have to bear with me here; this is a bit circuitous, but interesting nonetheless. Taking the phrase "WORTH THE COLD" you can spell CL TROOTH with WHED leftover. CL = 17th element. (The 9-<u>cl</u>ue Poem is on page 17 backwards) TROOTH (Truth?) CL TROOTH = Page 17 Truth.

The Oneida Indian word for "<u>Truth comes out</u>" is TOKΔ'. The actual letter at the end of the word is an Oneida Language letter that's a V turned upside-down. The closest I could come is a triangle, which works because if you slide the bottom of the triangle up (or add a sideways I to an inverted V) you have an A. Again, AI, except now you have VIA which means "by way of." If you combine the leftover WHED with TOKA you can spell HEAT DOW K. If you substitute AWIN for DOW you have HEAT A WINK. Isn't "a wink" a subtle way of letting someone know they're correct? A WINK - CL TROOTH - HEAT. <u>Your effort will be HEAT</u> derived from Worth the Cold." I'm still working on what HEAT.

Heat from Cold? Are things really the opposite? Above or below 5,000 feet? North or south? It could be north of Santa Fe, Texas and south of Santa Fe, New Mexico. Or the hidden Treasure Chest could be where everyone thinks it is; north of Santa Fe, New Mexico.

3. I suggest you buy Mr. Fenn's book "The Thrill of the Chase" and a U.S. map so you can see for yourself how the state-capital-formed Cross and the Harrisburg/Burbank slanted line work. I'm using a National Geographic 24" x 36" Lambert Conformal Conic Projection U.S. Political State map with quite a bit of detail. It has lots of Cities, State Roads, Interstates, and most importantly State Capitals (Stars).

4. It just hit me about the phrase <u>CON</u>MAN STORY from earlier. My map is a Lambert **Con**formal **Con**ic Projection. The "scale" for miles on the map is 300 miles long. (Mr. Fenn's statement that it's more than 300 miles west of Toledo becomes a little more interesting now.)

5. When I Tale. Conman Story. <u>When I</u> = A Memoir. <u>Tale</u> = Story. <u>Man</u> = Fenn. <u>Con</u> = Map. You have to find a two-part story that fits on the map. It just occurred to me that if you add AI to CONMAN STORY you can spell A COINMAN STORY.

6. I was about to stick a fork in it and call it done, when I realized that I should look at **Con**formal and **Con**ic. If you drop the CON from both words you have IC FORMAL. Maybe a prom is involved somehow. Again, kidding. Let's look at those eight letters. FORMAL IC

   a. If you add U you can spell FORMULAIC.

   b. If you change the C to a U you can spell FORMULA I. (Cu= copper. I = E/R?)

   c. If you change the M to a W you can spell C AIRFLOW. (Jet stream?)

   d. You can spell CAIRO (Egypt) with FML leftover. Add AI and you have A CAIRO FILM.

7. Of all those possibilities, "b" seems the most likely. There is a formula for making horseshoes on page 135 in Mr. Fenn's book. Horses will come into play in Phase Two.

8. As an interesting side note, in "The Santa Fe Interviews" (available on Mr. Fenn's website) Mr. Fenn is either sitting in front of windows (A WIN are the first four enlarged brown letters in "The Thrill of the Chase" plus the before mentioned DOW), or in front of bookshelves

with unmistakable Four Corners imagery. Make of that what you want. There are also hats hanging on the wall near the windows. UTAH in a mirror is HATU.

9. One last look at IN THE MOUNTAINS NORTH OF.

                                                                 NO TH

Another possibility is; IN THE US - AI FORM ⟨

                                                                 NO NT

In the third verse of the 9-clue poem there's NO PLACE and NO PADDLE. Place and Paddle start with the common initial P. Remove the P's and you have the words LACE and ADDLE or ADD LE.

NO TH + LACE = NO CHALET (KNOW CHALET?)

NO NT + LE = NO LENT (KNOW LENT?) (Fish on Fridays?) (The Fish Videos?)

Again, a two-part division. At this point I've no clue if Chalet and Lent are hints. Perhaps this is Formul**a I**. I just noticed the **AI** at the end of the last sentence.

Just before Mr. Fenn gave his 11th clue on The Today Show he said, "**I** don't have **a** clue." Not to put words in Mr. Fenn's mouth, but that could easily mean, "I have <u>No</u> clue." I'm just saying, No Place, No Paddle, No Chalet, No Lent, No Clue. Hmm. Of course, NO can be rearranged to spell ON.

Here's another bit of interesting wordplay. I looked at "A Memoir" and noticed that it also contained AI. I removed the AI and anagrammed N ROME or ROMEN (Roman, maybe?). Remember the 10th clue and the Roman numeral X. Then I decided that perhaps the A and I were actually already together: that the letter I was hidden in the M.

I pulled the <u>M</u> apart and made it <u>I N</u>. That gave me "A <u>I</u> NEMOIR." Those letters gave me AI NO RIME. Rime is a thin layer of ice, such as frost on grass. RIME rhymes with RHYME. AI NO RIME. (No Cold?) AI NO RHYME. NO CLUE? (9 no clues in a 6 verse poem?) The letter combination ON or NO appears 9 times in the 9-clue poem in the following words: g**on**e al**on**e cany**on** **no**t **no no** k**no**w d**on**e **no**w. Again, hmm.

10. To the countdowns…first, I had **four** state capital cities with <u>Carson City</u> being the exception to the rule. Then I had **three** words with <u>Waters</u> being the exception to the rule. Then I had **two** cities with <u>Burbank</u> being the exception to the rule. That leads me to believe that I'm looking for **one** point on the map that is "the rule" and "the exception to the rule" simultaneously. Possibly <u>a city</u>, that's <u>a star</u> and <u>an aphetic word</u> as well. I'm still working on that (B Fyrst) <u>**One**</u>. (Be Fyrst No?)

11. "AI" is apparently "code" for the Treasure Hunt and the Poem. In the 9-clue poem there are 5 capital A's and 9 capital I's. 59 is the 17th prime

number. Again, the number 17. Page 17 forward has a photo of Mr. Fenn's father. Page 17 backwards has the 9-clue poem. 17 is 7th prime. 7 is the 4th prime. 4 is 2^2. Page 22 shows a picture of Forrest at 13, the 6th prime starting grade 7, the 4th prime. Page 22 backwards is page 127. That's the page on which "Gold and More" (the treasure hunt) starts. 127 is the 31st prime. 31 is the 11th prime. 11 is the 5th prime. 5 is the 3rd prime. 3 is the 2nd prime. And 2 is the 1st prime. Countdown complete. Houston, we have liftoff. Look to the stars.

Maybe you'll figure all this out before I do and be the first one "Dancing With the Stars." Of course, I could be wrong about everything. I could have misinterpreted all the clues. It is, after all, just my opinion. Of course, it's been three years now since the book was published. No one's stumbled upon the hidden Treasure Chest so far. Maybe it's time to look at things with fresh eyes (I's). You'll have to decide for yourself if I'm correct. Good Luck.

Sincerely, C. G. Knight

Phase One is the cover story. Now for the real deal.

Phase Two.

CUT TO THE CHASE!

I'm going to take you to a place and tell you things that most of you will probably disbelieve. You'll surely think I've gone mad. I have evidence that Forrest Fenn's Treasure Chest hunt is really the second half (the finale) of a puzzle called "TREASURE" In Search of the Golden Horse. "Treasure" was published in 1984; 30 years ago. Forrest Fenn would have been around 50 years old at the time. The "Treasure" puzzle was written by Dr. Crypton - puzzle master. His real name is Paul Hoffman. Before you dismiss this notion, you should at least read what I have to say.

First, let's talk about "TREASURE" In Search of the Golden Horse. The "Search" ran for 5 years, from 1984 to 1989. (5 is an important number in this discussion.) It was never solved and no official solution was ever published, which left a lot of searchers angry. There was an unofficial solution which you can read at homepage.ntlworld.com/mparry/treasure/solution.

The unofficial solution (designed, I believe, to appease the masses and to help with the current Chase) is a convoluted tale that involves ciphers, some unbelievable reasoning, and some questionable details like how many steps were needed to walk to the exact spot where the Golden Horse was buried; as though everyone's gait is the same. In the unofficial solution, when describing how ciphers work, they show two alphabets (one regular and one scrambled) aligned one over the other as I've demonstrated here:

A B C D E F G H I J K L M N O P Q R S T U V W X Y Z

L K J H G F D S A M N B V C X Z P O I U Y T R E W Q

You'll notice that the only letter in the same place in both alphabets is the F. Two Fs? Forrest Fenn. Is that a coincidence or not? The unofficial solution was to "Try Route Two Dozen" or Route 24. Forrest Fenn's 9-clue poem has 24 lines. Back to the Chase.

I'm not saying that there wasn't actually a Golden Horse buried; legally there had to be. What I'm saying is that the solution was so convoluted and difficult that it was sure to <u>not</u> be solved in the given five year timeline. I'm saying that the whole Golden Horse contest was a "Red Herring" to disguise a Hidden Puzzle that would fire back up 21 years after it supposedly ended. "Red Herring" is even printed in Japanese in "Treasure" in Chapter Six, "Fish." (Remember the Japanese Haiku reference from Phase One?) Forrest's latest interviews are called "The Fish Videos."

"The Thrill of the Chase" was published 21 years after the end date of the "Treasure" contest. "Treasure" has 21 chapters. The $500,000 prize was to be paid out over 20 years.

On the back of the "Treasure" book is the statement, "Solve the hidden puzzle and lay claim to the most fabulous treasure in contest history." What Hidden Puzzle? The Golden Horse puzzle certainly wasn't hidden. It was all there in the pages of the book, it even said so in the Rules. So what was hidden? And $500,000 wasn't, even back in 1984, the most fabulous treasure in contest history.

The book "Treasure" ends with a 4-line poem that's most interesting. The poem is on page 79. Forrest Fenn's book opens with him saying that he's

79 years old, almost 80. There are 80 pages in the "Treasure" book. 79 is the 22nd prime. Page 22 backwards in "The Thrill of the Chase" is page 127 – the title page of the "Gold and More" section, the Treasure Chest section. The "Treasure" poem is as follows:

> Take all the clues, hidden here**in**
> Combine them and take their **full measure**
> **It**'s time for your search to beg**in**
> It **may** lead you to Treasure.

(**May** 26, 1989 was the end of the "Golden Horse" contest.)

"Treasure" In Search of the Golden Horse leaves off with a poem; Forrest Fenn's Treasure hunt starts with a poem, a 9-clue poem. Forrest Fenn claims to have written the 9-clue poem in 1987; smack dab in the middle of the "Treasure" contest. I've underlined and highlighted the letters f-e-n-n (Fenn) in the "Treasure" poem. You can see how they form a "cross" (like I described in Phase One) or an arrow (I added the lines), which I believe means that Fenn will point the way. Or perhaps he's pointing the wrong way. There is an arrow either direction in the above verse. In "The Thrill of the Chase" a pre-teen Forrest is looking away from the cross in the cemetery on pages 37 and 41. 37 and 41 are the 12th and 13th prime numbers respectively. Prime numbers play a large part in this puzzle.

Speaking of cemeteries. One of Mr. Fenn's Today Show clues is, "The trea-sure is not in a graveyard." Chapter Four in "Treasure" is called "Cemetery." In "Treasure," Amanda, the main character, is told by her magical Kite in

Chapter Three, "To find your Treasure you first must find your father's <u>grave</u>." A common form for kites is a "cross" covered with paper so they'll fly. Again, a cross. It just hit me about Forrest's "multi-colored ball of string" in the "Gold and More" section. Kites need string. On page 19 in "Treasure," a gold kite string leads to a multi-colored box kite, the tail of which leads into Chapter Four, "Cemetery;" a multi-colored connection to Forrest Fenn. Even in the box kite image, the outline of a cross is clearly visible.

Remember all the references to the number 17 in Phase One. Chapter 17 in "Treasure" is "Forest." Of course it's spelled with one R. However, in Chapter 6, "Fish," a trout is carrying away the letter R. Forrest is shown holding fish on the cover of The Thrill of the Chase. Forrest Fenn's latest interviews are titled, "The Fish Videos." In the <u>Table of Contents</u> in "Treasure," "Fish" is the sixth item forward, and "Forest" is the sixth item backwards (a reverse or mirror relationship.) Forest is tied to Fish carrying away the second R: F and F - Forrest Fenn.

Another 17: In the front and back of "The Thrill of the Chase," pictured on the rough brown paper that is glued to the hard cover, is a Forrest Fenn ID card. On that card it says he is 17. It also gives his address as 1413 N. Main St., Temple, Texas. In "Treasure," because the pages are intentionally misnumbered, pages 13 and 14 are the same page; or one of those pages is missing, depending on how you look at it. On that 13/14 page is a mirror. In that mirror, on a nightstand, is an "H" or an "I" depending on how you look at it. Also in that mirror is a cross in the window frame. Forrest Fenn calls his book a "mirror."

In a drawing in Chapter Eighteen, "Rehearsal," two dancers are in front of a mirror on a tile-covered floor. At the right edge of the drawing is a strange door that is partly opened. The tile floor continues through the door and then turns into a Forest. The part of the door that's visible could be construed to look like the letter F reflected downward, so two F's (Forrest Fenn). This reflection theme is repeated all through that drawing. The top of the strange door forms an angle with the door frame very similar to the one on the dust cover of "The Thrill of the Chase" in the way the three photos overlap.

The three just-mentioned photos also form a mirror image of Utah. The front of "Treasure" also can be said to show a likeness of Utah. One of Mr. Fenn's Today Show clues is, "The treasure is not hidden in Utah or Idaho." Idaho-shaped puzzle pieces are in "Treasure" in Chapter Seven, "Road," on page **36**, and in Chapter Ten, "The Signal," on page **45**. 7 + 10 = 17. Chapter Seventeen is "Forest." 36 + 45 = 81. Because the "Treasure" pages are misnumbered, page 81 is the last page of the book (the "Rules" page). 81 = 9 x 9. Forrest penned a 9-clue poem.

The other state shaped puzzle piece in "Treasure" is North Carolina. In North Carolina there's a city called Rocky Mount. Add "ains" and you can spell Rocky Mountains – another connection to Forrest Fenn. The added letters AINS can also spell SAIN. "Sain" means to "make the sign of the cross." There's the Cross in the "Treasure" poem with f-e-n-n as its endpoints. Forrest Fenn's 9-clue poem describes a Cross with state capitals as endpoints spelled out in the line, "just take the chest and go in peace."

The cover of "Treasure" and the title of "The Thrill of the Chase" are printed in identical fonts, not just similar fonts; identical fonts. The title "The Thrill of the Chase" is printed in gold lettering. The title "Treasure" is printed in white lettering with gold shadows.

Chapter Nine in "Treasure" is "Mr. Maps." As I demonstrated in Phase One, the 9-clue poem draws a map.

Speaking of maps, in "Treasure" there's a map that's in pieces scattered through the pages of the book that you have to copy and assemble. It's a very intricate map that was never used, even in the unofficial solution. It was said to have looked like a tree that was near where the Golden Horse was buried. That map doesn't resemble any tree I've ever seen. In fact it looks more like a stick figure of a horse with its front leg lifted, similar to the Golden Horse statuette. Though now that I think about it, saying that the map looked like "a tree" is a connection to Forrest. Forrest Fenn has said that the Treasure is surrounded by trees. A Forest by definition is Trees.

The lines of the "Treasure Map" end in arrows ⟶ like I've demonstrated here. In a sketch on page 99 in "The Thrill of the Chase" there's an arrow in plain view on a rock face. There is no page 99 in "Treasure." However, if you turn 99 upside-down it becomes 66. Page 66 in "Treasure" is in Chapter Seventeen, "Forest." The sketch on page 99 in "The Thrill of the Chase" has the initials JF signed at the bottom. "Treasure" was illustrated by Jean-Francois Podevin. I'm not saying that the JF in "The Thrill of the Chase" is the same artist in "Treasure," but at a minimum, it's curious. 99 is the number 9 used twice. The 9-clue poem draws a map. Two 9's, two maps; the 9-clue map and the unused "Treasure" map.

In Forrest's 9-clue poem there's the line, "If you've been wise and found the blaze." In the movie version of "Treasure," the Treasure Map that you have to assemble is on "fire" as the video opens. Actually the map burns in reverse, starting as ashes, and then rising from the ashes like a Phoenix. In the book version, the edges of the map pieces are all burned and singed. (In "The Thrill of the Chase" on page 60, Forrest describes "very wisely" wadding up and burning a map to get a fire started.) I believe you have to use Treasure's "burnt" map in concert with the map the 9-clue poem draws to find the hidden chest.

Speaking of the hidden chest, on page 54 in "Treasure" in Chapter Thirteen, "Lodge," there's a drawing that shows items from Amanda's memory. On the floor in that drawing, sitting in front of an upright piano, is an open chest very similar in shape and size to the Forrest Fenn chest. In the "Thrill of the Chase," the description of the hidden Chest does not fit the pictures of the Chest. Apparently there are two chests; being in two parts is a consistent theme throughout this analysis.

"If you've been <u>wise</u> and found the blaze." I've read other people's posts online at various sites about The Chase, and one fellow opined that perhaps Forrest had carved a blaze in the shape of an (wise) owl in a rock face. I thought that was interesting. I liked his thought process; one of the few I've seen that was thinking outside the box.

In "Treasure" an owl is part of the story. There's an owl on the cover of "Treasure" and owls scattered throughout the book. In Chapter Thirteen, "Lodge," on page 53 there is a carved owl on the banister of a staircase. In Chapter Nineteen, "Party," on page 71, (17 if you reverse the numbers) an owl in flight is looking in on the party; and in Chapter Twenty-One, "Horse," an owl startles Amanda when she enters her father's workshop. The owl is called "the watchman" in that chapter. "The Watchman" is a mountain in Zion National Park in Utah. Utah is on the cover of "Treasure" and "The Thrill of the Chase." (Interesting side note; 17 and 71 are both prime numbers.)

Also in Chapter Twenty-One, after Amanda is startled by the owl, she finds her father's tools, one of which is an "Iron" melting spoon flecked with gold. Remember in Phase One when I talked about the Iron Spur, and how in Utah there's an Iron City that's a ghost town. Chapter Nineteen, "Party," takes place in Amanda's dream. In that dream she goes into a house where all the people are ghosts. They all died when the house had been caught up in a fire, a blaze, a century before. The party is a "costume ball" and all the ghosts are wearing masks and are dressed as pirates (remember Captain Kidd), policemen and ladies of the court.

There are "masked aspects" to this puzzle. In fact, the whole thing is masked to look like something quite simple – a 9-clue poem that leads "simply" to a hidden chest. Even the clues have hidden clues. Mask after mask. I have not been able to visit Iron City, Utah to see if anything in that ghost town might be a clue.

Let's return to the Egyptian Ankh from Phase One. On page 62 in "Treasure" there are what appear to be Egyptian hieroglyphics on a wall in a drawing that is supposed to be in New Orleans; out of place as the Ankh is in Forrest's tale. Among those hieroglyphs are several owls.

I surmised in Phase One, once I found the Ankh, that you may have to look for pyramid shapes. On the cover of "Treasure," in the concentric-circle stone maze, there are several roofed structures. All the roofs are green except one; it's a brown pyramid. Two other green pyramid roofs lead over to the owl in the picture. The three roof pyramids are spaced similarly to the pyramids of Giza; not unlike the stars of the Orion Belt correlation theory. So here's a connection to the stars (state capitals) and pyramids (the Egyptian Ankh).

So, now what do you think? What if I'm correct about all of this? What could this mean?

Well, first, if indeed this is true, it's a historic and amazing puzzle spanning three decades. And who knows what it's worth. "Solve the hidden puzzle and lay claim to the most fabulous treasure in contest history." If an interest-compounding account was set up over 30 years ago, there's no telling how much it would be worth today. That was the deal with the original contest; inside the Golden Horse statuette was a key to a safety deposit box which contained a certificate worth, at the time, $500,000. Add the Treasure Chest and you have "the most fabulous treasure in contest history." Of course, all of that is strictly my supposition.

Mr. Fenn's first Today Show clue was, "The <u>treasure</u> is hidden higher than 5,000 feet above sea level." The cover of "Treasure" shows "sea level." "<u>Searchers</u> have been within 500 feet of the Chest." The original prize was $500,000. There are 5 cities named Toledo in the U.S. The "Golden Horse" puzzle ran for 5 years. Chapter 5 in "Treasure" is titled "Fortune." In that chapter there are images of cards, dice, coins, and bones. Forrest Fenn says that along with the treasure he wants you to find his bones. His bones are on page 26 in "Treasure." It seems you can make lots of connections between these seemingly unconnected puzzles. But let's go back to the "Treasure" (f-e-n-n forms a cross) poem.

The page just before the poem has a drawing of Amanda sitting on a horse in front of a full moon. If you hold that page up to a light, the Fenn/cross poem on the other side of that page is completely in the confines of the moon. "Home of Brown" can be anagrammed to say "Her Moonbow" with a leftover

F for Forrest. Her Moonbow in this case would be Amanda's. In the Epilogue of "The Thrill of the Chase" on pages 145 and 146 (the front and back of the same page), Forrest Fenn's father is staring at a crescent moon.

In Phase One I demonstrated how the word "moon" plays into the Treasure Hunt. The second Today Show clue was, "No need to dig up old outhouses, the treasure is not associated with any structure." Outhouses are famous for having crescent moons on their doors. On page 17 (again the number 17) in "Treasure" there's an image of a crescent moon surrounded by stars (again, images of stars). In Chapter Five, "Fortune," there's a crescent moon on one of the eight tarot cards shown on page 24. That card is titled "La Lune," which is French for "Her Moon." Indianapolis, one of the four "cross" points, has the name Diana in it. Diana in Roman mythology is the goddess of the moon and the hunt. The moon appears to tie all of this together.

Searchers and those interested in "The Thrill of the Chase" are always wondering just how Forrest Fenn knows that the treasure hasn't been found. "Treasure" was published in 1984. 1984 by George Orwell is a book famous for the phrase, "Big Brother is watching you." If I were to hazard a guess I would say that the Treasure Chest is under 24/7 surveillance. Big Brother is, in my opinion, watching.

There are horses on the cover of The Thrill of the Chase. Because "Treasure" was never officially solved and no official solution offered, it's been rumored for years that there was a silver (perhaps platinum) horse still hidden somewhere. "The Thrill of the Chase," is published by One Horse Land and Cattle Company. Chapter Twenty-One in "Treasure" is "Horse." Although, I heard on Chasechat.com that Forrest reportedly said that he'd change the name to Two Horses if he sold enough books. That last sentence is strictly hearsay.

Oh, if you want to accurately assemble the "Treasure" map, it's done by placing the pieces over the full moon image on page 78. The first map piece (from page 2) fits around the horse's head in the drawing and lines up with various points around the frame. If I get enough interest I'll publish that starting point on my website, cgknight.com. And if you're looking for the missing piece of the map, it's on the cover of the book.

Of course, I could just be crazy, seeing connections where there are none. It's a pretty good story, huh? As far as the original Golden Horse puzzle being a "Red Herring," the back of the "Treasure" book (showing the Golden Horse statuette) is red, and on the front of the book where the image of the Golden Horse is displayed in a <u>torn</u> away corner forming the likeness of Utah, the background is red.

I recently realized that in "The Thrill of the Chase" there is a <u>torn</u> page. The tear is on page 123. The tear is pointing at a photo of "Fish." In fact, the subject of every photo on that page is Fish. Fish is tied to Forrest in both "Treasure" and in "The Thrill of the Chase."

$123 = 3 \times 41$. Page 3 in "The Thrill of the Chase" shows a picture of the Chest; page 41 shows a drawing of Forrest sitting in a cemetery with a cross. Page 41 forward in "Treasure" is in Chapter Nine, "Mr. Maps." Because the pages of "Treasure" are intentionally misnumbered, it turns out that page 41 forward and backwards in "Treasure" is the same page; thus dividing "Treasure" into two equal parts. So if "The Thrill of the Chase" is one part, and "Treasure" is in two parts, that makes three parts; thus the above 123.

Page 3 forward and backwards in "The Thrill of the Chase" and in "Treasure" contain the following items:

1. A picture of the Treasure Chest (page 3);

2. Forrest's father staring at the moon and stars (page 146);

3. The opening of the book "Treasure" talking about "understanding the Map;" the words "story" and "tale" are included in that text (page 3). On page 4 in "The Thrill of the Chase," Forrest says, "the **story** about my treasure chest is true, and if it doesn't stir your spirit then I hope at least it brings a smile in one of your dreams." There are spirits in a dream in "Treasure." And let's not forget the Oneida Indian word for moon, Wehni•talé. There's the **tale** related to the moon.

4. And finally, the f-e-n-n forms a cross poem (page 79). "The Thrill of the Chase" opens with Forrest saying he's 79.

If I'm correct about all this, then the puzzle and map was conceived by Paul Hoffman, and who knows how tricky it will be to solve. He's a puzzle master; said to be the smartest man in America. So, it would appear that more than one person knows the answer.

Here's how I happened upon all of this. I became interested in the Chase and figured out the X or the Cross just before Forrest went on the Today Show and said he wasn't going to put an X on the map for you. And that's true, he didn't put an X, he put a cross.

Once I had the cross I kept working through the poem and other aspects of the puzzle, which includes ciphers, alphabet manipulation, and constructing more of the map (Luna, New Mexico was indeed part of that construction), when through a cipher and alphabet manipulation, I came to the terms "gold horse" and "doctor." You discover these things as you draw the map. Each step leads to the next.

Eventually, starting from the original cross, an image was drawn that I can only describe as a giant letter A over the U.S. that reaches, at a slant, slightly into both Mexico and Canada. The original Cross transformed into an A. Perhaps that's the significance of AI. The bottom of the A sits on a large circle of which the circumference passes through Brownsville, Texas. ("Put in below the home of Brown.")

Into the top of that A, a small circle is inscribed, the center of which puts you on a mountain top in Idaho. The center of the small circle falls on one of those small + signs that designates a high point on a map with the elevation printed next to it. The ratio of the small circle to the large circle is that of the moon to the earth.

I believe that the "mountain point" I found by working through the first part, is one of the points needed to draw the final Treasure Map. Chapter Twelve in "Treasure" is "Mountain." The maze of concentric "circles" on the cover of "Treasure," houses a Carousel with a picture of a mountain on it.

The more I worked on the "Chase" puzzle the more it seemed like a Paul Hoffman design. I'm somewhat of an expert on Paul Hoffman's "Treasure" as I have tried to solve it, off and on, for many years, always wondering if there was more to it. It would seem I'm correct about there being more. Now I know why I could never solve it; I didn't have all the information.

The original "Golden Horse Treasure" was "buried" somewhere in the whole of the continental U.S. You'll have to decide for yourself if you think the Chest is north of Santa Fe, New Mexico. I'm keeping an open mind about where it might be hidden. Of course there could be two Treasures even now; one north of Santa Fe, NM and one somewhere in the whole of the U.S. One, a Chest with a Platinum Horse; and one, a Chest of Gold. Maybe you have to find one to find the other.

Will I ever solve it? Who knows? I haven't been able to so far. But that doesn't mean I won't keep trying. I think I have a better chance than those who believe that you just need to read the 9-clue poem, wander around in the woods or the dessert, and stumble upon it.

I believe that Forrest Fenn is "the face" for the hidden puzzle, and perhaps he's Mr. Maps as well. Forrest says to start at the beginning. The beginning is the book "Treasure – In Search of the Golden Horse." Chapter 1 is "Creation."

Remember from "Where Warm Waters" the fifth clue, "A Rhyme Star." Maybe the "Treasure" poem is that star. Or perhaps it's A Rhyme Star**t**. The enlarged <u>Gold</u> Letter on a <u>red</u> background in Chapter One, "Creation," is the letter <u>T</u>.

A Rhyme (Star----T)ake all the clues, hidden here**in**

Combine them and take their **full measure**

It's time for your search to beg**in**

It may lead you to Treasure.

"Solve the <u>hidden</u> puzzle and lay claim to the most fabulous treasure in contest history." Forrest points the way to that hidden treasure. After all, that's what he keeps saying, the Treasure Chest is <u>hidden</u>. It is the "hidden puzzle." Forrest Fenn is pointing the way with a cross.

You can see how the four Today Show clues link to "Treasure." You can see how there are clues "hidden" in those statements.

Forrest Fenn's Today Show clues:

Clue #10 – The treasure is hidden higher than 5,000 feet above sea level. The cover of "Treasure" shows sea level. The number 500,000 on "Treasure's" cover is higher than 5,000 by a factor of 100. If the ratio stays the same then perhaps the prize is $500,000 x 100 or $50,000,000. I could live on that for a while. Again, this is all just conjecture. There is no proof that any of it actually exists.

Clue #11 – No need to dig up old outhouses, the treasure is not associated with any structure. Outhouses are famous for having crescent moons on their doors. There are images of crescent moons in both "The Thrill of the Chase" and in "Treasure." The most significant crescent moon image in "Treasure" is on page 17 in Chapter Three, "Kites." Kites are paper-covered crosses. One of the cross-shaped kites shown on page 17 shows an image of a fish. Fish is now clearly tied to Forrest Fenn.

Clue #12 – The treasure is not in a graveyard. Chapter Four in "Treasure" is "Cemetery." The kite or cross in Chapter Three tells Amanda to find her father's grave. Interestingly, there is no cross shown in the cemetery on page 18 in "Treasure." However, there is a small image of a "toy bear" on a tombstone in that image. It would appear to be the same "toy bear" image that is standing next to the Chest (the one that looks like Forrest's Chest) on page 54 in "Treasure." It occurred to me that the "toy bear" in a cemetery could imply "A Cross to Bear."

In "The Thrill of the Chase," the "toy bear" image is similar, but not perfectly so, to the arrangement of gold pieces sitting on a map on page 133. Those pieces include a frog as part of the arrangement. There are frogs on one of the cross-shaped kites shown flying over the cemetery in "Treasure." Forrest says that frogs are his specialty.

On page 21 in "Treasure" there is an image of Amanda's father's grave with a rose, placed by Amanda, lying on the stone. I always took that to mean "Arose from a grave" as in Jesus arose from a grave. Jesus died on a cross. There is a cross in the cemetery in "The Thrill of the Chase" on page 41. There are two crosses shown in the cemetery in the movie version of "Treasure," as well as Amanda touching a cross in the "Lodge."

There's a door in the "Lodge" that opens to the image of the Forrest-like Chest in that drawing. Like the reflected "F" door described earlier, the "Lodge" door features a cross reflected downwards, so two crosses, or a double-cross. You got to love that; a double-cross. That sort of goes with the "Waiting for ships that never come in" theme. Make of that what you will. So far, nobody's ship has come in; no one has found the hidden chest.

Clue #13 – The <u>treasure</u> is not <u>hidden</u> in Idaho or Utah. Utah is hidden in plain view on the covers of both "Treasure" and "The Thrill of the Chase." Idaho-shaped puzzle pieces are in "Treasure." The other state-shaped puzzle piece in "Treasure" is North Carolina. The city of Rocky Mount is in NC. As stated earlier, add "ains" and you have Rocky Mountains. The added letters can also spell "sain." The definition of "sain" is to make the sign of the cross.

Chapter Twenty-One in "Treasure is "Horse." Remember how I took BY FORREST FENN and represented each letter only once giving me BYFORESTN with the double letters left over being FERN. BY FOREST N FERN. The first paragraph of Chapter Twenty-One in "Treasure" talks about

Amanda following a stream through a "forest," the floor of which is covered by moss and "fern." "The sound of many waterfalls urged her on."

In the Chapter Twenty-One movie version, the narrator says, "Now she came to an enchanted forest that had slept these many years." How many years? It appears that Forrest Fenn has been a "sleeper" for twenty-one years. He published "The Thrill of the Chase twenty-one years after the end date of "Treasure," a book with twenty-one chapters. An enchanted forest? Forrest Fenn lives in New Mexico, The Land of Enchantment. Hmm.

In as far as the Treasure & Chest puzzle being broken up into two pieces that span 30 years, yeah, I'm a little bit pissed about that. I mean I worked hard to solve the first half, worked for years on the "hidden puzzle" with no luck; plus all the embarrassment and ribbing I took because I thought there was more to it than was being said. Now I find I had "no chance" to solve "Treasure's" hidden puzzle because all the information needed was not available until Forrest Fenn made the scene. I'm pissed and vindicated in the same breath. I knew there was more. Though, admittedly, all the work I did on the hidden puzzle was like going to puzzle-solving school; good, on the ground, in the trenches, Paul Hoffman puzzle treasure-hunting experience.

Oh, I almost forgot about "the north of Santa Fe, Texas" claim I made in Phase One. In "Treasure" Amanda makes a stop in New Orleans, except in the book it's called Old Orleans. Forrest's poem hints at riches new and old. Santa Fe, Texas is exactly west of New Orleans: both sit almost directly on the 30th parallel; so both are associated with the number 3. Remember "Cairo" from Phase One. Cairo, Egypt is also on the 30th parallel. More importantly, a line north from Santa Fe, Texas divides the U.S. into approximately two equal parts.

Let's look at all the two part items:

1. The Harrisburg/Burbank line divides the U.S. into two parts.

2. The IN THE US - AI FORM that splits into NO CHALET & NO LENT.

3. The apparent two book division; "The Thrill of the Chase," and "Treasure."

4. "Treasure" itself divides into two parts in "Mr. Maps" on page 41, a page that's the same number forwards and backwards.

5. In the "Unofficial Treasure Solution" the Golden Horse was buried on the Continental Divide (2 parts). The Continental Divide is where rivers either flow east or west. Chapter Fifteen in "Treasure" is "River." In that chapter on page 59 (the 17th prime) when Amanda works up the courage to speak to the captain he rings the ship's bell, "Once. Twice." Remember "I Captain" from the Cross formation, and "Waiting for Ships that never come in." Forrest Fenn specializes in making bells that he buries. The last page of the "Gold and More" section features Two Bells. "Once. Twice."

6. There is evidence of two different Chests; one described (with raised female figures) and a different one pictured (with a castle under siege).

7. The pile of coins on page 131 (the 32nd prime) in "The Thrill of the Chase" is composed of the same pile of coins imaged twice. Include

the same image from the dust cover and you have 1-23 images; three in two parts. That has to be a clue as to how the map works.

8. The coin, mostly hidden, on page 133 (the map page) is a 1904 "Double" Eagle Liberty Head gold coin. A Double Eagle lying on a map? Two maps?

9. Five of the images in "The Thrill of the Chase" are doubles; (1) Forrest and his father in school, (2) Forrest milking a cow, (3) Stout-Hearted Men, (4) Forrest holding a tombstone of a French soldier, and (5) Forrest's father looking at a crescent moon and stars. Again, the number five, this time associated with the number two. 2 and 5 are primes.

10. Forrest said he wrote the 9-clue poem in 1987, thus dividing the original "Treasure" contest into two parts.

11. The number 9 itself is the product of two primes, 3 x 3.

12. There are two images of mirrors almost evenly spaced in "Treasure;" one 13 pages forward, and one 14 pages backwards. The first image is on page 13/14.

13. "The Thrill of the Chase" ends with two Omega symbols. The term "Alpha" is in the book in three places; pages 40, 110, and 113. 110 and 113 refer to the same Alpha teacher; so again a 1-23 arrangement; three in two parts.

113, as it turns out, was a key number in manipulating a hopefully final code-breaking **Alpha**bet that I'm currently working on. This alphabet has been particularly tedious; clever and precise in its construction. 113 is also the longitude that runs next to "The Watchman" mountain in Zion Nation Park in Utah. 113 is the 30th prime; a connection to the

30th latitude associated with Santa Fe, Texas, New Orleans, and Cairo, capital of Egypt.

The page 40 and page 110 Alphas are almost evenly spaced page-wise in the book; nineteen physical pages (not page numbers) backwards and nineteen and a half physical pages forward before each Alpha page. The "half page" contains two images of "Silver," the Fenn's childhood horse (page 39); two horses. Page 39 in "Treasure" is in Chapter Nine, "Mr. Maps." Two horses; Two maps; a Two-part puzzle.

14. And the pièce de résistance; Forrest Fenn said that he hid the Treasure in two parts; that he made two trips from his car, and when he returned to his car after the second trip he started laughing because he couldn't believe what he'd just done. I can't help but feel that "laughing" is some sort of clue.

So, now you have to decide if I'm crazy or not. Is "The Thrill of the Chase" really Part Two of "Treasure – In Search of the Golden Horse?" Are they two sides of the same coin? Are they the same Hidden Treasure? Do you need one to solve the other? The answer seems obvious to me. "Solve the hidden puzzle and lay claim to the most fabulous treasure in contest history."

Of course, I'm keeping some secrets. I have a few hidden cards. After all, I want to find "The Treasure," if for nothing else, vindication. I've got years and a lot of hard work invested in the hidden puzzle. The money might be nice as well.

What I'd really like to know is who conceived such an elaborate puzzle? Was it all Paul Hoffman's idea? It sure seems like a team effort. How long was it in the making? How many people are involved? How many people know the answer? How could such a thing even be possible? And Forrest Fenn certainly plays his part well. How could he keep this secret for all these years? What was in it for him? Though, when I hit my 80s, I hope I have as much fun as Forrest seems to be having. What's in it for other "masked" individuals I believe to be involved? If it is true, it's certainly historic. It's certainly amazing. I guess I'm sort of stunned by it all.

I wonder what's going to happen when I publish this. Will Forrest admit to the existence of the hidden puzzle? Will Paul Hoffman? Or will it have to be solved and proven to exist? Most probably I'll be labeled crazy and ignored; and again ridiculed for believing such a thing. But that's okay; I got to call 'em like I see 'em. We'll just have to wait and see.

I'd like to say Thanks to Forrest Fenn and Paul Hoffman for such an intriguing puzzle. They've got me hook, line, and sinker. Though, don't get me wrong, I'm still pissed.

Interesting side note: Forrest Fenn has double consonants in both his names; Paul Hoffman only has double consonants in his last name, though he has double fs. Isn't that how Forrest signs things, with a lower case f? I guess that's why Forrest is "the face" for the hidden puzzle; he's the center of it all. Of course, there's the reference to Captain Kidd. In "Treasure," Amanda is told, "Though the path is simple, it is well concealed." "The Thrill of the Chase" ends with two Omegas, ΩΩ. All those double letters; a two-part puzzle…hmm.

The "simple path" quote is from Chapter Five, "Fortune;" again FF. (Fortune Five and Forrest Fenn both have 11 letters.) Attached to the "simple path" quote in "Treasure" is this warning - "Then beware the man who is also a bird. He will try to lead you away from where you want to go. He will lie with the truth, and make the true seem false."

Forrest Fenn is a birdman; he's a pilot. The term "birdman" is slang for an Aviator, and in the military it's an informal name for an Airman. Plus, the brightest coin on the dust cover of "The Thrill of the Chase" features an Eagle, and there's the Double Eagle coin on the map page.

The "birdman <u>truth</u> warning" is on page 26 in "Treasure." That page also features an image of two bones; another clue to two parts. Forrest says he wants you to find his bones. Page 26 in "The Thrill of the Chase" has the line, "you should always tell the <u>truth</u>, but you should not always tell A<u>LL</u> the <u>truth</u>."

So what is the Truth? Why all the references to Truth?

There is no proof that any of this actually exists. But the preponderance of the evidence is substantial. How would you vote? Is it real? Or am I crazy?

Of course the first line of the birdman warning could mean, "Then <u>be where</u> the man who is also a bird." Perhaps the Treasure is in New Mexico after all.

One last thought; Fortune Five easily leads to the term "Fortune Five Hundred." Forrest's statement that <u>two</u> groups of <u>Search</u>ers have been within "500" feet of the hidden Treasure suddenly becomes a little more interesting.

Along with the Fortune 500 thing, if you consider the original <u>X</u> over New Me<u>x</u>ico (two Xs), along with Phoeni<u>x</u> and Austin, Te<u>x</u>as (two more Xs), you have Four Xs in the formation of the Cross. Forex is the market for trading Currencies. So we have the Fortune 500 associated with the Forex? Sounds

C . G . KNIGHT

like money to me. "Solve the hidden puzzle and lay claim to the <u>most fabulous</u> <u>treasure</u> in contest history." Perhaps $50,000,000, a box of gold, and a platinum horse (again, that's all my supposition). Time to match wits with Paul Hoffman.

Paul Hoffman's initials are PH. Those initials relate to this analysis in the following ways: **Ph**oenix, **Ph**iladelphia, **H**idden **P**uzzle, and **P**latinum **H**orse. Hmm.

Good luck, you're going to need it. It's time to find the missing Omega Ω.

Sincerely,

C. G. Knight